# It Pays to Be a Senior

## 1,147 Incredible Discounts, Benefits, Sweet Deals, and Giveaways for Folks Over 50

# Publisher's Note

The editors of FC&A have taken careful measures to ensure the accuracy and usefulness of the information in this book. While every attempt was made to assure accuracy, some websites, addresses, telephone numbers, and other information may have changed since printing. All estimates were made with the best data available at that time.

This book is intended for general information only. It does not constitute medical, legal, or financial advice or practice. We cannot guarantee the safety or effectiveness of any treatment or advice mentioned. Readers are urged to consult with their personal financial advisers, lawyers, and health care professionals.

The publisher and editors disclaim all liability (including any injuries, damages, or losses) resulting from the use of the information in this book.

*We set our eyes not on what we see but on what we cannot see. What we see will last only a short time, but what we cannot see will last forever.*

2 Corinthians 4:18

# Table of contents

## Super savings at the supermarket

## Grow, eat, save

## Dining out on a dime

# Easy ways to earn extra money

# Fraud alert: don't get fleeced

# Make your bank work for you

# Make the most of your investment

# Tax tips: keep more of what you earn

# Estate planning: wise safeguards for your family & finances

## TV & Internet: new ways to save

## Buy & sell: how to profit from your home

## Online shopping secrets

## Save with alternate living arrangements

## Control your medical costs

## Health insurance money-savers

## Healthy living for less

## Stop wasting money at the pharmacy

# Pamper yourself for pennies

# Drive down car costs

# Best-kept computer secrets that save

# Cut your phone spending in half

## Thrifty ways to fill your clothes closet

## Powerful energy & water savings

## Appliances: fast fixes & real deals

## Home improvements: inside changes that pay off

## Cost-cutting cleaning solutions

## Laundry & linens: loads of money-saving tips

## Home improvements: outside fix-ups that make cents

## Budget-friendly backyard tips and tricks

## Home insurance: protection for less

## Auto insurance discounts & deals

## Keep yourself safe & secure

## Pay less & travel more

## Frugal fun

## Index

# Super savings at the supermarket

## Smart ways to save on produce

A simple, 10-second trick can cut your cost of fresh fruits and veggies. Supermarkets may spray produce with water to keep it fresh, but the water adds extra weight to foods you pay for by the pound.

Shake per-pound produce thoroughly before bagging, or find a store that doesn't spray its vegetables. And never buy root vegetables or cucumbers from stores that spritz them. Water can make them rot much faster, even overnight. Trim your bill even further with these tips.

**Buy direct.** Put farmers markets and farm stands on your list of stores to shop. These places let you buy direct from the folks who grow the food, cutting out the middleman and the markup.

**Shop late.** Hit the farmers market just before closing time. Few sellers want to haul their produce back home. Some may offer discount deals to late-day buyers. If they don't right away, nicely ask if they would be willing to bargain with you.

**Pay cash.** Set a fruit-and-vegetable budget, then bring only that much in cash to the farmers market. When money gets low, begin asking sellers what a dollar will buy. You might be surprised how much people are willing to bargain. Leave when the money runs out.

**Eat seasonally.** Supermarkets carry almost everything year-round, but you'll pay a premium for out-of-season produce shipped in from far away. Try to eat only what is in season, when fruits and vegetables are cheapest. You'll get the freshest fruit in the store when you shop on Friday afternoons and Saturdays. Stores put out their fresh produce then as they gear up for weekend crowds.

Buy extra of your favorite fruits and vegetables while still at their peak, and practice freezing them to last through the off-seasons. See *Secret to free produce all year long* in the chapter *Grow, eat, save* for advice on freezing vegetables.

**DEEP DISCOUNT**

These five ways to save will leave $2,473 in your pocket at year's end.

- Switch to a faucet-mounted filter and save $180 on bottled water over the course of a year.
- Opt for a good-tasting but affordable coffee rather than pricey gourmet brands, and cut $70 a year in grocery spending.
- Buy cleaning supplies and household items at the dollar store instead of the supermarket to save as much as $324 annually.
- Shop your own refrigerator once a week, avoid overbuying, and invest in a vacuum food sealer. That will help you save the $600 worth of food the average family tosses every year.
- Clip coupons and combine them with sales to trim your grocery spending by 20 percent and save up to $1,299 annually.

# Hunt for hidden bargains

Save money at the market by simply walking in the direction grocers don't want you to walk. Stores usually put staples like meat and dairy in the back, forcing you to walk through aisle after aisle of tempting foods in order to get there.

Don't let them tempt you. When you arrive, head straight to the back of the store, rather than walking around the perimeter the way the store tries to steer you. You'll finish faster and spend less on impulse buys.

That is just one of the ways you can beat supermarkets at their own game. Shop smart in these areas, too.

**Deli versus dairy.** You can find cheaper versions of the same food just a few aisles over. Deli and gourmet cheese costs much more than the same kind of cheese in the dairy section. Compare the cost of nuts in the produce versus the baking aisles, and check salsa prices on the chip aisle versus the condiment aisle.

**Center of the aisle.** Stores put everyday staples, like flour and coffee, near the middle of each aisle. Then they flank the ends with expensive, optional items, hoping you'll pick them up on your way to the necessities.

**Bakery.** Fresh-baked breads and rolls may cost less than commercial, prepackaged ones. Check the bakery, and compare prices there to shelved bread elsewhere.

**Back of the row.** When it comes to food with a short shelf-life, like milk, cold cuts, or cereal, grab them from the back of the shelf. Retailers stock the oldest ones up front.

# Outsmart supermarket spending tricks

You could be missing out on sweet deals every trip you take to the supermarket. Here is how to spot secret savings.

**Check per-unit prices on sales items.** Some stores change the shelf label when an item goes on sale to show the new, lower per-unit price. Other stores don't. That's a problem, because smaller-sized packages on sale may cost less per-unit than jumbo packages at regular price.

Make sure you are truly getting a good deal. Bring a calculator and divide the sale price by quantity (ounces, liters, or other) to figure the per-unit price yourself.

**Avoid eye-level items.** There is a "sweet spot" in supermarket aisles where the best bargains are most likely to hide. Hint – it's not staring you in the face. Shelves at eye level are prime real estate in supermarkets. Stores put more expensive, top-selling items there. Cheaper versions or store brands tend to hide on the shelves above or below this. Do a little looking, and you'll snag bigger discounts.

**Buy bagged produce.** Some vegetables and fruits tend to be cheaper by the bag – like potatoes and apples – than loose by the pound. That is especially true of produce with a long shelf life.

**Don't go by brand.** Go by ingredients, not brand name. For example, any dry pasta made with durham wheat semolina will probably taste good, regardless of its brand.

# Get wise to sneaky sales tactics

Stores try all sorts of cunning tricks to separate you from your money. Don't get duped by these four common ploys.

**10 for $10 buys.** You generally don't have to buy 10 of an item to get the $1-apiece price. Many stores sell one item for $1, unless the sale specifically says otherwise.

**2-for-1 deals.** A two-for-one sale isn't a good deal if you only need one but have to buy two to snag the discount. Some stores will let you buy just one and only charge you half price. Ask about the rules at Customer Service.

**Misleading endcaps.** Those end-of-the-aisle displays can be tricky. One displayed item may be on sale, while the related items around it are not. Chips may be $1 off, for instance, but the salsa and cheese dip next to them probably aren't. Check their prices on the main aisle before filling your cart.

**Discount bins.** The bins may scream "bargain," but the stuff inside isn't always priced for clearance. Grocers may dump items into these bins to get you to buy them.

Safe & Secure

Don't be fooled by flyer tricks. Not everything in a grocery ad is actually on sale. Manufacturers sometimes buy ad space in weekly circulars, which means some featured items aren't a good deal. Check the "sale" price against the regular price in the store before buying.

# Reap rewards for being loyal

Half of stores now offer loyalty cards, including supermarkets and drug stores. Signup is often free, and the savings are real. These loyalty cards typically:

- qualify you for special sales, like buy-one-get-one-free deals and members-only prices, as well as doubled coupons.

- earn you reward points good toward discounts on future purchases.

- snag you discounts and even freebies when you buy in bulk.

- generate coupons at checkout based on your shopping history.

- reward you with extra coupons by mail for items you buy often.

- allow you to save coupons on them electronically from websites like *www.shortcuts.com,* eliminating the hassle of clipping coupons and forgetting to bring them with you.

## When to never buy groceries

Never shop at the end of a long day or when you are hungry. Go early in the day, and you will have more willpower to resist all the tempting sales and samples. If you must go at the end of a long day, at least make a list — even if it only has three items on it.

The old standby advice still applies, too — don't shop while hungry. You'll buy more food on impulse when your stomach influences your decisions. If nothing else, grab a quick snack before you leave for the store.

## Everyday items at deep discounts

You should never buy some items at the grocery store, because you're guaranteed to overpay. Your neighborhood dollar store carries perfectly good household items, snack foods, and more for 40 to 90 percent less. If you normally spend $30 a month on these items in your supermarket, that is a savings of $12 to $27 a month, or $144 to $324 a year.

- Save cash and buy bargain brand cleaning products. They contain the same basic ingredients from one brand to the next.

+ Get your greeting cards, gift wrap, and gift bags on the cheap any time of year. No one will know the difference but you and your bank account.

+ Snag great deals on snack foods, which usually have a long shelf life. You'll often find the same name brands in dollar stores as in grocery stores, but at better prices. Look for food in tightly sealed containers.

+ Shop for off-brand shampoos and hair sprays at discount stores, and spend the extra cash on high-quality conditioner.

+ Save a mint on spatulas and other kitchen gadgets by foregoing the gourmet cooking shops in favor of dollar stores.

## Safe & Secure

Play it safe and don't buy these items at a dollar store. Their poor quality makes them either dangerous or a waste of money.

- **Batteries.** They're usually made from carbon zinc and won't last nearly as long as alkaline batteries.

- **Toothpaste.** An antifreeze ingredient was found in dollar-store toothpaste around the nation in 2007.

- **Holiday lights and other electrical products.** They are so poorly made they may pose serious safety hazards.

- **Kids' toys and jewelry.** These Chinese-made goods are more likely to contain lead.

- **Vitamins.** No-name discount brands may not contain the nutrients they claim or dissolve properly once swallowed.

# Crafty couponing cuts hundreds

"I can't claim to be a coupon master, but I shave at least 20 percent every week off my grocery bill," says coupon-clipping shopper Melanie Dewalt. "Some weeks, I save upward of 40 percent."

Those are no small beans. A two-person family over age 50 typically spends between $101.50 and $124.90 a week on groceries. Trimming just 20 percent from that could put an extra $1,055.60 to $1,298.96 in your pocket in a single year.

+ Peel off on-package coupons. Don't miss this grocery discount. Most people do. As many as 94 percent of coupons on packages never get redeemed. Peel it off as soon as you put the item in your basket. Don't count on the cashier to do it for you.

+ Check empty packages before chucking them. A box of oatmeal may have a coupon printed on the inside, good on your next purchase.

+ Snap up coupons from in-store dispensers. They're free. They're convenient. They're practically begging to be used.

+ Peer under labels. Soup cans may hide coupons on the backs of their labels.

+ Scan your receipt for coupons on the back or at the bottom. Some give sizable discounts if you take a short survey rating your last shopping trip.

+ Pick up a Sunday paper. The coupon circulars inside can more than pay for the cost of the paper.

Coupons can't save you money unless you use them. Stretch your dollars farther with this advice.

**Double up.** Shop at stores that double coupons. They may not double them every day, so ask about the rules at Customer Service.

**Deepen that discount.** Put coupons to work at discount stores for even bigger savings. Walmart and Target both accept manufacturer's coupons.

**Don't count on clubs.** BJ's Wholesale Club takes manufacturer's coupons, but other warehouse clubs don't. Sam's Club and Costco may offer their own coupons at in-store kiosks.

Stacking coupons and combining them with store sales can make some products absolutely free. You can't use two manufacturer's coupons on one item, but many stores let you combine a manufacturer's coupon with a store coupon.

A popular cleaner may cost $4, but you can bring the cost down to $2 by combining a $1-off store coupon with a $1-off manufacturer's coupon. Wait until that cleaner goes on sale at half price, and you'll pay nothing.

BJ's Wholesale Club even lets you use more than one manufacturer's coupon on multipacks of the same item. You may be able to use three Kleenex coupons on a 3-pack bundle of Kleenexes.

Get creative with your shopping. Treat it like a game, and compete with yourself to see how much you can save.

# New ways to discover great deals

Fall back in love with coupons. Companies are getting creative, wooing shoppers in new ways with coupons and fabulous deals on the Internet.

Online coupons are everywhere these days, from supermarket websites like *www.kroger.com* to manufacturers' sites such as *www.kraft.com* and *www.generalmills.com*. Some sites even specialize in finding and sharing coupon deals, like these:

+ *www.coupons.com*

+ *www.smartsource.com*

+ *www.redplum.com*

+ *www.shortcuts.com*

+ *www.coolsavings.com*

+ *www.mygrocerydeals.com*

+ *www.couponmom.com*

All you need to start saving is a computer, a printer, and an Internet connection. Go to each website, browse the "printable" coupons, and click on the ones you want. You can print them directly from the website, then use them at your local store just like regular coupons.

Some sites feature electronic coupons that you can save directly to your store loyalty card. Register your Safeway card name and number at *www.shortcuts.com*, and store coupons on it for the next shopping trip. No wasting paper or ink. Swipe your card at checkout, and the store will automatically apply your coupons.

Sign up at *www.cellfire.com* to search for coupons using your cell phone or computer. Save grocery coupons to your store loyalty card, and have coupons for nongrocery items like movie rentals sent to your cell phone. Simply swipe your store card at checkout or show the cashier the coupon on your cell phone screen to snag the discount.

## Put an end to impulse purchases

Don't blow all the money you save with coupons on items you don't need. Curb the urge to buy on impulse with these three fail-proof tricks.

**Plan your attack.** Write down a week's worth of meal ideas, along with the ingredients you will need, before heading to the store. You'll be less likely to buy things not on the list.

For just a small fee, the online services *www.savingdinner.com* and *www.e-mealz.com* will create a weekly meal plan for you, along with a shopping list. You can even add guidelines, like kosher, gluten-free, or low-fat foods.

**Keep moving.** Those narrow aisles with lots of endcaps are no accident. Grocery aisles are designed to make you slow down and stop. The more often you stop, the more likely you are to see something you want. Do your best to stay in motion, and don't browse when you do stop.

**Shop sparingly.** Make your grocery list thorough enough so you only need to shop once a week. People who make many quick trips tend to spend more on impulse purchases.

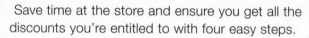

Save time at the store and ensure you get all the discounts you're entitled to with four easy steps.

- Scan the week's grocery ads before you go shopping.
- Make a list of things you need, and note which ones are on sale.
- Match up your coupons with the items on your list and in the sales circular to maximize savings.
- Move each coupon into a special envelope as you put that item in your grocery cart. Then hand over the envelope at checkout.

## Catch expensive errors

Watch the register like a hawk when you go through the checkout line. Mistakes happen, and plenty of people get overcharged. Maybe a sale item rang up at the regular price, or perhaps you were charged twice for one item. Review the receipt before you leave the store.

Head straight to Customer Service if you notice a problem. Some stores give you the item for free if it rings up wrong, so don't shrug it off.

## Try salvage markets for super savings

Salvage grocery stores sell items that are damaged, overstocked, out of season, or near or past their sell-by date at incredible discounts. You could get groceries up to 50 percent off. You'll find them if you know who to ask.

✦ Start with the Customer Service desk at your local supermarket. Ask what they do with their dented, damaged, discontinued, or out-of-date goods. They may dump them in the clearance section of their own store.

- **✦** Ask around. Word may spread about salvage grocers by mouth. Check with neighbors, fellow churchgoers, or people at your community center.

- **✦** Head to the Internet. The website *www.andersoncountrymarket. net/directory* lists salvage grocers around the country. Or try typing phrases like "salvage groceries" or "discount groceries" into the Google search engine at *www.google.com* to find locations near you.

Once you find a store, shop with a little common sense.

**Check sell-by dates.** Crackers, canned goods, and other "shelf-safe" items are fine even past their sell-by date. Meat is not. Fresh juice and dairy are also best before this date.

**Watch for damaged cans.** Minor dings are most likely OK, but severe dents, especially along the seams, are not. Also take a pass on cans that are:

- **✦** leaking or bulging, a possible sign of botulism.

- **✦** badly rusted.

- **✦** punctured or have visible holes in them.

- **✦** crushed or dented so badly that they can't be stacked or opened with a can opener.

**Inspect boxes carefully.** Damaged boxes are often fine, but look for rips or tears that could make the food unsafe. For example, crushed outer cardboard may not matter on a cereal box, but make sure the plastic bag inside is not torn open.

**Know your prices.** Not all goods at a salvage store will be a steal. Keep in mind what you would normally pay at a supermarket for each item.

# Score big deals on bulk buys

Spend 26 to 57 percent less with discount groceries from warehouse clubs like Costco, Sam's Club, and BJ's Wholesale Club, compared to supermarket retail.

These stores can boast huge savings on food and household goods, as well as pharmacy items, eye exams, car tires, and even glasses fittings. Their consistent discounts mean you don't have to work as hard scanning weekly circulars or clipping coupons.

Of course, you may have to buy in bulk to get these low prices, and warehouse clubs generally do not accept manufacturer's coupons. They also charge an annual membership fee.

**Bigger isn't always better.** In theory, the savings are so good that the membership more than pays for itself. That's not necessarily the case, though. Warehouse pricing does not always beat discount stores such as Walmart or Target. Clubs are known for their bulk buys, but smaller versions may cost less per-unit at a discounter.

**Shop the store brand.** Warehouse clubs like Costco offer their own store brands, just like supermarkets. And like supermarkets, a club's store brand may be a better buy. Look for:

✦ Kirkland at Costco.

✦ Member's Mark, Baker's, and Chef's at Sam's Club.

✦ Berkley & Jensen at BJ's Wholesale Club.

**Avoid overspending.** It's easy to do. Harvard researchers say that paying an annual membership fee may actually encourage you to overspend. People tend to assume they are getting a great deal because they're paying a fee. As a result, they spend more, even when prices aren't that good.

**Beware bulk savings.** Buying big quantities can be cheaper, but it can also waste money if food goes bad before your family can finish it. Only buy as much as you know your household can eat.

Take the pain out of paying for a warehouse club membership with these savvy tips.

**Find a free trial.** Clubs occasionally advertise free trial memberships through their websites, including *www.cost co.com, www.samsclub.com,* and *www.bjs.com*. One recent promotion promised a free 60-day membership trial to BJ's Wholesale Club.

**Nab a day pass.** Some clubs offer a one-day pass to people who just want to try them out or don't want an ongoing membership. They may tack on a small fee, say an extra 15 percent of your total purchase, but you may still net a better deal than paying full retail price.

**Upgrade for cash back.** A regular Costco membership runs $50. Upgrade to an Executive membership for $50 more, and you'll earn 2 percent cash back on most purchases. BJ's offers a similar deal.

# Smart substitutes for bottled water

Bottled water is no bargain, but the taste of tap water may be too much to bear. Consider cash-saving compromises that taste good, too.

**TOP DOLLAR:** Drinking only bottled water. You'll spend around $4.99 for a 24-pack of bottled water. Drink three bottles a day, and your bank account will be $229.95 lighter after one year. Renting a water cooler runs even more — around $10 a month, plus the $6.95 or so for each 5-gallon jug delivered to your door. Drink the same amount of water, and you could end up paying $500.51 each year.

**VALUE:** A basic faucet-mounted filter system from Brita or PUR starts around $19. Beyond that, you'll pay 18 cents for each gallon of filtered water you use. That's 78 percent cheaper than bottled water. You could spend as little as $49.28 in one year drinking the same amount of faucet-filtered water, a savings of $180.67 over bottled water and an amazing $451.23 over a rented water cooler.

**WHAT YOU GIVE UP:** The convenience of having chilled, portable bottles of water with you wherever you go. But you also give up the hassle of toting giant packs of water home from the store, or of lifting large, 5-gallon jugs onto a water cooler.

With a faucet or pitcher filter, you will also never run out of fresh water. Just keep an extra filter on hand. You won't sacrifice safety, either. Brita filters remove lead, chlorine, pesticides, herbicides, microorganisms, sediments, and other dangerous compounds. Look for an NSF-certified filter system, and replace the filter according to the manufacturer's guidelines.

## Shopping lists made simple

A grocery list can keep you out of trouble by saving time and money on every shopping trip. These days, though, you have more choices. The Internet can help you make a list fast and find the best prices.

Many supermarkets, including Kroger (*www.kroger.com*), Meijer (*www.meijer.com*), and Publix (*www.publix.com*), now have easy list-making features. You can view the latest sales circular, mark items you want to buy, then add them to an online grocery list and print it out.

The downside? You end up with a different list for each store. The website *www.grocerywiz.com* eliminates this problem. It lets you look at ads from many different stores and make one shopping list. Another site, *www.knotler.com*, allows different people in your family to add to the same list. You can even check your list on a cell phone while at the store, just in case you forget to bring the paper list with you.

Some websites go further, helping you find the best deals. For instance, *www.couponmom.com* offers a free service that matches coupons with store sales. You can search by product, store, or state. The site *www.mygrocerydeals.com* helps you compare product prices at different stores to find the best bargain. It will also filter the products you see based on limits you set, like "low sodium," or food allergies you have.

# Trick yourself into spending less

Trimming your grocery bills doesn't have to be rocket science. You can set yourself up to spend less automatically, without even thinking about it.

+ Listen to fast music on your way to the store or while making your shopping list. Fast-paced music helps you make decisions. Calm, slow music does the opposite, which may lead you to spend more than you planned.

+ Wear uncomfortable shoes while shopping, to discourage yourself from lingering at the supermarket. The more time you spend in a store, the more impulse buys you are likely to make.

# 13 smart uses for old grocery bags

Even grocery bags can save you money. Put them to work, with over a dozen uses for both plastic and paper.

+ Protect carpet from filthy shoes when you work in the yard. Slip a plastic bag over each foot and tie around the ankle before coming into the house. Don't wear while walking on slick surfaces, though. The bags have no traction.

+ Tie plastic bags over your feet when crossing puddles or muddy patches to keep shoes clean and dry. Again, don't wear them when crossing slick surfaces.

+ Cushion delicate items for shipping or moving. Use bunched-up plastic bags in place of packing peanuts.

+ Wrap packages for shipping, and save money on craft paper. Cut the bottom out of a paper grocery bag, and use the paper to wrap packages.

+ Remove wax from tablecloths and carpets. Place a brown bag over the wax, and run a warm iron over it. Wax should begin to seep through. Move to a clean part of the bag, and repeat until the wax is gone.

+ Make cooking cleanup easy. Double-line a bucket or pot with plastic bags. Peel vegetables or skin chicken directly into them. Simply lift out, tie, and toss when done.

+ Ripen peaches, avocados, pears, apples, and tomatoes faster by leaving them in a brown paper bag at room temperature.

+ Stop scraping snow and ice off car windshields. Cut open a large paper bag, spread across the windshield, and pin it beneath the wipers. In the morning, peel the bag away and go.

+ Treat chapped hands. Rub hands with petroleum jelly, then stick them inside plastic bags for 15 minutes.

+ Bulk up valances. Stuff them with plastic grocery bags for extra pouf.

+ Line small wastebaskets with either plastic or paper bags, and save on trash bags.

+ Keep a stash of plastic bags in your suitcase. Stow dirty clothes in them while traveling to keep clean clothes separate.

+ Pack work lunches in paper or plastic grocery bags instead of buying brown lunch sacks at the store.

## CASH SAVER

Clean out the refrigerator once a week, and make an effort to eat, cook, or freeze anything worth saving. Want bigger savings? Skip going to the store every few months, and shop your pantry, instead. Spend one week making meals only out of what you have in your freezer and pantry. You'll use up food you have already paid for, eat things you forgot about before they go bad, and save a whole week's worth of grocery money several times a year.

# 10 terrific money-saving cooking tips

Some things grocers just don't want you to know, like how to eat better while spending less at their stores. Slash your grocery bills with these 10 easy tips.

+ Trim back on meat. It's one of the most expensive parts of any meal. A diet rich in vegetables, fruits, and grains can cost 20 percent less than a meat-centered diet.

+ Stretch inexpensive cuts of meat further by putting them in casseroles and stews. Combine the meat with low-cost peas, beans, lentils, and seasonal vegetables to add bulk, flavor, and nutrients.

+ Think beans. They're an excellent substitute for meat in meals, thanks to their high protein content. Plus, they cost cents per serving.

+ Try brown rice. This whole grain is healthy, cheap, and versatile. Cook one batch, and use it as a base for several different meals.

+ Buy deli-sliced lunch meat for 60 percent to 80 percent less. Stores charge a premium for per-pound, freshly sliced deli meat. Purchase a sealed chunk of cooked meat from the meat department instead, and have it sliced for free at the deli counter.

+ Save gray meat. The plastic used to wrap meat lets some air through, making meat turn red. The center of the meat may stay gray because air can't reach it. It's still fine to eat. If meat is gray or brown throughout, however, it may be starting to spoil.

+ Ignore convenience foods. You pay a premium for someone else to chop the broccoli, shred the cheese, and shuck the corn.

+ Don't toss stale bread. Freeze it and use it to make French toast and seasoned bread crumbs.

+ Make your own fancy cereal. Buy a basic, high-fiber cereal, and dress it up yourself with sliced fruit and nuts.

+ Skip oatmeal in single-serving packets. Buy a carton of oatmeal, and season it yourself with cinnamon, raisins, and walnuts.

# Easy technique turns tough meat tender

Meat may be the most expensive part of daily meals. You don't have to go vegetarian just to watch your budget, though. You can transform cheap cuts of meat into tender, tasty morsels with a few cooking techniques.

The USDA grades red meat cuts into three main categories – Prime, Choice, and Select. Prime beef has the most fat marbling, making it the most tender, flavorful, and expensive. Select, on the other hand, is the leanest and least expensive. It has little fat marbling, so it tends to be tougher and less flavorful – unless you know how to cook it.

Buy a cut of select beef, and soften it by either marinading or braising it. To braise meat, first brown it to add flavor. Then cook it with a little liquid on low heat in a closed container, like a slow cooker, pot with a tight-fitting lid, covered casserole dish, or pan covered in aluminum foil. The goal is to trap both heat and moisture.

Enhance the meat's natural flavor by adding tomato paste or salt pork while cooking. Even better, try anchovies. They're top-notch at boosting beefy flavor. Anchovies contain glutamate and inosinate, two compounds known to heighten the taste of beef up to 15-fold.

# Fight spoilage with these storage secrets

Experts say a family of four throws out $590 worth of food each year. Slash that number with tricks to lengthen the life of your perishables.

**Milk.** Nearly double a milk carton's "shelf life" in your fridge with these sneaky little secrets.

+ Keep it cold. Refrigerate milk at or below 40 degrees.

+ Never pour unused milk back into the container.

+ Add a pinch of salt or a teaspoon of baking soda when milk nears its expiration date to get a few more good days out of it. Paul Stevens adds salt when he first opens the carton. "One gallon was still good two weeks after the sell-by date when I finished it off."

**Berries.** These delicate fruits go bad fast. If you don't plan to eat them right away, wash them in a solution of one part white vinegar and three parts water. This kills the bacteria behind rot. Dry as usual, and store in a sealable container lined with paper towels to absorb extra moisture.

**Lemons.** Prevent hardening and preserve their moisture by storing them in a sealable bag inside the refrigerator.

**Green beans.** Don't snap off the ends before storing. Instead, keep unwashed green beans in a sealed bag in the refrigerator.

**Onions.** Keep these in a dark, well-ventilated area, but do not refrigerate. And store them away from potatoes. The spuds speed up spoilage.

**Potatoes.** Moisture makes them sprout, so don't stick them in the refrigerator. Find another cool, dark place to put them.

**Mushrooms.** Put unwashed mushrooms inside a brown paper bag. The plastic they usually come wrapped in traps moisture and makes them spoil faster.

**Beets.** Cut off the green tops, then refrigerate the roots. Wash the tops and use in a salad or cook them as a side.

## Kitchen gadget keeps food fresher

Vacuum sealers save more than food. They save money, too. This "high-class" kitchen appliance pays for itself almost immediately, then keeps saving you money every week.

Researchers at the University of Arizona collected people's grocery receipts and then dug through their garbage to figure out how much food they threw away. The verdict – the average American family of four tosses nearly $600 worth of meat, fruits, vegetables, and grains each year.

Vacuum food sealers can cut that amount down to size. They help prevent spoilage by sucking the air out of plastic packages. This slows the growth of mold and bacteria and prevents freezer burn. Sealers could save you money two ways – by helping you throw away less food and by enabling you to buy in bulk, without worrying the food will go bad before you can eat it. Break large packages of perishables into smaller portions, then vacuum seal and freeze or refrigerate them.

These machines range from cheap ($20) to expensive ($400 and up). Your best bet may be a mid-range unit for $60 to $100. Also consider the cost of the special bags or plastic sheets the sealer uses. The cheapest unit may not use the cheapest plastic.

Handheld models tend to cost less, but they may not seal food as tightly. Countertop units may seal better, but you have to push down firmly on some machines. Look for a model that uses the thickest plastic sheets or bags if you plan to freeze a lot of food. The thicker the plastic, the better it protects against freezer burn.

**Freebie Frenzie**

Drugstores offer blaring deals on everyday items like shampoo, coffee, and toothpaste — sometimes better than grocery stores. Combine sales with coupons, rebates, and rewards, and you can walk out with free products.

- At Walgreens, certain items earn you register rewards, which you can use like cash toward your next purchase.
- The free CVS ExtraCare loyalty card gets you the sale price on advertised items and earns you 2 percent in store credit on each purchase.
- RiteAid's wellness+ card earns you UP+ rewards on certain items, used like cash for your next purchase. It also enables you to claim store rebates, mailed once a month, for certain items.

# Eat healthy for less

Good nutrition doesn't have to cost a fortune. The Affordable Nutrition Index ranked 300 common foods based on how nutritious they were and how much they cost. Those with the most nutrients for the least money ranked highest. These 16 foods grabbed the top spots.

- ✦ vegetable soups, including Campbell's line of Healthy Request vegetable soups, certified by the American Heart Association, as well as its lower-sodium tomato soup

- ✦ carrots, sweet potatoes, broccoli, oranges, and bananas

- ✦ peas, string beans, squash, lettuce, grapes, and apples

- ✦ raspberries, blackberries, strawberries, and nectarines

## Top-tasting coffee for half the cost

The best coffees are not the most expensive. Forget paying $14 per pound for gourmet coffee. At $6 per pound, Eight O'Clock Coffee's 100% Colombian blend proves that less is more. It easily won a recent Consumer Reports taste test. The group estimates that drinking an inexpensive, top-tasting brand like this could save you $70 or more each year.

Kenneth Davids, author of three books on coffee and editor of the website *www.coffeereview.com*, suggests looking for a coffee that says "100% Colombian" on the label. "That's going to be much better than the standard brands, which are full of robusto coffee," he says.

If you don't want to pay the high price of gourmet coffee — yet you enjoy a darker roast — try one labeled "para el gusto Latino," or "for the Latin taste." The Italian brand Medaglia d'Oro is a great inexpensive option, available at most grocery stores. For the most flavor, buy whole-bean coffee and grind it fresh daily at home.

## Get safer produce without the high price

Organic fruits and vegetables aren't treated with pesticides like regular produce, and you generally pay a higher price for that safety. Fortunately, you may be able to get the same effect without breaking the bank.

**TOP DOLLAR:** Organic produce typically costs 17 to 62 percent more than conventionally grown fruits and vegetables. You'll pay around 32 percent more for organic apples and 28 percent more for organic bananas. In all, your produce budget could rise by one-third or more if you switched to all organics.

**VALUE:** Make regular produce safer by washing away pesticides for just a few pennies. Skip fancy produce washes like FIT. Researchers with the Connecticut Agricultural Experiment Station found that a combination of friction and water does the job fine. Rubbing food for one minute under running water removed most pesticides from strawberries, lettuces, and tomatoes — better than dish soap or fruit and vegetable washes.

Take cleaning a step further by killing germs. Rinse produce with a solution of 10 percent vinegar and water. This killed roughly 90 percent of bacteria and 95 percent of viruses in one study, including the germs E. coli, Salmonella, and poliovirus. Simply washing fruit in warm water for two minutes will cut germs up to 90 percent.

**WHAT YOU GIVE UP:** The convenience of eating fresh fruits and vegetables straight out of the bag, the time it takes to wash them, and the knowledge that you are supporting organic farming methods.

## Wholesome food for a whole lot less

Save on organic goods the same way you do other groceries. A little savvy shopping can make these items a staple in your kitchen instead of a rare luxury.

**Join a club.** Community supported agriculture programs (CSAs) deliver fresh food directly from the farmers who grow it. Prices are competitive — you can buy a box of farm-fresh organic produce for as little as $25 a week. What you get varies by season and by farm.

Find a CSA near you with the website *www.localharvest.org*, or check with farmers at your local farmers market to see if they participate in a CSA program.

**Go local.** Unlike CSAs, the farmers market lets you pick and choose only the foods you want. Street vendors and local resellers may offer organic bargains, too.

**Dig for deep discounts.** Check the clearance carts in your regular supermarket. Soup, beverages, and other nonperishable organic groceries sometimes turn up there alongside other clearance items.

**Use your coupons.** Check weekly circulars for coupons on organic items like eggs, milk, and soup. Or get coupons directly from a manufacturer's website, such as *www.organicvalley.coop* or *www.seventhgeneration.com*, or a coupon aggregator like *www.mambosprouts.com*.

**Shop store brands.** Retail grocers are catching the wave with their own lines of lower-priced organic products. Publix carries the Greenwise Market line, while Kroger features Private Selection Organics, a branch of their Private Selections line.

**Buy in bulk.** Some warehouse clubs give better-than-average deals on organic as well as regular goods. Go in with a friend on bulk bags and packages.

Some foods are covered in more pesticides than others. Conventionally grown apples, for example, tend to have more pesticides on them than mangos. To save money, buy the low-pesticide regular produce and only splurge for the organic versions of the serious offenders.

**The dirty dozen.** According to the nonprofit Environmental Working Group, people who eat the 12 most-contaminated fruits and vegetables below take in an average of 10 different pesticides a day.

| | |
|---|---|
| celery | bell peppers |
| peaches | spinach |
| strawberries | cherries |
| apples | kale/collard greens |
| blueberries | potatoes |
| nectarines | imported grapes |

**The clean 15.** People who eat these 15 least-contaminated fruits and vegetables consume fewer than two pesticides per day.

| | |
|---|---|
| onions | cabbage |
| avocados | eggplant |
| sweet corn | cantaloupe |
| pineapple | watermelon |
| mangos | grapefruit |
| sweet peas | sweet potatoes |
| asparagus | honeydew melon |
| kiwi | |

# Why organic milk lasts longer

Organic milk can last a month or more, while nonorganic milk may only last a week. What gives?

Regular milk gets pasteurized, which kills some — but not all — bacteria. Organic milk undergoes ultrahigh temperature (UHT) processing. This kills all bacteria, giving the milk a longer shelf life. Some regular milk undergoes UHT processing, too, such as Parmalat. UHT milk may taste a little sweeter, since the high heat can caramelize some of its natural sugar.

Consider switching to organic milk if the regular stuff routinely sours before you finish it. Organic costs more, but you may save money by buying and throwing out less.

## DEEP DISCOUNT

Pet food is one area you can save money when it comes to groceries. Pricier doesn't necessarily mean better. Premium pet foods can cost three to four times more than grocery store brands, but they all have similar ingredients since they have to meet certain nutritional requirements.

Choose pet food labeled "complete and balanced" to be sure it follows guidelines set by the Association of American Feed Control Officials, a regulatory group. And for higher quality no matter what the price, look for protein as the first ingredient on the label rather than grains, vegetables, or byproducts.

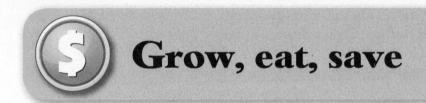

# Grow, eat, save

## Fresh produce at half the price

One in three households grows at least some of their own vegetables, fruit, berries, and herbs. Half do it specifically to save money.

They're on to something. Most gardens are small — less than 100 square feet, or 5 feet by 20 feet. Despite this modest size, home-growers still come out on top. They invest an average of $53 a year in their vegetable gardens. Yet a 100-square-foot garden can yield 50 lbs of produce worth $100 at in-season store prices.

It's like paying half price for produce. Plus, you know where it comes from and what pesticides have or haven't been used. Give gardening a try, and see how much you save.

## Grow more in less space

You can have all the garden vegetables you want in half the space. Follow these 10 tips for a cheap and easy container garden.

**Consider container size.** A container should generally be at least two-thirds as deep as the full-grown plant is tall, and at least as wide as the leaf spread.

**Pick the right plants.** Stick with vegetables that take up little space, like carrots, radishes, and lettuce. Even better, plant crops that bear fruit over a long period of time, such as tomatoes and peppers.

**Don't go too small.** Some gardening experts warn against dwarf or miniature varieties, saying they don't tend to produce as well as standard varieties.

**Look at lighting.** The amount of sunlight you get may determine what you can plant. Root crops and leaf crops can usually tolerate partial shade. Fruiting vegetables need at least five hours, preferably eight to 10 hours, of full, direct sun each day.

**Ditch bad dirt.** Don't fill plant pots with dirt from your yard. Sure, it's free, but most yard dirt is too heavy, coarse, and infertile for potted plant growth. It also tends to pack down in containers, choking the roots.

**Invest in potting soil.** It's lightweight and free of insects, diseases, and weed seeds. Avoid soilless mixes such as peat-lite, however. They contain few nutrients and are so lightweight they may not give enough support to plant roots.

**Double up.** Grow different vegetables together in one container to make the most of limited space. Plant lettuce, spinach, and herbs between tomatoes, peppers, and cabbage. Use tall, trellised plants like cucumbers to shade cool-weather greens underneath.

**Make adjustments.** Don't let shade end your gardening dreams. Boost the light your vegetables receive by placing reflective materials around them. Lay out sheets of aluminum foil, or paint surrounding surfaces white.

**Fight wilting.** Punishing heat can dry soil fast. If your plants wilt every day, consider grouping the containers together, so the foliage creates shade to cool the soil. Also, put pots on pallets or other structures to get them off a hot concrete patio.

**Grow fresh year round.** Lettuce, radishes, and small-fruiting tomatoes and peppers do especially well indoors. So do parsley, chives, cilantro, and thyme. Place pots in a bright, sunny, south-facing window during winter. For fruiting vegetables, supplement weak winter light with a fluorescent fixture.

# How to get a new garden for free

Forget about costly fertilizers and expensive seeds. Start your garden for free. It's so surprisingly easy anyone can do it.

**Look for free fertilizer, compost, and mulch.** One of the best fertilizers is absolutely free. Keep mowing your lawn, and you will never run out of it. Grass clippings break down fast, putting much-needed nitrogen and organic matter back into soil. They also reduce the need for other fertilizers.

- Spread grass mulch around plants in a 1-inch deep layer to discourage weeds, keep soil from drying out, and prevent erosion around plants.

- Work clippings directly into garden soil to put even more nitrogen back into the earth. Work 2 to 3 inches of cut grass into the top 6 to 12 inches of dirt. Don't use clippings loaded with weed seeds or mature grass, though. These could sprout later.

- Add grass to your compost heap, then turn the pile within 24 hours. Grass contributes both moisture and nitrogen and helps the pile heat up, destroying more weed seeds and speeding up the composting process. Clippings should not make up more than half the pile by volume.

Don't spread or mulch clippings from grass treated with weed killers. Compost them first. Most lawn herbicides break down quickly in the compost pile, with the exception of dicamba (Banvel).

Grass isn't your only free fertilizer. Call your city or county government and ask if they offer free compost to residents. It could save you the trouble of making your own.

**Stock up on free seeds.** Stop paying for common vegetable, herb, and fruit seeds. You can easily get them for free.

- Join a seed swap. Local gardening clubs sometimes hold seasonal seed-swapping events, sharing surplus seeds and growing tips. Or start your own through your church or community center. If you have access to a computer, join an online swap group and mail seeds to one another. You can find one at *www.seedswaps.com*.

- Save your own. For tomatoes, simply scoop out seeds and gently rinse away the jelly-like goo surrounding them. Spread them in a single layer on a paper towel to dry for several days.

To learn how to salvage other seeds, order a copy of *Basic Seed Saving* by Bill McDorman for $5.95. Write to Seeds Trust, P.O. Box 596, Cornville, Arizona, 86325, or call 928-649-3315. Computer users can get free instructions from the International Seed Saving Institute's website at *www.seedsave.org*.

Plants aren't picky, unlike people. They will grow in almost anything that holds soil. Don't blow your gardening budget on fancy planters. Make your own simple planter for free.

Old bread bags work great. Double them up for added strength, or use a gallon-size zippered plastic bag. Fill with potting mix to within a few inches from the top. Seal the bag and staple it shut. Lay the bag on its side in a waterproof tray, like an old baking sheet. Punch a few holes in the underside of the bag for drainage. Carefully slit it open across the top, insert your seeds or seedlings, and water thoroughly.

Lettuce, spinach, and radishes do best in these small self-made containers. For bigger plants like potatoes, pick up free feed bags, bulk food bags, or burlap bags at feed stores or farms that raise livestock.

# Repel pests for less

Who needs bug spray when you have sage, garlic, onions, and marigolds? Companion planting can protect crops against pests cheaply and naturally. While it's not an exact science, some gardeners swear by certain combinations.

**Kill pests naturally.** The roots of French and African marigolds contain a substance that kills nematodes. Plant a thick layer of them for one season before sowing crops, or plant them between rows of crops. They're especially good at guarding tomatoes.

**Set traps.** Put in decoy plants to draw bugs away from crops. Radishes planted among squash and cucumbers help catch cucumber beetles, while radishes near cole crops such as cauliflower, broccoli, Brussels sprouts, and kale attract flea beetles. Nasturtiums among cabbages catch the attention of caterpillars. You can kill the pests for good by selectively spraying the decoy plants once they have drawn bugs.

**Build up good bugs.** Not all insects are bad. Predatory wasps, spiders, ground beetles, lady bugs, pirate bugs, and the praying mantis attack common garden pests. Encourage the good ones to take up residence. Intersperse dill, parsley, carrots, coriander, angelica, and parsnip in your garden. Dill, in particular, attracts aphid-eating hoverflies and predatory wasps. Leave some parsley, carrots, and celery in the ground over winter. Next season, their blooms will bring in the good bugs.

**Mask your plants.** Some herbs and flowers give off strong odors that confuse pests or drive them away. Sage, carrots, and plants in the cabbage family all produce odors that ward off each other's pests. French marigolds drive greenfly and blackfly away from tomatoes. Here are a few more clever combinations.

| Plant this | To repel this |
|---|---|
| garlic at the base of peach trees | boring bugs |
| basil among tomatoes | tomato hornworms |
| nasturtiums near squash | squash bugs |
| tomatoes among asparagus | asparagus beetles |
| marigolds, mint, thyme, or chamomile | cabbage moths |
| carrots with leeks or onions | onion flies, leek moth, carrot flies |

# Save more with smart choices

Some vegetables and fruits are so cheap you're better off buying them at the store. Brussels sprouts, broccoli, green cabbage, cauliflower, and sweet potatoes are among the bargains you'll find at your local grocer's. Others are so expensive it may pay to grow them yourself. Here are some you may want to consider.

+ apples
+ blackberries
+ carrots
+ cherry tomatoes
+ collards

+ green peas
+ mustard greens
+ okra
+ raspberries
+ spinach

+ turnip greens
+ zucchini
+ kale

# Secret to free produce all year long

You pay a premium in stores for produce during its off-season. Freeze the extra from your garden for year-round food at a price that can't be beat.

**Start by blanching.** Nearly all vegetables must be blanched – scalded with boiling water or steam – before freezing. Blanching halts the work of enzymes in food, preserving flavor, color, texture, and vitamins. Begin by boiling one gallon of water per pound of vegetables. Lower a wire basket of vegetables into fast-boiling water, then cover with a lid. Start marking time as soon as the water returns to a boil.

Beets, pumpkin, winter squash, and sweet potatoes should be cooked rather than blanched before freezing. For the rest, follow the guidelines below for water blanching.

**Cool them quickly.** Remove the veggies and plunge them into cold water, below 60 degrees. Let them cool for roughly the time they took to blanch. Change the water or add ice as needed to keep it cold. Drain them thoroughly before freezing.

| Food | Blanching time (minutes) |
|---|---|
| Snap, green, or wax beans | 3 |
| Lima, butter, or pinto beans | 2 to 4, depending on bean size |
| Broccoli | 3 |
| Carrots, whole, small | 5 |
| Cauliflower flowerets | 3 |
| Corn on the cob | 7 to 11, depending on ear size |
| Eggplant | 4 |
| Collard greens | 3 |
| All other greens | 2 |
| Okra | 3 to 4 |
| Blackeye and other field peas | 2 |
| Green peas | 1 1/2 |
| Sweet pepper | halves, 3; strips, 2 |
| Summer squash | 3 |

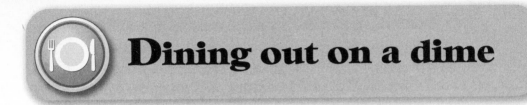

# Dining out on a dime

## Uncover hidden deals for seniors

Don't be shy about asking for a senior discount because you will be blown away by how many places offer them. Find out why businesses do not advertise their senior discounts and how you can reap the rewards of your age.

Businesses want to honor older citizens, but some 49-year-olds would be insulted if they were offered a discount that was obviously for people over 60. That is why businesses often do not advertise their senior discounts or other senior benefits. But they usually tell you if you know when and how to ask for your senior discount.

Your best bet is to call ahead and ask about senior discounts before you visit a restaurant. AARP members should also ask about AARP discounts and deals. If the restaurant does not offer a discount, ask if it has any other senior benefits such as a reduced-price senior menu, freebies, a designated night for senior deals, or early-bird discounts. Don't forget to find out the age requirement.

But senior discounts are not just available at restaurants. You may also find them at movies, pharmacies, department stores, eyeglass stores, toy stores, banks, insurers, supermarkets, and more. If you use the World Wide Web, visit *www.seniordiscounts.com* to find articles and information about senior discounts. Otherwise, be sure to ask for your discount wherever you go. Just keep these tips in mind.

+ Some locations of a chain restaurant or store may not offer a senior discount.

+ Comparison shop for travel bargains because the senior discount may not always be the deepest discount available.

Government statistics suggest people over age 65 spend more than $800 on food away from home every year. So even if your senior discount only saves a meager 10 percent at each meal, that may put up to $80 extra in your pocket every year.

# Get deep discounts at your favorite restaurants

Enjoy the bargains that others miss. Dine out for less with these money-saving secrets.

✦ Instead of going out for dinner, go out for lunch or breakfast. At lunch, you often get the same food for less, and breakfast is usually cheaper, too.

✦ Eat an appetizer as your meal.

✦ When portions are too large, ask for a doggie bag, and take half your food home for the next meal.

✦ When you are reading a menu or advertisement, keep an eye out for discounts on smaller portions, buy-one-get-one-free deals, early-bird specials, a weekly discount night, weekday specials, and freebies. Ask your friends and family to keep an eye out for these as well.

✦ Order takeout. Even some mid-priced restaurants now offer curbside service. You can save the cost of a drink, dessert, and maybe more.

✦ Restaurants often give freebies or discounts on birthdays, so be sure to tell your server when it is your special day.

✦ Ask about senior discounts, and clip coupons anywhere you can find them.

✦ Instead of high-markup drinks like tea, soft drinks, or alcoholic beverages, order water with lemon.

+ Take a poll. You may get a freebie, coupon, or discount by participating in a phone, online, or email survey for the restaurant's market research.

+ Join the restaurant's customer club by filling out a paper form or signing up on its website. You will get coupons and notices for discounts, specials, and freebies. For an extra discount or freebie, include your birthday if they ask for it.

+ Buy discount gift cards from websites like *www.restaurant.com* or *www. giftcardgranny.com*. You may get a $50 gift card for at least $20 less.

**Freebie Frenzie**

Keep an eye out for annual freebie days. For example, on National Donut Day, you may find free donut deals at shops like Krispy Kreme or Dunkin Donuts. Call ahead for details. Visit sites like *www.thefreebieblogger.com* to find out about upcoming free offers, or simply ask the servers at your favorite restaurant if they have a free giveaway on a particular day of the year.

## Beware sneaky restaurant tricks

"Would you like fries with that?" is just one way restaurants try to get you to spend more than you planned. But that is just the beginning.

**Be a menu skeptic.** Restaurants have done studies to find out how the design of their menu can tempt you to spend extra money. In fact, menu designers know the first-viewed and most-often-viewed parts of the menu, and that is where they put the expensive dishes. Skim over the entire menu to find the places where the cheaper dishes are hidden.

**Avoid boxes and ignore photos.** Drawing a box around items and their descriptions helps pricey items sell. So does a mouthwatering picture of the dish.

**Evaluate descriptors.** "Hand-breaded rainbow trout with authentic salsa cruda" sounds better than "breaded trout with salsa," but the extra adjectives help a high price tag sound worthwhile. The adjectives are usually accurate, but they may not always indicate a specialty product.

Be on your guard against these menu tricks, and take your server's friendly suggestions with a grain of salt. If you can resist buying an unplanned appetizer and dessert at just one well-known chain restaurant, you could save up to $19.

# Find terrific coupons in surprising spots

Once again, the restaurant coupons in the newspaper are not the ones you need. But you may find what you want if you know where to look.

Start by checking websites like *www.couponmom.com* to find local coupons. You can also try an entertainment book. Students sell these booklets of coupons and discounts as fundraisers. Make sure the book contains enough coupons for restaurants you already use before you buy.

But don't stop there. You may also find coupons at:

- ✦ your supermarket on the back of the sales slip.

- ✦ the phone book.

- ✦ rest stops.

- ✦ welcome centers.

- ✦ travel magazines.

- ✦ your city or state's tourism website.

# Know when to skip the tip

Experts recommend tipping 15 to 20 percent at restaurants, but not always. If you see a tip jar at your favorite deli or coffee shop or if you pick up takeout from a restaurant, tipping is optional. And, of course, always check the menu and your bill to see whether the tip is included.

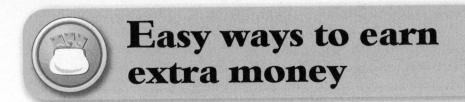

# Easy ways to earn extra money

## 15 ways to make $100 or more a month

Everyone could use a little extra cash. Check out these 15 ways to make $100 or more a month you've never thought of.

+ File papers. Companies may need help filing, making photocopies, and handling other office duties. While they may not offer full-time work, they may hire you as a part-time clerical assistant.

+ Sell on eBay. This auction website makes it easy to turn your surplus stuff into extra cash.

+ Provide editing services. If you live in a college town, editing term papers and other assignments can pay off.

+ Be a handyman. As long as you have the skills and the tools, fixing things can also improve your finances.

+ Deliver papers. The early bird catches more than the worm. Early risers can also make a quick buck with a paper route.

+ Shop professionally. People who are busy may hire you as a professional shopper around the holidays.

+ Teach workshops. Share your expertise with others – whether it's cooking, crafts, or computers – at a local community college or recreation center.

+ Tutor. Helping local students with their studies can help you pay the bills. Check with local high schools for opportunities.

+ Host a party. Home selling parties – where you peddle anything from candles to makeup – can be a social way to supplement your income.

- ✦ **Walk dogs.** If you don't mind scooping poop, you can earn money as a dog walker or pet sitter.

- ✦ **Rent a room in your house.** Whether you take in a tenant or just rent storage space, you can collect a monthly check.

- ✦ **Clean houses.** Tidy up after your neighbors to make a tidy profit. You can also find work cleaning office buildings after hours.

- ✦ **Direct traffic.** Working as a school crossing guard makes a good part-time job.

- ✦ **Sew for dough.** Put your seamstress skills to good use by making alterations to other people's clothing.

- ✦ **Drive.** Use your car as a vehicle for profit by running a carpool or driving service.

**No-Sweat Solution**

Want to find out how to make money by doing practically nothing? Try housesitting. When people go on a vacation or business trip, they may need someone to watch their house. That's where you come in. Just stop in once or twice a day to make sure everything is in order.

Possible duties include bringing in the mail and newspaper, watering the plants, feeding the pets, taking down important messages left on the answering machine, and turning the lights off and on in various rooms to make it seem like the home is occupied. Perhaps you can even stay at an upscale house while the owners are away. It could be a chance to live in luxury and get paid for it.

## Focus on finding extra cash

Your opinion may actually be worth something. Be part of a focus group, and you can make $15 to $100 an hour.

Businesses use focus groups to help improve their products, customer service, or manufacturing. At these sessions, which typically last three to five hours, you'll be asked for your opinions. The company gets some valuable feedback and, just by being honest, you get an honest day's pay.

To find a focus group, check your local newspaper's classified ads. You can also use these online resources to find focus group opportunities near you.

- *www.delve.com*

- *www.findfocusgroups.com*

- *www.marketsdirectory.com*. Click on Focus Group Facilities, then click on your state.

- *www.greenbook.org*

Another option is to search for "focus groups" in your favorite search engine.

## Track down missing money

Eight billion dollars of forgotten money is floating around out there. Is any of it yours? Your state could take your money if you don't claim it. Find out how.

Believe it or not, unclaimed funds totaling billions of dollars are just waiting to be reunited with their rightful owners. By law, financial institutions must try to track down the owners or heirs of these assets. But if they can't, the money may get turned over to the state government.

Unclaimed assets include forgotten bank accounts, insurance policies, stocks, bonds, mutual funds, contents of safe deposit boxes, trust funds, escrow accounts, and utility security deposits, as well as uncashed paychecks and dividends. Unredeemed savings bonds, unclaimed IRS refunds, and undelivered or uncashed retirement and Social Security checks also contribute to the billions of dollars in missing money.

Complications that may lead to lost money include a name change after a marriage or divorce, an unreported change of address or expired postal forwarding order, incomplete or illegible records, and an untimely death.

Find out if you or family members have any money coming to you. These online resources can help you locate unclaimed assets:

- ✦ MissingMoney.com at *www.missingmoney.com*

- ✦ National Association of Unclaimed Property Administrators at *www.unclaimed.org*

You can also call your state treasurer's office. Don't forget to search every state where you've lived. Check maiden names and those of deceased family members.

Beware of private services that want upfront fees to search or stake a claim on your behalf. These companies could be legitimate, but you may have to pay a large fee. That means less money for you — and the last thing you need is more lost money.

# Harness the selling power of eBay

Discover the hidden source of instant cash that's right under your nose. Your old stuff could be making you money. Whether you have old jewelry, antique furniture, electronics, model railroads, comic books, or sports equipment, you can turn your attic treasure into cash.

The best way to sell your collectibles to get top dollar is to make them available on eBay, the auction website that lets you reach countless potential buyers from all over the world. No matter what you have to sell, someone is bound to want it. Don't even throw away your old LP record albums — even if the record is in less than pristine condition, sometimes you can make money just from their covers.

Go to *www.ebay.com* and browse to get a feel for the site. Then discover the top 10 tips and tricks that savvy sellers use every day.

- ✦ Research. Find out what your item is worth and what similar items have sold for.

- ✦ Hook potential buyers with an attention-grabbing title.

- ✦ Write a good description of your item. Include lots of detail. Specify if the item is new or used.

- Use photos. Sometimes, a picture really is worth a thousand words.

- Be up front about the terms of the sale, including your return policy, shipping options, and accepted methods of payment.

- Price it right. Start the bidding with a low number. The price will climb.

- Consider extras, like a boldface title, that may boost your chances of selling your item. Keep in mind you'll have to pay extra for these upgrades.

- Build trust. You may want to buy and sell a few small things to build up positive feedback from other users before trying to sell something truly valuable.

- Respond quickly to any questions from potential buyers.

- Take advantage of convenient shipping options. You can get free shipping supplies from the U.S. Postal Service. You can even print your postage from home, saving you a trip to the post office.

## Cash in at consignment shops

They say one man's trash is another man's treasure. So it's no surprise that you can get big bucks for "junk." That's right — even the stuff piled up in your basement, attic, shed, or garage could be making you dough. Just take your unwanted stuff to a consignment shop or pawnshop.

Consignment shops act as a middleman. They display and sell used merchandise for individual sellers in return for a percentage, generally 50 to 60 percent of what they sell your item for.

You can also go to pawnshops for quick cash. At a pawnshop, you use your item as collateral for a small loan. Either repay the loan, with interest, in a certain amount of time or forfeit the item. Or you can just sell the item outright.

Secondhand and vintage stores, which pay cash on the spot, are other good options for selling your unwanted things.

# Boost your income as a consultant

You may be nearing retirement age, but all the knowledge, skills, and experience you've gained from years on the job can still come in handy. Train for post-retirement careers without going to college. Earn $50 an hour or more as a consultant.

As a consultant, you provide clients with advice, solutions, recommendations, or specialized work. You usually get paid by the hour, day, project or on commission. You work as an independent contractor — not an employee.

While consulting can be a lucrative job that lets you choose your own projects and set your own hours, it does not provide a steady paycheck or common workplace perks, like health benefits.

Depending on your field, you may need a special license or certification. Insurance, real estate, financial planning, and accounting are some areas where this applies. But in many cases, all you need is a client who needs your help.

Here are some steps to take when setting up a consulting business.

+ Collect contacts. Nurture relationships with current colleagues, suppliers, or competitors. They may come in handy. Don't forget family and friends when building a contact list.

+ Stake out your area of expertise. Note your strengths, then target your ideal clients.

+ Craft sales pitches. Talking points will help you sell your skills. But listening to clients and their needs is even more important. Remember, you're there to help them.

+ Set your price. Develop a pricing structure so you know what to charge, depending on the project. Be ready with proposals, contracts, and timelines, too.

The more you learn, the more you earn. Boosting your knowledge and skills is a good way to boost your paycheck. But higher education comes with a high price tag. Luckily, the Internet gives you access to free college courses and lectures from top universities and professors.

Go to these websites for informative and entertaining online classes.

- academicearth.org
- lecturefox.com
- www.free-ed.net

Another good resource is Open Courseware Consortium, a network of major colleges and universities from around the world. Go to *www.ocwconsortium.org* for free lecture notes, exams, and videos.

You won't end up with a degree from Stanford, Yale, Princeton, or MIT, but you can still gain valuable knowledge — at no cost.

## Easy ways to save money

Making extra money is great — but it doesn't do you much good if you just spend it. Making more plus spending less is the recipe for financial success. Here are the top 15 easiest things you can do to save money in hard times.

✦ Set something aside. Save some money — even just $5 — from each paycheck. It will add up.

✦ Stick to a sensible budget. Track your spending, then figure out better ways to divvy up your dollars.

✦ Dine out less often. Home cooking costs less — and often tastes better — than pricey restaurant fare.

✦ Save your pocket change and put it in a high-yield savings account. You could even do the same with dollar bills.

✦ Address your spending weaknesses. Whether you tend to splurge on shoes, clothes, books, or knickknacks, find ways to cut back.

- Pull the plug on cable and DVD rentals and seek out free entertainment.

- Change your stance on shopping. Instead of shopping for fun or to pass the time, go to the store only when you need something.

- Rarely pay retail. Do your best to avoid paying full retail price for anything. Take advantage of sales, coupons, and your negotiating skills to pay less whenever possible.

- Sell stuff you no longer need or want. As a bonus, you also clear your house of clutter.

- Pay less at the pump. Combine trips, plan your route, slow down, and keep up with your vehicle's maintenance. You'll end up saving on gas.

- Curb coffee and bottled water purchases. Buy a reusable bottle and carry your own instead.

- Buy fewer books, compact discs, and DVDs. Simply borrow them from the library.

- Cancel magazine and newspaper subscriptions. Read them at the library or online.

- Use cloth napkins and towels instead of constantly buying and discarding paper products.

- Waste not, want not. Pay attention to expiration dates so nothing goes bad before you can use it. And make sure to eat your leftovers.

## Four surprising sources of get-it-now cash

Sometimes you need money — and need it right away. When times are tough and money is scarce, what can you do? Here are some ways to get much-needed cash when you have nowhere else to turn.

**Peer-to-peer lending.** Borrow from family, friends, or acquaintances. You can even borrow from strangers, thanks to websites that facilitate peer-to-peer lending, like Lending Club at *www.lendingclub.com* or Prosper at *www.prosper.com*. You'll get lower interest rates and more flexible terms than you would from a bank.

But just because these loans don't come from a financial institution doesn't mean you can blow them off. They're still legitimate loans, and you should take them seriously. Fail to repay them, and you could still be reported to credit bureaus. You may also strain friendships and put a damper on family get-togethers.

**401(k) loan.** Borrow money from yourself by dipping into your 401(k) account. Your employer may let you access up to 50 percent of your vested balance or up to $50,000 – whichever is less. Keep in mind that you need to repay the loan – with interest – usually within five years. And, by taking money from your 401(k), you're taking away from your future retirement savings.

**Emergency and worthy cause use of IRA.** If you need to pull money from your IRA, you can avoid the 10 percent penalty for early withdrawal in some situations. Taking out money to handle an emergency, such as medical expenses that exceed 7.5 percent of your adjusted gross income, is OK. You can also put your money toward a worthy cause, such as a college education for yourself or a close family member or a down payment on your first home. Check IRS guidelines before dipping into your IRA.

**Life settlement.** It may sound ghoulish, but you can sell your life insurance policy to investors in a transaction called a life settlement. You must be at least 65 years old and have a whole-life policy with a face value of at least $250,000. You'll receive more than the policy's cash surrender value, but less than the death benefit. The older and sicker you are, the more money you'll get. Investors take over the premiums for as long as you live, then collect the death benefit when you die.

Think of this only as a last resort. It may seem like a good idea if your premiums are high and you really need the money for other expenses, like medical bills. But, by selling your policy, you're leaving your former beneficiaries high and dry.

Looking for work can be a full-time job. Mailing out resumes, responding to ads in newspapers, calling companies, and networking for leads can be exhausting. And discouraging. Fortunately, you can cut to the chase by going online.

Tens of thousands of jobs are available — and one website puts you on the road to employment. Just go to *www.usajobs.gov* to search for federal jobs near you. At this government website, you can refine your search by salary, occupation, agency, and work schedule. You'll find openings in medicine, accounting, maintenance, security, forestry, social work, sciences, human resources, and more.

## Helpful hints for a home business

Danielle White, a stay-at-home mother of three from Fairport, N.Y., recently combined her baking talents, time-management skills, and peculiar love of cleaning and organizing into a successful home business. She calls it "Every Woman Needs a Wife," and its focus is simply on making other people's lives easier.

"My goal is to help busy individuals, families, and both large and small businesses manage their lives by taking care of everyday tasks and errands, as well as out-of-the-ordinary tasks," White says.

Her services include organizing and cleaning, planning parties and events, preparing gourmet appetizers and desserts, and shopping for gifts. For some clients, she puts up and takes down Christmas decorations. For others, she might wait at their home for a furniture delivery or a service call from the cable company.

"The feedback I am getting is great, and my business is actually busier than I can handle right now," White says. "I am thrilled at the fact I can really make this happen."

One challenge has been "figuring out how to price things, especially being married to the accountant who wants everything figured to the penny to make sure what I am doing makes sense financially," White says of her husband, Paul. "My goal is to make a minimum of $20 per hour with what I am doing, and so far it is working."

To make your home business work, too, follow these tips.

**Take advantage of your talents.** Whether it's woodworking, auto repair, graphic design, or cooking, your particular skill can make you money. Find your niche. Then find clients in need of your skills.

**Remember time is money.** Even if you don't have a special talent, your time can be valuable. Use your extra time to run errands for others, walk dogs, baby-sit, or provide in-home elder care.

"I think multi-tasking is my best quality," says White, who deftly balances childcare, laundry, housecleaning, baking, and grocery shopping on a typical day. "My brain doesn't turn off much."

**Start slowly.** Don't expect big bucks as soon as you launch your business. "My advice would be to start on the side. Don't try to do it and make money right away," White says. "Paul is always saying, 'You don't know what you don't know,' and that is so true. Things came up that I didn't expect and didn't think of. I am glad I am easing into this."

Safe & Secure

Working from home can be a fulfilling career choice. But many work-from-home opportunities are nothing more than scams. Beware of any ad that mentions typing, clerical work, data entry, payment processing, repacking, or assembly work. More often than not, it will be a bogus offer. Other popular work-from-home scams include ornament assembly, postcard labeling, rebate processing, envelope stuffing, and medical billing.

Avoid any offer that requires you to pay upfront fees for information. Also stay away from offers that provide few details about how you will earn money or those that rely on high-pressure tactics to make you act quickly. Skip any offer that comes in your email inbox, especially ads that begin with the words "work from home."

Before pursuing any work-from-home offers, ask exactly what the job entails, how you get paid — and by whom, when you can expect your first paycheck, and what is the total cost of the program, including supplies, equipment, and membership fees.

# Common mistakes that can doom your business

A home business can be very rewarding – and profitable. But it can also be disastrous if you fail to take precautions. Make sure to avoid these common mistakes when setting up your home business.

+ Not asking for help. Rugged individualism can be noble, but there's nothing noble about ignoring potentially helpful advice. Pick the brains of others in the business. Work or volunteer for a similar business first, join a trade association, or simply take an experienced businessperson to lunch. Free online resources include the Service Corps of Retired Executives (SCORE) at *www.score.org* and the Small Business Administration at *www.sba.gov*.

+ Not doing enough research. Talk with people who may be future clients to find out what they want in a business. Check out businesses that offer similar products or services to find out what they offer and what they charge. Include both local and out-of-town businesses in your research.

+ Not having enough cash on hand. You should have enough money to cover at least four months of expenses and preferably twice that. Don't underestimate the cost of those expenses, either. Similarly, have an exit strategy in case your business isn't working.

+ Not pricing your product properly. Be like Bob Barker and make sure the price is right. If you set your prices too low, customers may suspect that you're peddling a shoddy product. Aim for prices slightly lower than your competitors, but high enough to make a profit. Or you can charge more and stress how unique or superior your product is.

+ Not having a website. You'll miss out on countless potential customers who search for businesses online.

+ Not spending wisely. Don't blow your savings. Just because you don't pay overhead doesn't mean you have to buy the most expensive equipment.

+ Not having a business plan. Like any business, a home business needs a plan. Consider what happens if you need to expand.

+ Not promoting your company. Take advantage of email newsletters, conferences, industry gatherings, and local Chamber of Commerce events to get the word out.

+ Not separating your home from your office. Designate part of your home as office space. It will help you stay motivated and maintain a client friendly environment.

+ Not obeying the law. Make sure your business doesn't violate any local zoning rules.

## Safe & Secure

Many people often fall for the latest fad diet that promises quick results with little effort. If you're in debt or looking to strike it rich, you run a similar risk of being ripped off. Shell out money for an expert's debt reduction "system," and you'll end up with overpriced CDs or DVDs full of unrealistic advice. Credit card debt relief hotlines often charge high fees and leave you in worse shape than you were before you picked up the phone.

Looking to make some quick money? Beware of free lunch investment seminars. You'll get fed — but you'll also get bombarded by salespeople looking to earn commissions by making misleading claims about investment products. As with losing weight, getting out of debt or making more money is usually a slow, steady process — not a quick, easy gimmick.

## Save on business startup costs

Starting a business always requires some money up front. But how much you spend to get your business up and running doesn't necessarily correspond to how much money you'll make. As always, research any business opportunity to make sure it's legitimate before jumping in.

**TOP DOLLAR:** Invest big money in a retail store, pay a large franchise fee for an established franchise, or put your cash toward marketing a new idea. Besides the big upfront costs, these kinds of businesses also come with big risks — but there's also the chance for big profits.

**VALUE:** Choose an established work-from-home business instead. Host parties or sell items person-to-person. You will still have to pay some startup costs, but the price would be far less than the big-money options. Legitimate franchises, like Avon, Pampered Chef, Party Lite, Simply Fun, Tupperware, Mary Kay, and Amway, are popular choices — but you can sell almost anything this way. For more information on direct selling, go to *www.directselling411.com* or *www.dsa.org*.

**WHAT YOU GIVE UP:** The potential to earn big bucks if you succeed. But you also give up a variety of hassles, including expensive inventory, employees, leased commercial property, and long hours. For less money, you can pursue a safer, less-stressful home business.

# Rent rooms for regular income

Now that your kids have grown up and moved out, your house may be feeling kind of empty — but your pocketbook doesn't have to be. Extra rooms can bring in extra cash. Whether you take in a tenant or just rent out storage space, you can collect a nice monthly check.

**Bring in a boarder.** Nationally, a furnished room yields an average of $400 to $550 a month — even more if it features a private bathroom. Of course, prices vary depending on location.

Need help finding a tenant? Check out the National Shared Housing Resource, a free service that matches homeowners with renters, at *www.nationalsharedhousing.org*. Rent includes utilities, plus kitchen and laundry privileges. You can even reduce the rent in exchange for help with chores, such as gardening or cooking.

Before taking in a tenant, always check references or hire a screening agency. You'll also want to get proof of income and make sure the tenant signs a month-to-month contract.

**Offer spare rooms as storage space.** If you don't want a stranger living in your house, you can always rent spare rooms as storage space. Your garage, attic, basement, and backyard can also come in handy for this purpose.

These online resources can help you list your available storage space.

+ SpareFoot at *www.sparefoot.com*. This site lets you list your space for free, along with the available dates and asking price. When your space is booked, the site gets a one-time transaction fee of $75. You can also reach SpareFoot at 877-687-9771.

+ Store at My House at *www.storeatmyhouse.com*. This site provides a similar service, but it doesn't charge any fees.

**Safe & Secure**

Your two-week vacation could earn you big bucks. That's because you can rent out your home for up to 14 days a year without having to declare any rental income. If you happen to live in a prime tourist location or near the site of a major sporting event, you could end up with thousands of tax-free dollars.

# Mysterious way to make money

Go undercover to earn some extra bucks. Becoming a mystery shopper can help you solve some of your money woes. Here's how it works.

As a mystery shopper, you simply act as a customer to size up a business either in person or by phone. You may be asked to provide feedback about the attitude or competence of the store's employees, the place's appearance, the availability of merchandise, or how long it takes to be served. Usually, you complete an online survey about your experience.

You may find yourself evaluating a wide range of businesses, including restaurants, department stores, health and fitness clubs, car dealerships, pizzerias, banks, hotels, small retail stores, grocery stores, coffee shops, time shares, golf courses, convenience stores, and gas stations. You won't be hired by these businesses directly. Rather, businesses rely on a third-party vendor that hires the mystery shoppers.

Each assignment typically pays between $8 and $50, depending on how complicated it is. Hundreds of companies hire mystery shoppers, so you can register with several companies to land more opportunities. Keep these tips in mind when seeking work as a mystery shopper.

✦ Consider the distance. If your assignment takes you too far, you may spend more on gas than you earn.

✦ Bundle assignments. Try to fit several mystery shopping jobs into one convenient time period — like a weekend.

✦ Beware of scams. Never pay to be a mystery shopper, and do not respond to unsolicited requests by phone, mail, or email.

✦ Find legitimate opportunities near you through the Mystery Shopping Providers Association at *www.mysteryshop.org*.

## Great tips for a successful garage sale

Even if math was not your favorite subject in school, it's hard not to like the mathematics of a garage or yard sale. Subtract clutter from your home and add cash to your wallet with these surefire strategies.

✦ Check for any neighborhood or local government restrictions on yard sales and signs before you get started.

✦ Time your sale right. Avoid holding it on a holiday weekend, when most people have other plans.

✦ Lure people in by displaying more interesting items at the end of your driveway. A "free" box also does the trick — and helps you get rid of stuff you don't want but are unlikely to sell.

✦ Keep browsers shopping by playing background music. The longer they stay, the more likely they are to buy something.

- Put prices on everything, and make sure the price is clear. Do not overprice items.

- Combine your sale with other households in the neighborhood. When there's more stuff to sell, more potential buyers show up.

- Make sure you have enough small bills to make change. When making change, leave customers' bills out until after you give them their change so they can't claim they gave you a larger bill — $20 instead of $10, for instance.

- Watch out for eager beavers. No matter what time your sale officially begins, some bargain hunters will show up earlier. Be prepared.

- Advertise. How will anyone know about your sale if you don't publicize it? Place ads in your local newspaper and post signs on street lamps and telephone poles. Make sure your signs can be read from a moving car.

You can also go high-tech and advertise your sale online for free. Craigslist at *www.craigslist.org* is a good place to start. As a bonus, when you advertise on Craigslist, your ad automatically appears on a website called Yard Sale Treasure Map. Shoppers who go to *www.yardsaletreasure map.com* will be able to get driving directions to your sale. You can also post details about your sale at *www.garagesalehunter.com*.

## Super jobs for workers over age 40

Age has its privileges. Unfortunately, those privileges don't include a high demand for older workers in a tough job market. While most employers seem to prefer younger — and cheaper — employees, some fields actually welcome more mature workers.

Occupations like accounting, Internet security, nursing, home health care, pharmacy assistance, and aging-in-place remodeling — which includes installing ramps and grab bars in the homes of older people — are among the best bets for people over age 40. That's because these jobs often involve dealing with older people, who are more comfortable working with someone closer to their own age.

As the country's population ages, more and more jobs taking care of the elderly should open up. That's good news for over-40 workers. In the meantime, these websites can help older workers find jobs.

- ✦ Workforce50.com at *www.workforce50.com*

- ✦ Jobs4.0 at *www.jobs4point0.com*

- ✦ RetiredBrains at *www.retiredbrains.com*

- ✦ RetirementJobs.com at *www.retirementjobs.com*

- ✦ Seniors4Hire at *www.seniors4hire.org*

- ✦ RetireeWorkforce.com at *www.retireeworkforce.com*

## DEEP DISCOUNT

Looking for a job can pay off — or at least not cost you. That's because job-hunting expenses may be tax-deductible as miscellaneous deductions. You may be able to write off things like fees paid to employment and outplacement agencies, the cost of preparing and mailing resumes, and travel expenses related to your job hunting.

But there are a few catches. You must be looking for a job in your current field, and the expenses must exceed 2 percent of your adjusted gross income. Deductions do not apply if you are looking for a job for the first time, if you change occupations, or if there is a large break between your last job and your current search.

## Golden advice for selling gold

All that glitters is not gold. And not all cash-for-gold offers are golden opportunities. You've probably seen countless commercials and advertisements offering cash for your gold. While these offers may be tempting, they're not always a good idea.

Here are some smart steps to take if you want to turn your gold jewelry into cash — without getting ripped off.

**Research prices.** Get an idea of what your jewelry is worth. You can check the market value of gold at *www.goldprice.org*. Another good resource for gold prices is Kitco at *www.kitco.com*, a site used by most jewelers. Keep in mind that you may be dealing with unfamiliar terms, such as troy ounces and pennyweights.

**Act locally.** Local jewelers, who want to maintain their reputations, are more likely to offer you a fair deal – especially if you trade in your gold toward a new piece of jewelry. Show your wares to at least three local jewelers to see who offers the best price. You may even want to pay a trusted jeweler for a seller's advisory, which costs less than a professional appraisal.

**Sidestep shady sources.** Stay away from gold-selling parties and mail-away businesses, which pay based on scrap value, or the value of the gold content melted down. Some shady dealers offer as little as 11 percent of the jewelry's appraised value.

Unless you're an experienced seller, stay away from eBay, too. If you do choose to sell online, go to *www.top-10-cash-for-gold.com*, which ranks online gold buyers. Express Gold Cash, at *www.express goldcash.com*, currently ranks No. 1.

**Invest wisely.** Shady gold offers work both ways. In addition to cash-for-gold offers, you may see several ads urging you to buy gold. While gold may be a good investment during a financial disaster, historically it has not been. Investing in gold is probably not the best move.

# Live off your land during retirement

Saving big during your working years can help finance your retirement. Here's one creative way to live a life of luxury as a landlord.

If you have a large amount in your Roth IRA and you're older than 59 1/2, you can use a "self-directed" Roth IRA to buy a home in full with cash. Then you can collect any rental income tax-free, as long as you don't live in the home.

Before you decide to do this, make sure the rental income will easily cover any expenses, including maintenance of the property. Also make sure the rental income will exceed what you'd earn from a portfolio of the same size.

If you don't have enough money in a Roth IRA, you can convert your traditional IRA into a Roth — but you'll have to pay income taxes on any amount you convert.

## Collect cash for your collectibles

Instead of collecting dust, your collectibles could help you collect some extra money. Here's how to go about evaluating your collection.

**Think hard.** Ask yourself some questions about your collection. Does it bring you joy? Or do you just continue to collect out of habit? Could you comfortably part with it? At the very least, consider paring down your collection by selling duplicates or items you no longer use.

**Gauge its value.** If you do decide to sell your collection, will it bring in much money? An item's authenticity, condition, rarity, and historical significance all help determine its value. Consider also size, medium, subject matter, fashion, and quality when estimating your collectibles' worth.

**Know more to make more.** The more you know about your collection, the more likely you are to buy and sell at the right price. Take advantage of these resources.

+ your local library or bookstore, where you can find books explaining what makes certain items valuable as well as pricing guidelines.

+ official websites for brand name collectibles.

+ clubs or organizations specializing in the items you treasure.

+ guides for rare books.

+ coin collecting resources, including newsletters, websites, and price guides.

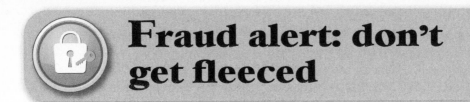

# Fraud alert: don't get fleeced

## Sidestep shady service

You need to get your car repaired and get your finances in order. But how can you find reliable people to do these jobs right? How can you be sure you won't get ripped off? Find service people such as mechanics and financial planners you can trust — and know how to spot those you can't.

In general, follow these tips to find trustworthy businesses. After all, service should come with a smile — not a swindle.

**Ask friends and family for references.** Let the people you trust the most tell you who they trust to handle their auto repairs, finances, and other matters.

**Get a second opinion.** When seeking a second opinion about your car, do not tell the second shop what the first one said. Just tell them the problem, and listen to their diagnosis and price.

**Look around.** A mechanic's garage should be clean — not littered with empty oil cans, old tires, and dirty rags.

**Check affiliations.** Professional organizations, like the Better Business Bureau, keep lists of their members. See if a company belongs to an appropriate — and legitimate — association. For financial professionals, check with the Financial Industry Regulatory Authority or the Certified Financial Planner Board of Standards. You can even do a background check on your broker with BrokerCheck at *www.finra.org.*

**Verify licenses and registrations.** Make sure auto technicians are ASE certified. Look for AAA certification and state licenses, too. Reputable shops should display them proudly. Beware of financial planners calling themselves senior advisers — the title may not mean anything. Do not do business with unlicensed professionals or plumbers, electricians, and other tradespeople.

**Seek online reviews.** The more, the merrier. Keep in mind that some positive reviews may be planted by the company, and some negative reviews may be the result of an isolated incident.

**Confirm contact information.** Make sure any company you deal with has a valid telephone number and street address – not just a website.

**Read policies and contracts carefully.** Know what you're getting into in terms of refunds, handling disputes, warranties, and online companies' privacy policies.

Safe&Secure

You may be more likely to trust someone your own age. Unfortunately, you may also regret that trust. As the population ages, so do the con artists. Because of the poor economy, some aging financial planners can no longer afford to retire. So they prey on their fellow seniors, pushing risky or shady investments.

These senior scammers use their age as a selling point, stressing something that you have in common. They may also flash credentials in order to look legit. Many of these titles have the word "senior" in the name — but many are also easy to get and essentially meaningless.

Before making important financial decisions, run them past a younger relative. Never attend a free lunch or dinner seminar hosted by financial advisers — especially not alone. Report any fraud to federal or state investigators. Do not be afraid to speak up.

# PINpoint potential problems

Debit or ATM cards certainly make life more convenient. But if you don't take some precautions, they can also put your hard-earned money at risk.

Here are two places you should never use your ATM card. You'll protect your PIN – and your money.

**Gas stations.** Scoundrels often slip devices called skimmers into gas pumps. These sneaky devices swipe your magnetic stripe and keypad information so thieves can create counterfeit cards. When you enter your PIN code, you may be handing it over to thieves. Use your credit card instead of your debit card when pumping gas. If you must use a debit card, choose the screen prompt that lets you use it like a credit card, so you don't need to enter a PIN.

**Sketchy ATMs.** Stick to ATMs found in banks. Those in convenience stores, airports, and isolated locations are prime targets for skimmers or hidden cameras. Be careful whenever using any ATM. Familiarize yourself with the appearance and feel of your ATM, so you can spot a recently attached skimming device. Use your hand to shield your PIN when entering it.

Skimming can take place anywhere – even in a restaurant. When the waiter takes your card, he could run it through a hand-held skimmer once he is away from your table. You may want to limit transactions where your card leaves your sight. And never use your card to buy anything from a website that is not very well known or secure.

These are just some of the instances when you should never "pay with plastic" – it could cost you your life savings.

Safe & Secure

Downgrade your debit card to upgrade your security. Consider asking your bank to replace your debit card with an ATM card. An ATM card can only be used for cash withdrawals and always requires your PIN code. Even if someone steals your card, it won't be much use to them without your PIN. A debit card, on the other hand, can be used like a credit card as well as an ATM card. A crook wouldn't need your PIN to wipe out your account. He would just need to forge your signature when making purchases.

# 10 terrific tips to avoid ID theft

Identity theft can happen to almost anyone. Possible victims include anyone who has a credit card, bank account, mortgage, car loan, debit card, driver's license, Social Security number, phone service, health insurance, or a job. Paying bills and using the Internet also puts you at risk.

Once someone steals your identity, they can use it to wipe out your bank account, take out loans in your name, or adopt it as an alias while committing other crimes. You may be denied credit, charged for purchases you didn't make, harassed by collection agencies, or even arrested.

Use these tips to protect yourself from identity theft.

+ Check your credit report regularly.

+ Don't give out your Social Security number.

+ Protect your computer with passwords and virus protection. If you use a wireless connection, make sure it's encrypted.

+ Keep track of billing cycles. A missing bill may mean an identity thief changed your address.

+ Examine financial statements carefully to make sure all the purchases are legitimate.

+ Invest in a shredder. That way, thieves who rummage through your garbage looking for personal information will find only confetti.

+ Be suspicious of calls or emails from a business asking for personal information.

+ Keep an eye on your credit card when shopping or dining out. Make sure salespeople and waiters don't have a chance to copy your card.

+ Use safe checks, from your bank, and use them sparingly.

+ Watch your back at the grocery store. The person behind you in line can use a cell phone to snap a photo of your credit or debit card when you pull it out to pay.

# Protect yourself with an ID score

How likely are you to be a victim of identity theft? Now you can find out. Just go to *www.myidscore.com* to get your free ID score. Used by financial institutions and other creditors, ID scores calculate the risk that customers are actually who they claim to be. At the website, you just provide your name, address, phone number, and birth date to get started. Social Security number is optional.

A high-tech database looks for unusual activity, such as a Social Security number attached to more than one name or several credit card applications made on the same day by the same person with multiple addresses. It also looks for reports of fraudulent transactions.

When it's done, you'll get a score between 1 and 999. The higher the score, the higher your risk for identity theft. If your score is high, you can follow a link to the nonprofit Identity Theft Resource Center for tips on how to protect yourself.

# Guard your secret code from identity thieves

To protect yourself from identity theft, guard this number. It's not your credit card or Social Security Number. It's the three-digit code on the back of your credit card. Once a thief has this number, stealing your identity can be as easy as one-two-three.

In a typical scam, you'll get a phone call from an official-sounding person claiming your card was flagged by security because of an unusual purchase. The caller is really a thief who has already obtained your credit card number somehow. When you deny making the purchase, the caller says that a credit will appear on your next statement. Then he'll ask for the three-digit number on the back of your card to prove that it is in your possession.

If you give out that secret number – usually called the CVV (Card Verification Value) number, but sometimes called the DVV2, DVD2 or CID number – the thief will be able to go on a spending spree in your name without being questioned. Never give out this number over the phone. A credit card company will never ask you for it.

# Keep a healthy eye on your medical records

Your next doctor's appointment could be even costlier than you think. In a sickening scam called "medical identity theft," thieves may pilfer your medical records. That is because these records contain everything a crook needs to steal someone else's identity, including your Social Security number, address, and billing accounts.

How does it happen? Some thieves work as "moles" in clinics and insurance offices to steal patients' records, then sell them. Some shady doctors may even submit fraudulent claims to boost profits. Computerized health records have several upsides — but they also open the door to computer hackers who can access this sensitive information.

Besides the usual risks of identity theft, medical ID theft poses extra dangers because it could impact your health as well as your finances. Thieves may use your identity to go on a shopping spree, but they could also use it to get medical treatment they can't otherwise afford.

As a result, you may end up having to pay for health care you didn't receive. You could also lose your health insurance or need to pay higher premiums to restore it. When someone else gets treatment under your name, it could even alter your medical records, putting you in danger when you need care. For instance, your records could list the wrong blood type, a medical condition you do not have, or medication that you're actually allergic to.

To protect yourself from medical identity theft, take these steps.

+ Keep an eye on your insurance card. Contact your insurance provider if you lose it.

+ Every year, ask your insurer for a list of benefits paid in your name. Also request an "accounting of disclosures," which shows where your records were sent. You have a right to a copy under the federal Health Insurance Portability and Accountability Act (HIPAA).

+ Read every letter you get from insurers, especially the explanation of benefits (EOB). If you see treatments you never received, call your health care provider and your insurer.

+ Ask your doctor's office to make you a copy of your medical records. The HIPAA health privacy rule also covers nearly every health care provider.

+ Check your credit report every year for medical billing errors. You can request a free report at *www.annualcreditreport.com*.

## DEEP DISCOUNT

Identity theft and other scams have one silver lining — losses from theft are tax-deductible. You can claim theft loss as an itemized deduction on Form 1040, Schedule A. Make sure to include all your costs, including your time. You can also report theft losses on Form 4684, *Casualties and Thefts*. Some complicated rules and calculations apply.

For instance, the loss must be reduced by any salvage value and by any insurance or other reimbursements you receive or expect to receive. Improvement or depreciation is also factored into the cost. Talk to your tax preparer, or visit the IRS website at *www.irs.gov*, for more information.

## Stamp out mail theft

The postman always rings twice — but so does the thief. Your mailbox can be a prime target for criminals. Here is how they operate.

Thieves cruise neighborhoods looking for upraised flags on home mailboxes. If they find an envelope containing a check, they're in business. Using a piece of tape and a pan of chemicals, they "wash" the check, leaving them with a blank check with your signature and bank account number.

Besides stealing your bills, crooks can raid your mailbox for boxes of new checks, bank or credit card statements, and pre-approved credit offers. Now they can empty your bank account, ruin your credit rating, and even steal your identity. Tax season doubles as hunting season for these thieves. Not only might they find checks to wash, they can find all sorts of information – like your Social Security number – that facilitates identity theft.

Take steps to protect yourself from these types of mail scams.

+ Put outgoing bills in a blue U.S. Postal Service drop box instead of leaving them in your mailbox. You can also deliver mail inside the post office or hand it directly to your mail carrier.

+ Look for a good location. Drop boxes outside a post office are often under video surveillance.

+ Deposit your mail as close as possible to posted collection times.

+ Do not put your bills in a mailbox that is overstuffed, which allows thieves easy access.

+ Use a gel pen to write checks. For example, Uniball pens contain a special ink that is more resistant to check-washing.

+ Pick up your checks from your bank rather than having them sent to your mailbox.

+ Remove mail promptly from your mailbox.

+ Put a hold on your mail if you go on vacation.

+ Use a locked mailbox for incoming and outgoing mail.

+ Go high-tech. If you have a computer, you may want to consider moving your financial transactions online. That way, you avoid mailing checks to pay bills or deposit funds.

# Put a stop to postcard ploy

Your mailbox probably contains an assortment of bills, catalogs, and junk mail. But watch out for an innocent-looking postcard that could drain your bank account.

The Do Not Call list helps prevent shady salespeople from contacting you – unless you opt out. Marketing companies mail postcards to seniors that trick them into doing just that. These phony postcards may say you have a problem with your Medicare or Social Security benefits. They may even feature an AARP logo or a government address to make them look more official. If you respond to the postcard, you remove yourself from the Do Not Call list.

Insurance companies pay the marketing company for the rights to your phone number. Then they contact you to pitch shady investments that earn the salespeople big commissions. Fall for these pitches, and you could lose thousands of dollars.

## Avoid quick-fix credit repair tricks

Your credit score may be bad — but credit repair scams are worse. Big promises only lead to big fees and big trouble.

Shady companies make false promises to appeal to people with bad credit. They may say they have inside connections and know legal loopholes to clean up your credit. They may promise to erase bad debt, bankruptcies, or foreclosures from your credit history in record time. And they will charge you a hefty fee upfront.

Once you pay them, you may never hear from them again. At best, they will file a number of frivolous disputes to make debts temporarily disappear. But that does nothing to boost your credit score. They may even suggest you apply for an Employer Identification Number to use instead of your Social Security number so you can invent a "new" credit identity. This gimmick could land you in prison.

Instead of falling for a quick — and fraudulent — fix, try these tactics to improve your credit.

**Be patient.** Contact your creditors and stick to a repayment schedule. It takes time and effort to pay your debts and improve your credit score.

**Seek real help.** A legitimate credit counseling service can set up a organized repayment or consolidation plan for a small fee — or even for free.

**Learn the law.** No one can remove accurate negative information from your credit history. Under federal law, debt remains in a credit report for seven years, and bankruptcy remains for 10 years. It is also illegal for credit repair companies to charge a fee before providing any service.

**Keep tabs on yourself.** You can get three free credit reports each year at *www.annualcreditreport.com*. Check for any fraudulent debts. If you spot anything suspicious, contact the three credit reporting agencies – Equifax, Experian, and TransUnion – to have it legally removed at no charge.

> **Time is Money**
>
> Get a quick heads-up before someone sends your credit rating down the tubes. Sign up for fraud alerts at your credit card issuer's website. You can receive these helpful alerts by text or email.
>
> In the past fraud alerts may have taken hours or even days, but newer options let banks warn you of suspicious activity almost in real time. Possible red flags include transactions exceeding a certain amount, denied transactions, ATM withdrawals, and transactions made overseas, online, or by phone. You can choose which types of alerts you would like to receive.
>
> While there is no charge for this service, text messaging rates may add up, depending on your cell phone provider and plan. Check with your credit card issuers to see if they provide real-time fraud alerts.

# Hang up on phony calls for help

The phone rings, and a frantic voice on the other end says, "Grandma, I need help." Only the caller is not your grandchild – and if you fall for this common scam, you'll be the one in trouble.

Here is how the scam works. The caller, posing as your grandchild, claims he or she is stranded in Canada after an accident, hospitalization, arrest, or some other misfortune and asks you to send money quickly.

The con artist could be a local acquaintance who knows your grand-child's name. Or the scammer could have gathered the information from a recent family obituary or from social networking or genealogy websites on the Internet. In some cases, they may not know your grandchild's name at all, but may ask leading questions to discover it. Or you could just give it away by guessing the name of one of your grandchildren.

Seniors lose millions of dollars each year in this type of scam. Most victims don't report the fraud because they're embarrassed that they didn't recognize their own grandchild's voice.

Don't let yourself be conned by an impostor. Take these steps to foil this telephone trickery.

+ First of all, be suspicious of any requests for money. Never give out an account number over the phone.

+ Put the caller on the spot. When the caller says, "It's your grandson" or "It's your granddaughter," ask "Which one?" rather than guess at a name. They might just hang up.

+ Verify the caller's identity by contacting your real grandchild directly, or check the story with a trusted family member.

## Steer clear of shady surveys

It sounds like easy money. Just answer a few questions and get paid. But beware of bogus survey scams, which are nothing more than the latest attempts to steal your identity.

The emails look like they come from well-known companies, like Walmart or McDonald's or even the U.S. Census Bureau, and they promise a nice chunk of change for completing an online customer survey. When you finish taking the survey, you are asked to provide your credit card or bank account number so the money can be credited to your account. You may even be asked for your PIN or electronic signature. Of course, con artists – and not legitimate companies – are behind these schemes.

Just like phony emails claiming to be from your bank, eBay, or PayPal that ask you to update your account information, these fake survey emails help crooks steal your information, identity, and money.

Your best bet is to ignore these email surveys. Companies may value your opinion – but this is not how they go about getting it. Do not give out your bank account or credit card information. And don't open any email attachments – they could expose you to a computer virus.

**Safe & Secure**

You want to lower your credit card interest rates – but going through a middleman just raises your risk of being ripped off.

Shady companies leave automated messages on your answering machine or voicemail that promise to negotiate significantly lower interest rates with your credit card issuers. When you call them back, they may demand an upfront fee for their services. Worse, they may ask for your credit card number and other personal information. Needless to say, you won't get anything for the fee – and they will use your personal information to commit fraud.

Never give your credit card number to a company you don't know. Instead of dealing with these fraudulent middlemen, call your card issuer yourself and ask for a reduced rate. Be calm, patient, and persistent. The worst they can do is say no. And it won't cost you a cent.

# Carry a 'smart' wallet

You can't guarantee you'll never lose your wallet or have your pocketbook stolen. But you can lessen the damage by being smart about what you carry in it.

**Reduce the clutter.** Remove everything you don't need on a daily basis. This includes things like gift cards, business cards, receipts, and other random scraps of paper.

**Protect your identity.** Do not carry your Social Security card. Just memorize your Social Security number. Do not carry blank checks, which have your address and bank account number printed on them.

**Make photocopies.** Copy the front and back of every card you keep in your wallet, including your driver's license, credit cards, insurance cards, video rental memberships, and library cards. This will help you remember what was in there. Plus, the back of the card often lists important information, like security codes and contact information to report loss or theft.

**Keep a backup.** Make sure at least one credit or debit card stays home. You'll have one less card to cancel if your wallet is lost or stolen – and access to funds while you sort out the situation.

**Get cute.** Carry a picture of a smiling baby or cute puppy in your wallet, and you have a better chance of having your lost wallet returned. According to a recent study, nearly 9 out of 10 people returned a wallet with a baby photo, and just over half returned one with a puppy picture.

# Secret to protecting your online activities

When it comes to computer passwords, one size does not fit all. Having just one password for everything may make it easier for you to remember, but it also makes it easier for crooks to figure out.

On the other hand, creating – and remembering – a unique password for every site you visit is difficult. So here is secret recommended by technology experts – create just three different passwords based on your online activities. You'll need a separate password for:

+ financial institutions, such as your bank or brokerage firm.

+ retail sites that store your credit card information and for sites that feature information related to your identity, such as social networking sites.

+ sites that don't ask for detailed user information, such as entertainment and news sites.

Keep in mind that a good password should have at least 12 characters in order to thwart encryption-cracking software. It should consist of randomized letters, numbers, and symbols. Don't use obvious words, dates, or patterns of symbols.

Once you create your passwords, don't store them on a document on your PC or on a mobile device, which can be easily lost, stolen, or accessed by others.

## Guard against gift card glitches

When you're stumped while holiday shopping, a gift card may seem like the perfect present. But, thanks to all the fine print, a gift card may be the gift that keeps on taking.

Take time to read the fine print. Chances are it's chock-full of mysterious fees, including purchasing and processing fees, transaction fees, inactivity fees, and fees to check the card's balance. Gift cards also often come with expiration dates and other restrictions.

But the drawbacks don't stop there. If you lose a gift card, you probably can't get a replacement unless you know the card's ID number. Of course, there is probably also a replacement fee. A gift card may become worthless if the company goes out of business or declares bankruptcy. And, even without all these obstacles, there is a good chance the gift card will simply go unused.

So, how can you avoid these tricks and traps? If you receive a gift card as a gift, take these steps.

+ Know the rules in case you need to replace your card.

+ Photocopy both sides of the card, and make sure the ID number is readable.

+ Report a lost card as soon as possible, so you won't be held responsible for any transactions.

+ Make a swap. You can sell your unused gift card for cash or trade it for a different gift card for a comparable amount at websites like *www.swapagift.com* or *www.cardavenue.com*.

Gift card buyers should try these tactics.

+ Stick to cards issued by retailers. They usually have fewer expiration dates and fees compared to bank cards with the MasterCard or Visa logos.

+ Steer clear of gift cards from retailers in questionable financial shape. They may go out of business or just close some stores, making it tougher to use the cards.

+ Consider giving cash instead. It's accepted everywhere, without restrictions or hidden fees.

# Bury debts with the deceased

When a loved one dies, you're already in mourning. You don't want to end up in debt, too. But that is what could happen if you give in to pressure from creditors or collection agencies to pay the debts of the deceased.

**Sidestep scams.** In some cases, a bogus collection agency will call a few days after the funeral and claim your deceased relative owed money and you have to pay. They may threaten legal action to frighten you into settling with them quickly. Often, crooks target older people with this scam and may even try to get you to provide your bank account or Social Security numbers.

**Stand up to pressure.** Even legitimate creditors, like credit card companies, will stoop to shady tactics. Creditors and collection agencies may try to coax you into paying your deceased relative's debt. They will use empathy, persuasion, misleading statements, and outright lies to get your money. Do not agree to pay anything. Check with a lawyer first.

**Learn the law.** Unless you cosigned a loan for your deceased relative, you are not responsible for the debt and should not pay. Children do not have to pay for a deceased parent's debts. Depending on your state's probate laws, a surviving spouse may be liable for the debt. Creditors must be paid from money in the estate. If the estate does not have enough to cover the amount owed, the debts remain unpaid.

**No-Sweat Solution**

Worried about your credit card number falling into the wrong hands? Now there is a simple, high-tech way to thwart thieves.

Instead of using your real credit card number when shopping online or by phone or mail order, you can use what is called a "virtual credit card." When you sign up for this free service, you receive a randomly generated 16-digit number for one-time use. Of course, this virtual card won't work for any transactions where you have to show your actual card.

Call the customer service number on the back of your credit card, or check your card issuer's website, to find out if your card issuer offers this service.

# Make your bank work for you

## Smart ways to beat bank fees

Stop letting the bank whittle away your income. Watch for these needless charges on your next statement.

**New checks.** A box of checks can easily cost $15 or more. Skip the fancy artwork and order the most basic checks available to trim the cost. You should never have to pay for checks with misspellings or other major errors.

**Wire transfers.** You could lose another $10 for wiring money from one account to another. Call your bank and ask about free ways to transfer funds. If you send money to the same person often, have them open an account with your bank. Transfers between accounts at the same bank are often free.

**Transfer limits.** Some banks limit the number of transfers you can make between accounts each month. Go over, and you could pay another $10 penalty. Plan your money moves in advance to stay under the limit, or look for a bank that doesn't limit fund transfers.

**Debit card purchases.** Shop with a debit card and you may pay a charge each time you use it. Ask the bank if it levies a fee on debit purchases. If so, simply choose "credit" instead of "debit" at check-out to dodge the extra charge.

Go over your monthly account statement with a fine-toothed comb to spot sneaky fees. Call the bank if you have questions about any charges. If all else fails, consider switching banks. Some have fewer fees than others.

# Hidden cost of 'free' checking

Read the fine print on those supposedly free checking accounts. Some banks require you to keep thousands of dollars in an account. Drop below the required minimum balance (RMB), and you'll get slapped with a fee. Just $5 a month still adds up to $60 wasted each year.

Never open a checking account that charges a monthly maintenance fee or penalties for falling below the RMB.

+ Ask your current bank if they offer any no-fee accounts.

+ Ask if they will waive the fee on your account if you have your Social Security check or paycheck deposited directly.

+ Shop around. Call or visit other local banks and ask about free checking, or use a website such as *www.bankrate.com* to find a truly free account.

+ Get the details before making any switch. In addition to RMBs, banks may charge extra for checks or ATM withdrawals on "free" accounts.

**Freebie Frenzie**

Cash in your coins for free at Coinstar machines by putting the money toward a gift certificate. Coinstar charges 9.8 cents per dollar to count your coins and give you cash. That's a service charge of nearly 10 percent. Ask for that money on a gift card or eCertificate, and the service is free.

• Press the "Cash in Coins" button, then the "Free Coin Counting" button.

• Choose a gift card from a store such as CVS pharmacy, JCPenney, Lowes, Starbucks, Amazon.com, iTunes, or Regal Cinemas.

• Pour in your coins.

Many credit unions provide coin counting services free for members if you'd rather have cash than a gift card. Pour in your change, then take the receipt to the teller for cash or to deposit.

# Put an end to overdraft charges

Your bank may be sneaking money out of your account through outrageous overdraft fees. The average big bank hits you with a $35 charge every time you overdraw your account. Some banks even charge a second fee if you don't pay the overdrawn amount plus the first fee within a few days.

Banks used to sign you up for "overdraft protection" automatically, unless you specifically told them not to. Now, you must ask for it, or "opt in." It's a small difference, but this switch can save you hundreds in fees.

Opt in, and your bank will allow you to overdraw your account, "loan" you the money, and charge a hefty price for that convenience. Opt out, and your bank will deny ATM withdrawals and debit card purchases if you don't have enough cash to cover them.

Say you don't realize your account balance is low. While running errands one day, you make four purchases with your debit card, each of which overdraws your account.

If you opt in to the protection, the bank won't warn you that you are overdrawing your account. It will let the purchases go through. Four overdrafts in one day could cost $140 in fees alone, according to the nonprofit Consumer Federation of America.

If you opt out of the protection, your card will get declined the first time you try to use it. No fees, just a little embarrassment.

You don't need the bank's help. You can guard against overdrafts for a whole lot less.

+ Keep your checkbook balanced and up to date.

+ Maintain a cushion of extra cash in your checking account, just in case you forget a charge or a deposit gets delayed.

+ Sign up for email or text message alerts that warn you when your account balance gets dangerously low.

+ Carry a back-up credit card for emergencies.

+ Have the bank link your checking account to a savings account, credit card, or line of credit. When you overdraw your checking, the bank will use these sources to cover the charge instead of "loaning" you money.

+ Opt back out of overdraft protection if you have already opted in. You can opt out, by law, at any time – but be careful. You will still be able to overdraw your account by check, preauthorized payments, or recurring debit card transactions, like bills set for autopayment.

## Outsmart ATM fees

Are you throwing away $200 a year? You are if you withdraw money just once a week from an out-of-network ATM.

According to Bankrate.com, people pay an average of $3.74 every time they use an ATM machine that doesn't belong to their bank. First, their bank dings them for using another bank's ATM. Then, the ATM itself slaps them with a separate charge. The result – you could pay $4 or more for each withdrawal. Do that once a week, and you'll easily waste nearly $200 a year in fees alone. Keep more cash in your pocket with this advice.

**Stick with one bank.** Only withdraw money from your own bank's ATMs or tellers. Take out cash once a week. Once it's gone, refuse to spend more. You'll save on fees and cut spending.

**Ask for cash back.** Get fee-free cash at supermarkets and drugstores. Buy something you need with a debit card and ask for $20, $40, or $60 in cash back, drawn from your bank account.

**Change banks.** A small number of banks now offer checking accounts with no fees for using out-of-network ATMs, such as online-only accounts at Ally Bank and HSBC Direct, as well as checking accounts at Fidelity and Schwab. An out-of-network ATM may still charge you, but these banks will reimburse the fees.

**Save on surcharges.** Allpoint ATMs in Target, Kroger, CVS Pharmacy, 7-Eleven, Costco, and some Walgreen stores do not levy surcharges. However, your bank may still pin you with an out-of-network ATM fee.

**DEEP DISCOUNT**

Checking your bank statements carefully for unexpected fees, like "free" checking, out-of-network ATM, and overdraft fees among others, could save you $66 or more each month. Add that to these five other simple steps, and you could save an average of $550 a month in household spending.

- Forgo $30 of weekly splurges to save $120 each month.
- Cut grocery spending. Clip coupons, shop sales, and eat leftovers to shave $158 off your budget.
- Call your insurance agent. Ask about discounts, bundling policies, raising your deductible, and dropping collision coverage on older cars to keep another $100 in your pocket each month.
- Ditch your landline telephone for $50 in monthly savings. Switch to a cell phone or an Internet phone system such as Vonage or magicJack.
- Add attic insulation and get free weatherization help through your state government to cut $55 off monthly utility bills.

# Never pay another late fee

Put an end to late fees. Let technology help you pay bills on time. With a computer, an Internet connection, and a few clicks of your mouse, you can pay bills from the comfort of your chair and never miss another due date. Besides late fees, paying bills by computer could also save:

✦ $18 a year on checks, at an average cost of 10 cents a check.

✦ $79.20 a year in stamps, assuming you pay 15 bills a month and postage costs 44 cents.

That's almost $100 in savings each year. Arranging your payments is so easy, you'll wonder why you didn't do it sooner.

**Set reminders.** Head to the websites of your credit card, mortgage, or utility companies. There, you can tell the company to send you a reminder by email or text message when a bill comes due. That little nudge could help you remember to pay.

**Schedule payments.** The moment you get a bill, schedule it to be paid through either your bank's website or the payee's website. Simply select a date and type in the amount you want to pay. The money will be withdrawn from your account on the specific day you choose.

**Put bills on autopilot.** Don't want the hassle of scheduling a payment every time you get a new bill? Visit your bank or payee websites and arrange to have bills paid automatically as soon as they come due. Keep a close eye on your bank statement and balance so you aren't caught off guard by billing errors or an unusually high bill.

However you decide to pay your bills, remember to write the amounts in your checkbook as if you had written a check for them. Otherwise, you might overdraw your account. And never sign into your bank, utility, or other payment websites using a public computer – at a library or senior center, for instance.

Also, avoid clicking on the links in emails that claim to come from your bank, credit card company, or similar source. Scammers may send fake emails in an attempt to steal your bank account or credit card information.

# Say goodbye to greedy banks

Tired of banks taking advantage of you? Try a credit union. Whereas banks aim to turn a profit for their shareholders, credit unions are nonprofit groups owned by the members themselves. As a result, credit unions often pay higher interest rates on deposits, charge fewer and smaller fees, and offer better rates on car loans. Of course, ditching your bank for one does have some disadvantages.

+ Credit unions tend to have fewer branches and ATMs than big banks.

+ Most, but not all, are insured up to $250,000 through the National Credit Union Administration, the equivalent of the FDIC. However, 3 percent are not. Make certain yours is.

+ Credit unions may not offer as wide a range of loans or financial services as banks, so be sure the ones you consider have everything you need.

+ You may not get canceled checks returned with your statement. Consider ordering a checkbook with carbon copies for record keeping.

Credit union members generally share something in common, like where they live, work, or attend church. These days nearly everyone is eligible for membership somewhere. Ask around within your church or job, or check with family and neighbors about nearby credit unions. For fast answers, visit the website *www.creditunion.coop* and search for one near you.

## Supercharge savings with high-interest accounts

Regular savings accounts pay so little interest you may wonder why you even bother. Make your money grow faster by switching to an online-only, higher interest savings account.

**TOP DOLLAR:** A brick-and-mortar bank with tons of branches, a large network of ATMs, and friendly tellers makes for pleasant banking, but it also eats into your bottom line. A savings account at a regular bank may pay as little as .05 percent interest. At that rate, you would earn a measly $1.50 a year on $3,000 in savings.

**VALUE:** Internet-only banks, such as INGdirect.com and HSBC.com, may lack nice lobbies and real tellers, but they trounce the interest rates of traditional banks.

When a well-known national bank was only offering .2 percent on its savings accounts, HSBC was touting a 1.85 percent yearly rate. If you keep $3,000 in your savings account, that higher rate could earn you $49.50 more interest in just one year, and a whopping $543.05 more over 10 years.

**WHAT YOU GIVE UP:** Internet-only banks have no ATMs or walk-in branches. You can withdraw your money using another bank's ATM, but you may pay a fee to do it. What's more, you cannot visit a bank branch to deposit money. You can mail in your deposits, but mailing takes time.

Consider having your paychecks or Social Security checks direct-deposited for less hassle. Or link your local checking account to the online savings account, then transfer money between them. Check with both banks to make sure you won't get hit with transfer fees.

Before you open an account at an Internet-only bank, be sure it's legitimate. Check the bank's website for a customer service phone number, and see if the Federal Deposit Insurance Corporation (FDIC) insures the accounts. Look through the bank's Web pages for the FDIC logo and visit *www2.fdic.gov/idasp* to search for the bank's name in the FDIC listings.

# Free help managing your money

Keeping track of your finances is one thing you must do to continue living in your own home as you age. Help managing your money could be right around the corner, and free, if you're a senior. A Daily Money Manager (DMM) can keep you independent longer in retirement.

Maybe you can't see well enough to read bills and pay them anymore, or you have a condition like arthritis that makes it hard to write checks, sign your name, or get to a bank. Perhaps you lost a spouse who used to handle the finances. You may find yourself forgetting to pay important bills like the mortgage, rent, or utilities.

A good DMM can help. They can also benefit loved ones who can no longer handle their daily finances or who have become vulnerable to scam artists.

Daily Money Managers can help you organize and keep track of financial and medical insurance papers, as well as write checks, pay bills, balance your checkbook, and make deposits for you. DMMs can even call companies regarding incorrect bills, organize your tax records, and negotiate with your creditors. Some will go over your medical insurance papers and make sure your claims get processed correctly, too.

You can hire a DMM, usually by the hour, but some groups offer DMM services for free or at reduced-cost to cash-strapped seniors.

✦ AARP's Money Management Program links seniors with DMM services. You can learn more online at *www.aarpmmp.org* or by calling 888-687-2277.

✦ Your local Area Agency on Aging can put you in touch with free and low-cost DMMs. Call 800-677-1116 and ask for information on agencies that provide basic Daily Money Manager services. Or find them online at *www.eldercare.gov*.

Bear in mind, state and federal governments do not regulate DMMs. Take extra care in choosing one you trust. Get referrals from family and friends, or from a nonprofit or government source like the Area Agency on Aging. Double-check any names you get with the American Association of Daily Money Managers to make sure they are certified. Call 877-326-5991 or visit the website at *www.aadmm.com*.

Don't let arthritis cripple your financial independence. Ask someone you trust to set up an online bill payment system, so you can pay your bills from a computer instead of writing checks.

Pay bills from your bank's website or the websites of utility companies. You can even schedule bills to be paid automatically each month. Be sure to review your statements carefully to catch errors before you pay them.

## Tricks to find the best credit card

Credit cards aren't one-size-fits-all. There's a dizzying variety, offering everything from cash back to airline miles, all with different fees and interest rates.

Ask yourself two questions to narrow the field. First, do you carry a balance on your card from one month to the next, or do you pay it off in full each month? Second, do you use it to pay for everyday items, or only for emergencies? If you:

+ sometimes carry a balance, focus on finding a card with the lowest possible interest rate, as well as a low introductory rate on new purchases.

+ pay the balance in full each month, the interest rate really doesn't matter. Look for a card with no annual fee and a long grace period, instead.

+ use your card to pay for almost everything, find a card with a high credit limit and generous rewards program.

+ use your card for emergencies only, get a basic, no-frills card with a low interest rate and low or no annual fees.

Shopping around is a cinch. If you have Internet access, you can compare credit card offers on websites such as *www.creditcards.com* and *www.lowcards.com*. Watch your mail for offers, too. Compare the materials you receive, and call the companies if you have any questions about the fine print. Avoid cards that charge extra for their rewards program or levy high fees.

**Safe & Secure**

The worst credit card to have in your wallet — a business, or professional card. The Credit Card Act of 2009 banned banks and credit card companies from many sneaky practices. Unfortunately, the law doesn't apply to business cards.

As a result, banks and credit card companies are pushing people to sign up for business credit cards, which allow the companies to:

- put your payments toward debts with the lowest interest rate first, instead of toward more expensive, higher-interest debts.
- change the terms and conditions of your contract with no advance notice.
- charge huge fees when you go over your credit limit.
- set a grace period shorter than 21 days.

All of these practices are illegal now with consumer credit cards. Don't fall for the sales pitch. Just say no to professional credit cards, and stick with the regular ones instead.

# Pay cash for incredible discounts

Paying with cash instead of a debit or credit card is an old-fashioned way to save. You not only spend less when you have to hand over cash, but you can also snag some terrific discounts.

Credit card companies such as Mastercard, Visa, and American Express charge stores a fee every time someone pays with a credit card. Retailers hate it because it cuts into their profit. Some hate it so much they will cut you a deal if you pay cash.

+ Gas stations may give you 5 cents off per gallon of gas. You could save $41 a year, depending on your driving habits.

+ Restaurants and eateries that offer delivery or takeout may shave 10 to 15 percent off your bill. Eat out regularly, and you could save $150 in one year.

+ Doctors' offices and hospitals love cash. They may trim 10 to 20 percent off your bill for paying cash within 30 or 60 days.

+ Jewelry stores may knock 5 to 20 percent off the total for cash purchases.

Other places may offer deals, too. You'll never know if you don't ask. Be willing to speak up, and get ready to save.

## A better way to buy

Layaway is making a comeback as a better way to buy the things you want. Credit cards give you instant gratification but at a high price – high interest, annual fees, and late fees. Layaway doesn't.

More retailers now offer it as an option, including Kmart, Sears, TJ Maxx, Toys R Us, Best Buy, Meijer, and many more. Call your local retailers and ask if they offer a layaway plan.

+ Find out what happens to your money if you decide you don't want the item. You may owe a cancellation fee, but most reputable stores will return your payments.

+ Ask what fee, if any, the plan charges. Look for a plan where the fee totals less than 10 percent of the item's price. Otherwise, you are better off saving up and buying it outright.

Stores count on you picking up a few extra items each time you come in to make your layaway payments. Resist the urge to shop if you want to maximize your savings.

# When 'junk' mail is a must-read

Watch out. Important credit card mail can look just like junk mail. Toss it without reading it, and you could get a nasty surprise in the form of new or higher fees.

Companies must notify you when they add a new fee or change others, but these notices may come in plain white envelopes. Unfortunately, the fine print on these letters may be the only way you find out about key changes to your card's terms, fees, and even interest rate.

Your credit card company must tell you about changes like these 45 days before they go into effect. They also must give you the choice of "opting out." When you opt out, you refuse the rate hike. You can never again put any new charges on the card, but you will keep your current interest rate on the existing balance until you pay it off.

**DEEP DISCOUNT**

High credit card balance? Paying just $20 more than your minimum monthly payment could save you almost $9,000 in credit card interest.

The secret — treat your minimum monthly payment as a starting point. A little extra goes a long way. Say you owe $9,000 on a card that charges 18 percent interest. If you only pay the minimum each month, around $225, it would take nearly 28 years to pay it off, plus $12,923.13 in interest on top of the original $9,000 debt.

Simply put $20 more toward that monthly payment, and the numbers change dramatically. At $245 a month, you'll pay off your debt in under five years and owe $4,177.53 in interest, nearly $9,000 less.

# Secrets to saving with balance transfers

Credit cards should not be your first choice for purchases. If you have already run up a big balance, a balance transfer could save you money.

Transfers move debt from one credit card to another. Find a good deal, and you could save big bucks by moving debt from a high-interest card to one with a low interest rate. Most balance transfers only lock in a low rate for a limited amount of time — say six or 12 months. The key is to pay off your debt before the low rate expires and to stay out of debt afterward.

Watch for traps before taking the plunge. These "gotchas" can turn a good deal into a real stinker.

**Big balance transfer fees.** Most cards charge a fee ranging from 3 to 5 percent of the money being transferred. You could pay $150 to $250 just for moving $5,000 to the low-interest card. Generally, the longer the low-interest period lasts, the higher the transfer fee. Credit union credit cards may be best. Many charge no or low transfer fees.

**Teaser rates.** Only people with a good credit history typically qualify for zero-interest introductory rates. Call the card company to find out what you qualify for before transferring your balances.

**Expensive annual fees.** Don't sign up for a credit card with an annual fee, no matter how good a deal the balance transfer seems to be. Any annual fee will simply eat into the money you save on interest.

**Missed payments.** Even low-rate cards require minimum monthly payments. Pay late, and your interest rate could zoom to outrageous levels.

Read the fine print of your balance transfer agreement to find out when the introductory rate expires. Mark it on your calendar, and have a plan to pay off the balance by then. Whatever is left on the card will be subject to a big rate increase after that date. Credit union credit cards tend to have longer low-rate periods. Consider these if you need more time.

# Haggle to cut high-interest cards

Everything in life is negotiable, and credit cards are no different. Don't put up with high interest rates. Fight back with a little planning and some smart bargaining skills.

+ Start by gathering the last credit card bill you received, and highlight your interest rate.

+ Save any recent credit card offers that have come in the mail. Highlight their promised interest rates and fees. Or go online to *www.bankrate.com* and *www.creditcards.com* to see current offers.

+ Count up the number of years you have been a customer of your credit card company.

+ Have your credit score on hand if you know it.

Call your card company's customer service number. Explain that you are a longtime customer in good standing and that you are considering switching cards. Tell them about the recent offers you have received. Point out the low interest rates and fees these other cards promise, and ask if they can beat these deals.

If you get a 'no,' ask to speak with a supervisor or with their customer retention department. Repeat the same process, and remember to be courteous.

Find out in a snap whether your credit card charges too much interest. Go to the website *www.indexcreditcards.com* to see the average interest rate on credit cards. For the rates on specific types of cards, like rewards cards, click on "More on current credit card interest rates."

If you pay more than the average, call your credit card company. Use these numbers as a bargaining tool to bring your rates back to earth.

# Credit or debit: tips to choose the best card

Different shopping situations call for different cards. Debit cards are great for budgeting and helping control your spending. They're great for everyday shopping at grocery and drugstores, and you can get cash back when you can't find an ATM. They aren't always the best choice, however. Consider swiping a credit card in these instances.

**Big purchases.** Credit cards allow you to withhold payment if the purchase goes wrong. With debit cards, on the other hand, the cash gets deducted immediately from your bank account.

The credit card company will often investigate the issue for you. But if you paid with a debit card and something goes wrong, you will likely have to fight with the merchant yourself.

**Gas, car rentals, hotel reservations, and dining out.** Your bank account can be "frozen" by hotels, restaurants, even gas stations for days. These merchants may put a hold on the money in your bank account when you pay by debit card.  In fact, they may freeze much more money than the cost of what you actually buy. That makes it easy to rack up overdraft fees. Prevent these bounced-check fees by paying with a credit card.

**Online buys.** Debit cards have different liability rules than credit cards, which can make online identity theft especially dangerous. With credit cards, you are only liable for the first $50 in fraudulent charges. With debit cards, you're liable for $500 or more. It's also easier to dispute fraudulent charges made with a credit card than with a debit card.

In addition to these benefits, some credit cards also insure your rental car against loss or damage; offer price protection by refunding the difference if the same merchant sells it later for less; automatically extend the warranty on purchases; and provide trip and baggage protection. Call your credit card company to learn about your specific benefits.

# Earn rewards that work for you

Credit cards offering rewards like cash back or airline miles may sound tempting, but they aren't for everyone. Rewards cards only work if you pay off the balance each month. That's because they tend to charge a high interest rate. That interest will devour your "rewards" if you carry a balance.

Beyond that, experts suggest choosing a rewards card based on your lifestyle. People who:

+ travel often should consider a card that earns airline miles or other travel rewards.

+ drive a lot should look into a card that gives discounts on gasoline.

+ don't do either, or prefer cash, can search for cash-back rewards cards.

+ want more flexibility should look at hybrid cards that let them mix and match rewards.

Rewards programs can be pretty confusing, so read the fine print carefully. You may have to spend a certain amount of money before you even begin earning rewards, or there may be a limit on the amount of rewards you can earn. Paying late, on the other hand, can void your rewards.

Check the expiration date on the points you earn. Look for a card that gives you plenty of time to spend your rewards before they expire. And beware of fees. They can offset an otherwise generous program.

# Foolproof steps to raising your credit score

Lenders have a super-secret way of deciding whether to loan you money. It's called your credit score, and it tells them how likely you are to pay back a loan.

You want them to think you will. Otherwise, you won't be able to refinance your mortgage, take out a car loan, or even get a credit card.

Thankfully, your credit score is not based on your income or assets. You don't need to make more money to boost it. You only need to pay your bills and be responsible with your debt. Follow these tips for a sky-high score.

+ Pay your bills on time. All of them, not just credit card bills. Experts say payment history has the biggest impact on your credit score.

+ Keep the balance on credit cards to less than half their limit, preferably to below 30 percent of their limit.

+ Cut back on credit card use for two to three months before applying for a car loan or mortgage.

+ Establish a credit history if you haven't already. Start by opening a secured credit card, where you send the credit card company a deposit, and they send you a card with a credit limit of the same amount.

+ Request a free copy of your credit report from each of the three reporting agencies. Check it for errors, and work to correct any you find.

Of course, some things can tank your score, too. Avoid these sure-fire ways to lower it.

+ Avoid closing your oldest credit accounts. Some experts recommend you stop using them, if you no longer want them, and let the creditors close unused accounts for you.

+ Don't apply for a bunch of store credit cards all at once. A 10-percent discount on your purchase may sound tempting around the holidays, but each credit application dings your score a little.

+ Don't take out a big loan right before you apply for a mortgage. Lenders don't like to see you take on several big debts at once.

You are now entitled to a free copy of your credit report every year from the three major credit reporting agencies — Experian, Equifax, and TransUnion — thanks to the federal government's Fair Credit Reporting Act.

Lots of commercials advertise "free credit reports," but they generally come as part of a pricey service you must pay for, like credit monitoring. Only the website *www.annualcreditreport.com* gives you a truly free report, no strings attached. Type in your name, address, Social Security Number, and date of birth to see it immediately on your computer. Or call 877-322-8228 and request a copy by mail.

The law entitles you to one free report from each of the three agencies. That's three reports total, and you don't have to get them all at once. Space them out. Request one report from each agency every four months. This will help you keep a closer eye out for errors and signs of identity theft.

# Free peek at credit scores

Annual credit reports are free, but finding out your credit score will still cost you. New websites can help you dodge the fees with free estimates.

**TOP DOLLAR:** Federal law requires credit reporting agencies to give you one free copy of your credit report each year. But that report does not include your credit score, the number lenders look at when deciding whether to loan you money. The score itself will cost you. Equifax, Experian, TransUnion, and Fair Isaac charge around $8 each.

**VALUE:** Head to websites that estimate your score for free. The numbers may not match your exact score, but they will give you a good idea of where you stand. Secure websites like *www.quizzle.com*, *www.credit.com*, and *www.creditkarma.com* produce an estimate based on information you provide, including your Social Security Number.

The sites may offer services for sale such as credit monitoring, or products like credit cards, but you don't have to buy anything to get your estimated credit score.

**WHAT YOU GIVE UP:** Knowing the exact score your lenders see. The estimator websites may also try to sell you goods or services. There's no obligation to buy, but you may feel hassled.

## Wise way to cancel cards

Closing a credit card account can actually lower your credit score. Your score is based partly on your credit utilization ratio – how much credit you have available, and how much of it you are currently using.

If you carry high balances on your credit cards, you are using a lot of your available credit. Close one card, and the available credit you have actually goes down. Since your debt hasn't gone down, your credit utilization ratio goes up.

Smart planning can stop this from happening. Pay down your balances first, so you are using less of your available credit. Then close the account.

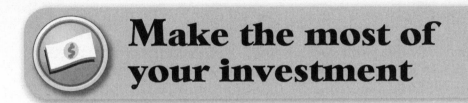

# Make the most of your investment

## Supercharge your Social Security benefits

Five easy-to-miss provisions can help you get all you deserve from Social Security. Decide which situations apply to you, then learn how to boost your benefits.

**Spouses.** If the highest-earning spouse waits until full retirement age to draw benefits, then the lower-earning spouse can collect half the other's Social Security benefits. However, if the higher earner claims Social Security early, then spousal benefits are cut up to 35 percent.

**Widows and widowers.** You can collect survivors benefits if your spouse or ex-spouse dies and you don't remarry until after age 60. Remarry before age 60, though, and you can't claim survivors benefits as long as you remain in the new marriage. You must have been married 10 or more years to collect on an ex-spouse.

To earn the most money over your lifetime, wait until your full retirement age to collect. Claiming before then could trim your benefits by more than one-quarter.

**Divorced couples.** You are entitled to part of your ex's benefits if you two were married for at least 10 years and you are at least 62 years old. However, you can't be married to someone else and collect on your ex, so your remarriage must have ended.

**Not-quite-retirees.** You can still work while collecting Social Security. But begin collecting before full retirement age, and you'll lose $1 in benefits for every $2 you earn over $14,160 a year (in 2010). The year you reach full retirement age, you'll lose $1 for every $3 earned over $37,680 a year (in 2010). The month you reach full retirement age, you can begin claiming benefits and working without penalty.

**First-year retirees.** The year you retire, you will probably begin drawing Social Security benefits in the middle of the year, not on January 1. By then, you may have exceeded the earnings cap. You'll still get benefits, however, for each month you fall below a certain income – $1,180 a month in 2010 – through the end of that year.

The rules can be complicated and do change. Contact your local Social Security office to meet with someone and go over your options.

## Increase your benefit for life

Make one mistake, and you could get 76 percent less in benefits each month. You can start collecting Social Security at age 62, but your benefits will be one-quarter lower than they could have been, for life, had you waited until full retirement age. Wait until age 70, and benefits will be about 76 percent higher than they would have been at 62.

For every year you wait to collect after age 62, your future payments go up by 8 percent. That's not just better for you. It's better for your spouse, too. If you pass away first, your spouse's survivors benefits will also be bigger for life, more than 20 percent larger if you claim at 66 instead of 62, and 60 percent larger if you claim at 70.

You can undo your decision within one year of applying for Social Security. Just meet Social Security Administration Form 521, your new best friend. File it within 12 months of when your payments begin. It withdraws your application, so you can restart your benefits at a later date.

## Stretch your savings in retirement

Experts recommend that most people try to delay taking Social Security benefits for as long as possible, so their payments grow as large as possible. Consider:

+ living off tax-deferred retirement accounts first, such as 401(k)s and IRAs.

+ then shifting to tax-free accounts, like a Roth IRA, at least until you turn 70.

However, if you get laid off and are still years away from collecting Social Security, think carefully about drawing down your IRA and 401(k) to pay mortgages, bills, and other debts. The money in these accounts is protected from bankruptcy. If you drain them and are still forced to declare bankruptcy, you have lost your retirement savings, too.

## Maximize your married income

Married couples can take their benefits in many different ways. The best strategy depends, in part, on each person's life expectancy and lifetime job earnings.

Social Security benefits are based on lifetime earnings, specifically the 35 highest-earning years of your life. In many families, one spouse earns more than the other and can expect a bigger benefit each month. Couples in this situation can boost benefits in one of two ways.

+ The lower-earning spouse begins collecting benefits early. The higher-earning spouse, on the other hand, waits to claim until full retirement age or later, even until age 70. This ensures the survivors benefit will be as big as possible if the higher earner dies first.

+ The higher-earning spouse applies for benefits upon reaching full retirement age. Then the lower-earning spouse applies only for spousal benefits. The bigger earner then files Form 521 to suspend their own benefit until age 70. This allows one person in the couple to draw benefits while the other person's benefits keep growing until age 70.

Couples who earned about the same amount of money can take a different tack. The older spouse can file for Social Security benefits once hitting full retirement age. Then the younger spouse can file for spousal benefits upon reaching their own full retirement age, while allowing their own benefits to keep growing. Once the younger spouse reaches age 70, they can switch to collecting their own benefits. This strategy works best if the younger spouse expects to live to a ripe old age.

Keep in mind, this only works if the younger spouse waits until full retirement age to claim spousal benefits. Any earlier, and they will only be allowed to claim the larger of the two benefits – theirs or their spousal.

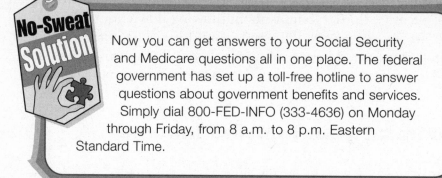

# Beef up your bond income

They're easy to take for granted, but your bonds could be working harder. Follow these simple strategies to squeeze more from your bond investments.

**Check prices.** Don't just buy whatever your broker offers you. Do your homework to find out if you're getting a good deal. Get the broker's price on a bond, then go to the website *www.investinginbonds.com*, or for municipal bonds, *www.emma.msrb.org*. Look up the bond's number to see what it last sold for. Take this price back to your broker to negotiate a better deal.

**Build a ladder.** Invest in several bonds with different maturities to ensure a steady source of income. It's a strategy called "laddering," where each bond represents one rung on the ladder.

By owning, say, a one-year, three-year, five-year, and 10-year bond, you stagger the interest payments and protect yourself against ups and downs in the bond market. For the highest return, always own one bond with at least five years left until maturity.

**Spread your wealth.** Don't place all of your nest eggs in one bond basket. Experts warn against putting more than 15 percent of your money in any one industry, in case it takes a dive. For instance, don't sink all your money into auto or financial bonds. If possible, avoid investing more than 5 percent of your total savings in any one bond.

**Shop for discounts.** Zero-coupon bonds can be bought for cents on the dollar. Unlike regular bonds, they don't pay any interest until they reach maturity. You pay a discounted price for them in the beginning, then redeem them for full face value at the end.

Even though you don't receive interest payments while you hold a zero-coupon bond, you pay income tax on it as if you did. The good news — by paying the tax now, you won't owe taxes when the bond matures.

**Dodge the tax man.** You can buy zero-coupon bonds through tax-deferred retirement accounts, such as an IRA, to avoid the tax hit for now. The interest earned will accrue tax-free until you withdraw your money. Or invest in municipal zero-coupon bonds outside of your retirement account. You won't owe any federal tax, and in some cases no state or local tax, either.

Keep in mind, however — you may not pay taxes on municipal bonds, but you must report the interest you earn from them as income to the Social Security Administration.

**DEEP DISCOUNT** Cut out the middleman. Buy your U.S. Treasury bills, bonds, and inflation-protected securities directly from the federal government. You'll save around $50 per trade in commission costs.

Simply call the U.S. Treasury at 800-722-2678 to buy securities. Internet-savvy folks can set up an account online at *www.treasury direct.gov* and buy them over the Internet.

# Cash in on forgotten bonds

Billions of dollars in matured U.S. Treasury bonds are floating around, forgotten, unredeemed, and no longer earning interest. Many bonds have matured recently, including Series E, EE, H, HH, A, B, C, D, F, G, J, K, and Savings Notes. A few minutes spent checking your old bonds could literally pay off.

The federal government's Treasury Hunt database can help you find matured Series E bonds issued after 1974. Head to the website *www.treasurydirect.gov*, and click on the link "Check Treasury Hunt to see if you own matured savings bonds." Then, click on the "Start Search" button. Enter your Social Security number, and the system will pull up your matured bonds.

## Free yourself from bad annuities

Like marriage, annuities come with binding contracts. Unfortunately, they're even harder to get out of. Try these tricks to free yourself.

**Take a look.** Most states require annuities to offer a trial period of 10 or more days, called a "free look," during which you can cancel the contract without penalty and get your money back. Find out if your state has this trial period, and make the most of it.

**Read the fine print.** Some annuities let you withdraw 10 to 15 percent of your principal without penalty under certain circumstances, for instance, if you become disabled, enter a nursing home, or develop a terminal illness.

**Switch your investments.** A variable annuity allows you to choose how the company invests your money. If you're unhappy with the returns, try changing how the money is invested. It may be cheaper and easier than getting out of the annuity altogether.

**Try a 1035 exchange.** It lets you roll money from one annuity to another without owing taxes, and it can help you trade out a real stinker for a better one with lower fees, different payout options, or a wider variety of investment choices. Make sure you have owned the first annuity long enough to escape any surrender penalties. Have a financial or tax professional look over the exchange first to make sure you won't owe taxes on the cash you transfer.

The new annuity may come with a new surrender period. Find out how long you will have to wait before withdrawing money. You may be better off keeping the old one, unless you plan to hold the new annuity for a long time.

## Collect fair share of old insurance policies

Tracking down the life insurance company when you need to collect may not be easy. The company that issued the policy may have merged, changed names, or even sold the policy to another insurer.

The National Association of Insurance Commissioners has set up a system to help, via the website *https://eapps.naic.org/orphanedpolicy*. Answer five questions, and the Life Insurance Company Location System will help you find the insurance company backing your policy. Don't have a computer? Do it the old-fashioned way.

✦ Find the full legal name of the insurance company as listed on the policy or binder. Also look for a mailing address and phone number.

✦ Figure out which state the policy was bought in, and when.

✦ Call the state insurance department in the insurance company's home state. This office should be able to track name changes or mergers the company underwent.

✦ If that doesn't work, find out where the policy owner lived when they purchased the policy, and call that state's department of insurance.

The American Council of Life Insurers may also be able to help. Many insurers belong to this trade association. Simply call 202-624-2000.

You could slash your life insurance premiums in half just by quitting smoking or losing weight. Premiums for smokers can run twice as high as for nonsmokers. Being overweight can ding you in a similar way. That's because rates are based on life expectancy, along with risk factors such as lifestyle, overall health, and medical history.

According to the website Insure.com, these 10 conditions are the ones most likely to raise your rates:

- high blood pressure
- high cholesterol
- depression
- asthma
- type 2 diabetes
- sleep apnea
- cancer (except skin cancer)
- heart disease
- coronary artery disease
- mitral valve prolapse

Many of these can be prevented or treated. Already bought a policy? Ask for a rate reevaluation once your health improves. Don't wait for January 1. Make resolutions now to change your habits, get healthy, and start saving big money.

# Outsmart expensive investments

Investing in mutual funds is one of the easiest ways to grow your money. Mutual funds pool people's money and use it to buy a wide variety of stocks, bonds, or other financial products. That diversity tends to make them safer than other investments. Not all mutual funds are made the same, however, and the ones you choose make all the difference.

**TOP DOLLAR:** Actively managed funds hire a team of investment advisors to research and analyze companies to invest in. The goal — to "beat the market" by out-earning one of the stock market indexes, like the S&P 500.

Sometimes they succeed. Most of the time, they don't. Still, the possibility of big returns tempts lots of people into investing in actively managed mutual funds. They pay a premium for the chance. These funds typically charge 1 percent more in fees than passive index funds. After all, someone has to pay those investment analysts.

**VALUE:** Index mutual funds, on the other hand, are known for low fees. That's because they operate on autopilot. Instead of trying to beat the market, they try to match it. It takes a lot fewer investment professionals to run an index fund.

**WHAT YOU GIVE UP:** A shot at beating the stock market. Most actively managed funds don't perform as well as index funds, however, in part because of their higher fees.

A 1-percent difference between funds may not sound like much, but it adds up over time. Say you invest $10,000 in an actively managed mutual fund that charges a 1.4 percent fee. If the fund earns 6 percent a year, you'll end up with $24,583.06 after 20 years. However, had you put that money in a lower-fee fund, like an index fund, that charged only 0.4 percent a year, you could have earned $5,152.63 more.

## Save thousands on sneaky fees

Your 401(k) fees aren't the only ones that can eat away your savings. Sneaky fees on your monthly bills could be costing you thousands.

+ "Free" checking accounts that charge $5 a month for maintenance, or $60 each year. Beat this fee with help from *Hidden cost of 'free' checking* in the chapter *Make Your Bank Work for You*.

+ Overdraft charges. At around $35 a pop, you could spend $420 a year just by overdrawing once a month. Learn how to *Put an end to overdraft charges* in *Make Your Bank Work for You*.

+ Paying car insurance premiums in installments. Insurers charge up to $100 a year for breaking your insurance premium into monthly payments. Save up and pay the lump sum every six months, instead.

+ Inessential phone add-ons. Caller ID, call waiting, and call forwarding can add $18 a month to your phone bill. Cancel them and pocket $216 a year.

+ Fraudulent charges on phone bills. Third-party companies may stuff your bill with fake fees, potentially $16 or more each month, or $192 a year. Block them before you get hit. See *Stop 'cramming' from fattening your bill* in the chapter *Cut Your Phone Spending in Half*.

+ Not-so-free 411 calls. Now phone companies may charge $3.49 per 411 call. Make four calls a month, and you'll pay $167.52 in one year. Discover the new free 411 services in *Cut Your Phone Spending in Half*.

+ Credit card late fees. At $25 to $35 apiece, they're bad enough, but paying late can send your interest rate skyrocketing. You'll pay $857 in interest on a $5,000 balance the first year if your low introductory rate zooms from zero to 19.85 percent.

Take the money you save on fees, and tuck it away for a rainy day or future retirement.

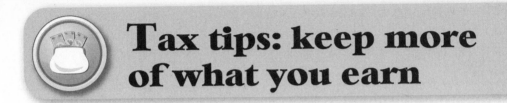

# Tax tips: keep more of what you earn

## Slash your property taxes to the bone

Thousands of people have already cut their property tax bills to rock bottom, and you can, too. Just follow this step-by-step process to appeal your property taxes.

**Ask how taxable value is figured.** It may be based on cost to rebuild, percentage of your home's estimated value, recent sales of similar homes, or something else entirely. Call the tax assessor's office and ask what methods or percentages they use — and when you are eligible to file an appeal.

**Visit the assessor's office.** Request the property card and other documents used to value your home, and ask how to calculate your property tax bill from the assessor's value.

**Review your property card.** This describes characteristics of your home that affect its taxable value, such as square footage and number of bathrooms. Check for mistakes like math errors or the wrong number of rooms.

**Audit your home value.** You may also reduce your property taxes if homes similar to yours sold or assessed for at least 10 percent less value. "Similar" means a similar-size home and lot roughly the same age, preferably with the same number of bedrooms and baths. Find 10 similar homes nearby that sold either recently or the year your home was assessed. A realtor can help you get this information, but some may charge a fee. Look up the valuations of these homes at the assessor's office.

**Prepare your case.** If you found mistakes on your property card, or discovered similar homes valued at least 10 percent lower for tax purposes, gather supporting evidence. For example, take pictures to show how your property card is wrong. Meanwhile, keep paying your property taxes to avoid penalties.

**Meet with your assessor.** Quickly explain the problems you found, and ask if the assessor can lower your tax bill himself. If so, request a written copy of his decision. Otherwise, ask how to appeal.

**Prepare and appeal.** Follow the assessor's instructions. Also, prepare a five-minute presentation and a one-page letter with attachments to explain why you should pay less. If you win your appeal, you will be rewarded with lower property taxes.

Even if you do not win, you may qualify for property taxes that never go up. Ask the assessor's office about property tax relief programs, exemptions, or freezes you could be eligible for, based on age or other characteristics.

# Exciting new answer to property tax woes

Millions of seniors can eliminate property taxes. Are you one of them?

You may be – if your county or town offers a property tax work-off program for older adults. People who participate in these programs may erase their property tax bill by working part time or temporarily for their local governments.

Available jobs have included answering phones, landscaping, manning an information booth, doing research or data entry, stacking library books, or even painting fire hydrants. Some programs even try to match the job to the skills, location, or limits of the person available for work.

A number of programs limit the amount of property taxes you can work off, so you may not be able to wipe out the entire bill if property taxes are high. But you could still save a lot of money, and you may have fun doing it.

To find out whether your local government offers a property tax work-off program and how to apply, contact its Human Resources department, Senior Citizen or Elder department, Tax Assessor's office, or Taxpayer Assistance office.

You can get free help with your taxes from the IRS.

The IRS provides prerecorded tax information 24 hours a day at its Teletax number. Available topics include deductions, tax credits, IRAs, 401(k) plans, and more. Just call 800-829-4477, and have pencil and paper ready so you can take notes. For a directory of topics, listen to topic 123.

For more complicated questions, call the IRS toll-free tax-assistance hotline at 800-829-1040.

To order free tax forms or free IRS publications that explain how the tax laws affect your taxes, visit *www.irs.gov* or call toll-free 800-829-3676. If you order by phone, be ready with the names or item numbers of the forms or publications you need.

For more details on free tax information and services from the IRS, order IRS Publication 910.

# Cut your taxes to the absolute lowest

A big tax refund may mean you temporarily paid more taxes than you owed, simply by withholding too much from your monthly paycheck. But during the months you lived without that money, the government probably earned interest on it. So make sure your withholding amount is as low as legally possible.

Gather your latest pay stub, current W-4, and most recent income tax return, and then decide which of the following methods to use.

+ If you have a computer, let the IRS Withholding Calculator do the heavy lifting. Just visit *www.irs.gov*, and click on the link Estimate your withholding.

+ Order IRS Publication 919, and fill out its worksheets to help determine the correct withholding amount.

If you are withholding too much, ask your employer for a blank W-4 form, use your IRS calculator or worksheet results to help fill it out, and return the form to your employer. When the increase shows up in your paycheck, you can put that new savings to work earning interest or profit for you, instead of the government.

**CASH SAVER**

You just increased your withholding but cannot decide how to invest your new savings. Be careful — investments or an interest-bearing bank account may not give you the most bang for your buck. If your credit card debt is piling up and you pay 20-percent interest, you can save 20 cents for every dollar you pay off. That is like earning a 20-percent return on an investment. So before using your new savings for investments, pay off any credit card debt you have. That is one investment that guarantees a great return.

# Beat high taxes with perfectly legal maneuvers

Make sure you only pay your fair share of taxes and not one penny more. But do not wait until you fill out your return. Discover legal ways to protect yourself from paying more taxes than necessary, and start cutting your taxes right now.

Pretax money can help slash your taxes by reducing your taxable income. It comes out of your paycheck before income tax, Social Security tax, and Medicare tax are subtracted. If you are in the 28-percent tax bracket and can pay for something with pretax money, you may save up to $55 for every $100 you spend. Here are some of your options for stashing pretax money.

**401(k) plan.** Many companies offer this retirement plan, which accepts contributions of pretax dollars from your salary. You can only contribute as much as the IRS allows, $16,500 for 2010, but that money grows tax-free until you withdraw it. Many employers also match this contribution up to a point, and that is free money.

**FSA or HSA.** If you chose a high-deductible health insurance plan and are not currently enrolled in Medicare, you may contribute pretax money to a Health Savings Account (HSA). In 2010, your insurance must have a deductible of either $1,200 (single coverage) or $2,400 (family coverage) and a high out-of-pocket maximum to qualify. You can contribute up to $3,050 (single) or $6,150 (family), and any money left at the end of the year can be used next year.

Interest or other earnings on money in your HSA are usually tax-free. Withdrawals from the account are also tax-free if you spend the money on qualified medical expenses. If you don't qualify for the HSA, you can put pretax dollars in a Flexible Spending Account (FSA). You can contribute as much money as your FSA's prescribed limit allows, but you must spend all of your contributions by the year-end date set by your plan – or lose what is left.

Remember to only use this money to cover out-of-pocket, qualified medical expenses. These are expenses that qualify for a tax deduction according to IRS Publication 502.

**Cafeteria plan.** Your employer may offer a cafeteria plan that allows you to pay for benefits with pretax dollars.

## DEEP DISCOUNT

The government keeps trying its darndest to find more ways to raise your taxes, but it still cannot tax some kinds of income. If you are in the 25-percent tax bracket, that means you avoid 25 cents of taxes on every tax-free dollar in your income. So when making financial decisions, remember that you do not pay income tax on items like these.

- the "cash back" you receive from cash-back credit cards
- earnings within health savings accounts and distributions from health savings accounts as long as the distributions are used for qualified medical expenses
- some scholarships and fellowships
- interest on most municipal and state bonds. Ask the bond issuer or purchasing organization if the interest is taxable.
- part of the profit from selling your home
- most life insurance proceeds

# Clever way to pay less to the IRS

You could hold a yard sale to get rid of your clutter, or you could turn those items into tax deductions by donating them to charity. Remember, even bulky or expensive items like furniture can be donated to organizations that will come and pick them up.

To turn your charitable donation into a money-saving tax deduction, you must be careful to follow the rules. Start with these.

+ Make sure you donate to a qualified organization such as the Red Cross, Salvation Army, religious organizations, war veterans groups, or nonprofit schools or hospitals. See IRS Publication 526 for more details, or call the IRS toll-free at 877-829-5500 to find out if an organization is qualified.

+ If you donate clothing, furniture, linens, or other household items, they must be in good used condition or better to qualify for a deduction.

+ You can only deduct the fair market value of a donated item. This is not always equal to the price you paid for the item. For example, the fair market value of used clothing is usually the price you would pay at a consignment or thrift store. For more details on determining the value of donated property, see IRS Publication 561. Estimates of fair market value may also be available at *www.goodwill.org* or *www.salvationarmyusa.org*.

+ You must document your property donations, but the rules vary depending on the size of your deduction and whether you receive anything from the charity. For deductions under $250, for example, you need a letter or receipt from the organization that lists the name of the charity, the date and location of your contribution, and a reasonably detailed description of what you donated. You should also keep additional records such as the name and address of the charity, the item's fair market value, and how you figured that value. See IRS Publication 526 for more details.

+ You must itemize on your tax return instead of taking the standard deduction.

## Escape the gift tax legally

You want to help your children pay for college, medical bills, or a house down payment, but you doubt you can afford the gift tax on that money. According to the 2010 gift tax rules, you can give up to $13,000 to each of your children every year without paying gift tax. You and your spouse can raise that amount to $26,000 if you each separately give $13,000 to each person during the same year.

You can give even more if you want to help pay for tuition or medical bills. You can pay an unlimited amount of someone else's medical expenses or tuition – without paying any gift taxes – as long as you pay the educational organization or the care provider directly. For the latest information about gift tax rules, check IRS Publication 950.

## Get more for your tax-prep money

Six out of 10 U.S. taxpayers hire a tax preparer to help make that April 15 deadline every year. But you can enjoy expert tax advice and save at least $50 if you use tax software to help prepare your own taxes.

**TOP DOLLAR:** Estimates of the cost of using a tax preparer range from $129 to $258.

**VALUE:** Popular tax software such as TurboTax or H&R Block At Home costs between $15 and $70 for home users. Each software package comes in several versions, cheaper versions with fewer features for simpler tax returns, and more complex versions with extra features for more complicated returns.

**WHAT YOU GIVE UP:** You may not receive as much expert assistance from the software as you get from a tax professional. Tax software uses a question-and-answer format to help you figure out your taxes, but those questions sometimes contain jargon that is hard to understand. A good tax preparer can ask questions, help you cut through the jargon, and may find tax deductions you would miss. Also:

+ you may forgo the free extra help you would get from a tax preparer if you were audited. For example, one tax software package offers a free Audit Support Center to help you face an audit on your own, but you pay extra for a human representative.

+ the more complicated your tax return is, the more likely you are to need a professional. For example, you may benefit from help if you have complex investments, a home business, or a recent major life change. Using a preparer may also save you the time and misery of doing your own taxes.

On the other hand, many tax returns do not require the expertise of a tax preparer and can easily be done with tax software. You do not have to leave home to prepare your taxes, you save money, and you can make sure your tax return receives the care and attention it deserves.

## Easy tax-return savings

You might be surprised at the extra money you pay to file your tax return. Whether it is postage to mail the return or extra dollars that sneak into your tax preparer's bill, you probably spend more than you would like. Try these tips to help.

**Trim your tax preparer's bill.** Never give your tax preparer a pile of papers and expect her to sort through them. If your tax preparer is paid by the hour, you may pay extra for anything that slows her work on your taxes. That includes hunting through papers for information or tracking down missing forms. So provide everything your tax preparer needs, and organize your papers into labeled categories.

**Use IRS Free File.** Stop paying to mail your tax packet to the IRS. If your adjusted gross income is $58,000 or less, you may qualify for IRS Free File, a way to file your taxes electronically using the Internet. Just visit *www.irs.gov*, and click the Free File link.

The site offers links to companies that let you use their software to file your federal tax return for free. Be careful, though. Filing your state tax return may not be free, depending on where you live and which company you choose. So check the cost of filing your state return before using a particular company's software.

If you do not qualify for Free File, you can use the Free File Fillable Forms. These are the same as the paper forms you usually fill out. The online forms help with your calculations and allow you to file your federal taxes using the Internet instead of the mail.

**Call for free help with your taxes.** Find out if you qualify for one of these.

- ✦ If you are age 60 or older, the Tax Counseling for the Elderly (TCE) program offers help preparing basic returns. To discover where to go locally for TCE, call the IRS toll-free at 800-829-1040.

- ✦ AARP Tax-Aide helps middle- and low-income taxpayers — especially those age 60 and up. You can meet with trained AARP Tax-Aide volunteers for tax counseling. Call toll-free 888-227-7669 to learn more and to find an AARP Tax-Aide site near you.

Remember, signing your tax return means you agree with everything on it. Before you sign, review the return, and ask questions until you understand its contents.

# Avoid tax surprises when moving

Many retirees consider moving to a "tax friendly" state to stretch their retirement dollars. But make sure you do your homework before relocating. States with little or no income tax are not necessarily tax friendly. A state with a minimal or zero income tax may make up for it with high sales taxes, property taxes, gas or auto taxes, or other taxes. Here is what you need to know.

+ Find out the property tax rate for the city, county, part of the county, and state you're considering – and ask what percentage of a property's assessed value gets taxed.

+ Check for property tax breaks and exemptions, especially those for seniors and veterans.

+ Examine the estate tax laws of any state you consider.

+ Learn how high the state, city, and county sales taxes are.

+ Find out whether the state taxes Social Security benefits, IRA distributions, and pensions.

+ If the state has income tax, find out how it defines income and what its tax rates and tax brackets are.

+ Check whether the state offers tax breaks for retirees.

To find this information, contact the local and state tax departments of places where you would like to move – or visit their websites.

**DEEP DISCOUNT** If you move to take a new job, you may be eligible for an income tax break on your expenses provided you meet a 50-mile distance test and work at least 39 weeks in the new location. You can usually deduct the cost of moving your household and personal goods plus the cost of travel. For more information, go to *www.irs.gov* and search for IRS publication 521.

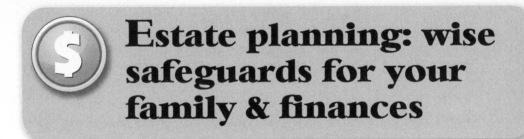

# Estate planning: wise safeguards for your family & finances

## 6 practical alternatives to a high-priced funeral

You may be in mourning, but you don't want to be in the poorhouse, too. Try these six practical alternatives to a high-priced funeral.

**Shop around.** Compare prices for funerals, as you would for any major purchase. Call a few funeral homes in your area. By law, they must provide you with a detailed price list – no questions asked.

**Skip a step.** Don't pay extra for embalming. This procedure is not required in most cases. Choose direct cremation or immediate burial instead.

**Opt for a cheaper container.** You don't need to buy a casket for cremation. That's literally setting money on fire. Buy an inexpensive alternative container made out of pressboard, cardboard, or canvas.

**Sidestep service fees.** Funeral homes may tack on extra fees for items such as flowers, obituary notices, pall bearers, organists, and soloists. They must let you know about these fees, as well as any discounts or rebates you're entitled to. You may be able to save by making your own arrangements.

**Pay less for a casket or urn.** Funeral directors may push for costlier vessels, but don't feel pressured to pay full price. Ask to see cheaper options. You can even buy one from another source. The funeral home can't refuse – or charge extra – to handle it. Remember, no casket keeps out water, dirt, and other substances forever.

**Plan your own funeral.** While your family will still grieve when you die, you can lessen their burden by making your wishes known ahead of time. This also spares your family from emotional over-spending. Don't keep your funeral plans in a safe deposit box with your will. The box may not be opened until after your funeral – when it's too late.

When planning a funeral – either a relative's or your own – make sure you know your rights and your options. One good resource is the Funeral Consumers Alliance at *www.funerals.org*. You can also contact them at 800-765-0107.

The Federal Trade Commission's pamphlet "Funerals: A Consumer Guide" also has helpful information. Order it online at the government site *www.pueblo.gsa.gov* or by calling 888-878-3256. You can also find help at *www.ftc.gov*.

**Safe & Secure**

Planning your own funeral may be a smart move — but prepaying for it may not be. Here are some drawbacks to a prepaid funeral plan.

• Not all states make funeral homes guarantee their locked-in rates. Changing your plan may also void any price guarantees you were given.

• You may pay more in premiums for burial insurance than the actual cost of services.

• The mortician may keep up to 30 percent of your money as commission.

• Prepaid plans don't change with your needs. Many are irrevocable, so you're stuck with them.

Ask these questions when considering a prepaid funeral plan.

• Which parts of the funeral are included and which are not?

• Can the policy be canceled or transferred to another funeral home? Are there penalties for doing this?

• Are there substitutions if something you've chosen is no longer available?

• What happens if the funeral home changes hands?

Here's another thing to keep in mind — sign a contract only after a lawyer has reviewed it.

# Get the verdict on free legal advice

Estate planning comes with a host of legal issues. Writing a will, setting up a trust, and taking stock of your estate can be tricky. It's enough to make you plead guilty to feeling overwhelmed. Luckily, the following resources offer free expert legal advice for seniors — including taxes, benefits, housing options, and more.

+ Legal hotlines. If you're over age 60, your state may offer free legal advice over the phone. The lawyers who staff these hotlines can answer legal questions, mail pamphlets containing the information you need, or refer you to a special, low-cost group of attorneys or to a free legal services program. Contact your state's bar association or Area Agency on Aging to find out about legal hotlines in your area. You can also go to *www.legalhotlines.org* to find legal hotlines and websites for your state.

+ Government hotline. Have a question about U.S. government benefits and services? Call this toll-free hotline at 800-333-4636 (800-FED-INFO). You can also get information at *answers.usa.gov*.

+ American Bar Association at *www.abanet.org*. Click on Public Resources, and this website will help you find a lawyer, get definitions of legal terms, find free legal help, learn about the court system, and read about topics like family law, real estate transactions, wills, and more. There's even a search tool where you can type in a topic and read various free articles.

+ Nolo at *www.nolo.com*. This one-stop provider of legal information sells several things, like legal forms, software, and books. But it's also a great resource for good, free legal information. Read articles about wills and estate planning, patents and copyrights, property and money, family law and immigration, and rights and disputes. There's even a lawyer directory to help you find legal help.

+ SeniorLaw at *www.seniorlaw.com*. This site provides legal information in plain language that anyone can understand. Features include basic explanations of Medicaid and Medicare, links to resources on elder abuse, and information about wills. You can also find attorneys in your area who specialize in elder law.

✦ Eldercare Locator at *www.eldercare.gov*. This public service of the Administration on Aging connects older Americans with information on senior services, including national and local legal resources. You can also call 800-677-1116.

# Tips and tricks for titling your assets

What's in a name? When it comes to estate planning, plenty. Part of estate planning includes putting your assets in order, so it's important to title your assets correctly. Whose name is on your car title, your insurance policies, your mortgage? Listing the wrong person could cost you thousands.

**Consider your car.** To limit liability in case of an accident, you may want to list only the car's primary driver on the title. That way, lawsuits won't wipe out both you and your spouse. On the other hand, if you and your spouse own everything jointly anyway, you may choose to list both of your names on the car's title in order to get a better deal on auto insurance.

**Inspect insurance policies.** If the name on your homeowners insurance policy does not match the name on the home's title, it could affect your estate. Say you put your home in a trust in order to avoid probate and limit estate taxes – but you leave the insurance in your name. If you die in a home fire or other disaster, the insurance claim will go to your estate rather than the trust, leading to probate, estate taxes, and all the complications you were hoping to sidestep.

**Manage your mortgage.** To get the best terms, two-income couples should usually list both names as borrowers. However, if one spouse makes all or most of the money and has a much better credit score, you might want to list just that person's name.

**Handle your home.** Your home is likely your most valuable asset, so having the right name on the title is very important. Listing you and your spouse as "joint tenants" allows the house to pass to your spouse without going through probate when you die. But it may be a better move to put your home in a living trust, which makes it easier to pass on to your children later.

If you or someone you live with is facing bankruptcy, lawsuits, or a long stay in a nursing home, keeping that person's name off the title might provide some asset protection. Don't put your child's name on your house's title. Your child must report this as a gift, pay taxes on their portion of the home's value, and possibly pay extra taxes if the home is sold.

# Wise ways to write a will

Everyone needs a will, but not everyone needs to pay big bucks to prepare one. Consider these options when writing your will.

**TOP DOLLAR:** Hire a lawyer who specializes in estate planning to draw up a will and comprehensive estate plan. This could cost $300 for a simple will and $1,000 or more for the comprehensive plan.

**VALUE:** Prepare a basic, no-frills will by yourself. It's legally valid and can cost less than $50. Software, websites, and do-it-yourself kits and books can help walk you through the will-making process.

+ Nolo's Quicken WillMaker Plus program costs about $40 on CD or to download at *www.nolo.com*.

+ BuildaWill offers a customized will for just $19.95 on its website *www.buildawill.com*. For an extra $9.95, you can make unlimited changes to your will, which will be stored online on a secure server.

+ LegalZoom's standard will costs $69 at *www.legalzoom.com*. There are also more expensive options, depending on your needs.

Basic, do-it-yourself wills are a good option for people with typical assets – house, car, savings, investments – especially if you're leaving your entire estate to one or two heirs with no strings attached.

**WHAT YOU GIVE UP:** Expertise. Lawyers can come up with more hypothetical situations and solutions than you would think of on your own. They also know more options for setting up trusts, avoiding probate, and minimizing estate taxes.

While a basic, do-it-yourself will can save you money, it may not be for everyone. If you have a complex family situation, own property in more than one state, or have assets worth more than $2 million, you may want to consult a lawyer. Professional advice can also come in handy if you're disinheriting a child, setting up a trust for a special needs child, or expect your will to be contested.

**DEEP DISCOUNT** You don't have to wait until you're dead to give money to your children or grandchildren. Take advantage of tax loopholes to help them now. Current rules allow a single person to give up to $13,000 per recipient to any number of people without paying gift taxes. Couples can give up to $26,000 per recipient. Best of all, recipients pay no taxes on the money received. For information about how much you can give, visit *www.irs.gov* or call 800-829-1040.

If you want to give away more money than the limits allow, you can pay an unlimited amount for current — not future — tuition expenses or medical expenses. You can also give money to your heirs through trusts, such as irrevocable life insurance trusts and charitable annuity trusts. Talk to a financial professional to learn more.

# Bypass probate with these accounts

Probate can be problematic. This complex process can keep your estate tied up in court, leaving quite a hassle for your heirs. Luckily, it's easy to pass property to your heirs without going through probate. Keep things simple with transfer-on-death accounts.

With a payable-on-death bank account, you can keep even large sums of money out of probate. Simply fill out a form naming the person you want to inherit the funds in your account.

Transfer-on-death securities registration works the same way for stocks and bonds. Request to take ownership in "beneficiary form," and your beneficiary's name will also appear on your ownership papers. When you open a retirement account, such as a 401(k) or IRA, you can name a beneficiary who will inherit the account when you die. Some states even offer a transfer-on-death registration for vehicles.

In all these cases, your designated beneficiary has no rights or access to your money or property while you're still alive. When you die, the beneficiary simply provides proof of your death plus proper identification and inherits it. No probate, no problems.

## Pass on your riches with a Roth IRA

Individual retirement accounts are a great way to save money. They can also be a great way to leave money to your heirs. To maximize their inheritance, choose a Roth IRA.

Unlike a traditional IRA, a Roth IRA does not feature mandatory withdrawals after you reach your 70s. So there could be more money left in the account to pass on to your family. As a bonus, your heirs won't owe income tax on withdrawals from the account.

As with other IRAs, your heirs must withdraw a percentage of the funds annually, based on age. So the younger your heirs are when they inherit an IRA, the longer they can stretch out withdrawals, leaving more time for tax-free growth of investments. You can even set up a trust to withhold all but the minimum distribution until your grandchildren reach a certain age.

Consider converting your retirement account to a Roth IRA. Keep in mind that each dollar you convert will be taxed as ordinary income. You can contribute up to $5,000 a year to a Roth IRA until you reach age 50. After that, you can add up to $6,000 a year.

## Low-cost living wills give you peace of mind

If you have a will, you know what becomes of your house, car, and other valuable possessions after your death. But what happens to your most prized possession – your own body – if you are incapacitated by severe injury or illness?

That's why you should also prepare an advance directive, or living will. In this legal document, you state the type of life-prolonging medical intervention you want or don't want if you become terminally ill and unable to communicate.

You can find several free or cheap resources to help you create a living will. Here are some useful websites.

- ✦ Caring Connections at *www.caringinfo.org*. You can download your state's advanced directive forms and instructions from this site, a program of the National Hospice and Palliative Care Organization.

- ✦ Aging With Dignity at *www.agingwithdignity.org*. For $5, you can order this organization's popular living will called Five Wishes, which meets the legal requirements in 42 states.

- ✦ U.S. Living Will Registry at *www.uslwr.com*. This source answers all your questions about living wills. You can also store it and make it available to health care providers across the country. The site even provides resources for preparing a living will and links to download the appropriate forms in your state.

- ✦ LegalZoom at *www.legalzoom.com*. Create a living will with help from this site, which specializes in legal documents. Prices start at $39.

**No-Sweat Solution**

Make sure to keep a copy of your IRA beneficiary-designation form. While your bank or brokerage likely keeps it on file, it could end up missing — and your heirs could miss out on some money.

With the form, your heirs can stretch withdrawals over their life expectancy. Although they have to pay taxes on the withdrawals, the balance in the account would still draw interest. Without the form, your heirs would have to empty the account sooner, costing them much more in taxes.

Remember, the names on these forms supersede those in your will. If you need to change your beneficiary, you can probably do it online. You can also ask for a beneficiary-designation form from your bank or brokerage.

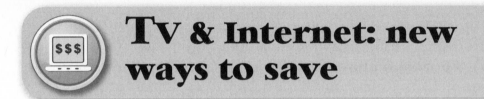

# Tv & Internet: new ways to save

## 7 easy ways to get rid of old electronics

Your new television arrives next week, so you need an easy, cheap way to get rid of your old one. This problem crops up with most electronics because many states have passed laws against tossing old televisions and gadgets in the trash. Here's what to do instead.

**See what your seller says.** Any time you buy a new television or other gizmo, ask the seller what it charges to haul off your old one. The service may be free and could be particularly helpful with large TVs and other items that are too heavy to lift.

**Consider the Internet.** Your old electronics may help you make cold, hard cash. Recycling websites like *www.gazelle.com* and *www.wireflytradeins.com* appraise the value of your electronics and pay you accordingly. For example, Gazelle can pay you by check, PayPal, or even with Amazon or Walmart gift cards. Items accepted by Gazelle include cell phones, digital cameras, computers, video games, calculators, MP3 players, gaming consoles, camcorders, and computer monitors.

**Make a deal with your favorite retailer.** Some retailers may give you a gift card in exchange for your old electronics. For example, if you turn in electronics through Walmart's trade-in website, you may get a Walmart gift card. Other retailers, like Sears, Best Buy, and Costco, have similar programs. Visit these websites to learn more.

✦ *walmart.gazelle.com*

✦ *sears.gazelle.com*

✦ *costco.gazelle.com*

✦ *www.bestbuytradein.com*

**Check nearby stores.** Some electronics and office supply stores, like Staples, let you drop off small electronics for recycling.

**Ask the manufacturer.** Which company made your old television or gadget? Visit the manufacturer's website or *www.mrmrecycling.com* to find drop-off locations that collect electronics for recycling.

**Find the right local recycler.** Surf to *eiae.org, electronicsrecycling. org*, or *earth911.com* to find electronics recyclers near you.

**Ring your local government.** Call your city or county government to ask whether they offer a place or event to drop off electronics for recycling.

Just remember this – any time you visit a recycling website or call a potential recycler, check whether you must pay fees to recycle your item. Some services are not free. And some free services may charge you a small fee for televisions with cathode ray tubes.

**DEEP DISCOUNT**

Don't miss out on annual discounts on your cable bill or other monthly bills. Make a list of the companies you pay every month. Call each company and ask if it offers a discount for paying once a year instead of every month. Some companies may even advertise this discount on their websites.

# Pay less for satellite, cable, and more

You want to pay less for cable or satellite television. Yet, you don't want to give up your favorite channels, and you don't know which providers are available. Fortunately, a website can do all the work for you.

Visit *www.billshrink.com* and click on the Television service option. BillShrink asks you a few questions like where you live, how much you pay now, which channels you want to keep, and your approximate credit score. You may also be asked to sign up for a free BillShrink account.

BillShrink reviews the possible providers, supplies you with a list of plans that may save money, and estimates how much you can save. Be a savvy consumer and visit each provider's website to discover the details of the plans in your list. This extra research can help you avoid any unpleasant surprises BillShrink is not yet designed to spot.

BillShrink also has options that can help you save money on cell phone service, gasoline, credit cards, and more. If you sign up for an account, BillShrink can even notify you when a new offer could save you even more money.

# Get better results from customer service

Your cable service, Internet service, or a product seller has let you down. Don't get angry – get results. Secrets like these can help your complaint story have a happier ending.

**Reduce your on-hold time dramatically.** According to Lucyphone, you need never wait on hold again. Just visit *www.lucyphone.com*, type in a company's toll-free customer service number, enter a phone number where you can be reached, and click on Start. When your phone rings, pick up and Lucyphone connects you to the number you wanted. After you navigate through the phone menu and are put on hold, you press a special key sequence and hang up. When a customer service representative picks up, your phone rings.

*Consumer Reports* tested Lucyphone and found it usually works well if no one picks up during the first minute you are on hold, but it does not work as well when you call government agencies.

**Be polite.** People yell at customer service representatives all the time. To truly get their attention, be polite but don't compromise on what you want.

**Be prepared.** State your problem briefly, have your supporting documents ready, and know exactly what resolution you want.

**Go higher up.** If the person does not have the authority to give you what you want, ask to speak to a supervisor. Move up the ladder until you get results. If that doesn't work, write or send an email to the public relations department.

**Ask for advice.** If your phone call has reached a dead end, ask the customer service representative what he would do in your situation.

**Write an effective complaint letter.** If a call or email has not helped, write a complaint letter using these guidelines.

+ Address your letter to the director of customer service or another person with enough authority to help.

+ Give details about the product or service involved and clearly, but briefly, describe your problem.

+ Specify the result you want and when you expect that result. Make the deadline reasonable.

+ Include copies of any documents related to the problem.

+ Provide your contact information and any account numbers, serial numbers, or model numbers that identify the product or service you are writing about.

+ Keep the tone of the letter courteous and free of sarcasm or anger.

## Beat the automated phone system and talk to a real person

Call any customer service hotline and you will probably hear one of those annoying automated phone systems telling you to "Press 1 to reach customer service." But here is a secret customer service hopes you never find out — you can confuse the automated system and bypass all its options. Try these 10 ways to speak to a real person — fast.

- When the automated system asks what you want, say each of these phrases until one works — "transfer," "operator," "customer service," "help," "get human," "agent," or "representative."

- Press the pound key, star key, zero, or some combination of these keys.

- Press a bunch of keys quickly, one after the other, or rapidly press one key repeatedly.

- Mumble or speak gibberish to stump the phone system so it will forward you to a live person.

- Don't respond. This may trick the system into thinking you have a rotary phone. Rotary phone calls may be automatically forwarded to a real person.

- Visit *www.gethuman.com* or *www.dialahuman.com* to look up the business you are calling. These websites keep databases of effective phone shortcuts for specific companies.

- See if you can "speak" with customer service using online chat.

- Call from a friend's phone or a work phone to convince the phone system to treat you as a new customer. Sometimes, new customers are moved to the front of the line. If the company keeps a separate number for new customers, phone that number instead of the customer service line.

- Call the company's main phone number, especially if it is toll-free.

- Choose the option for Spanish and hope you reach a bilingual agent who can help you.

## Save hundreds each year with a simple phone call

You can slash your cable bills, Internet bills, and more without giving up the services you like. Here's how to get started.

**Discover an insider secret.** Call the cancellation department instead of customer service. Businesses know that retaining an old customer costs far less than bringing in new ones. That is why many businesses have a cancellation or retention department. Agents in these departments often have more power to give you better deals than regular customer service representatives. You just have to know how to approach them.

**Watch the competitors.** To start earning a better deal on your cable package, monitor your junk mail for offers from cable competitors. When you find an offer you like, call your current cable company and ask to speak with the cancellation department or choose the cancellation option from the automated phone system.

Whether you are routed to the cancellation department or the customer service department, tell the representative about the competitor's offer and say you are thinking of switching unless the cable company matches that offer. If the representative offers you a discount that is weaker than the competitor's offer, thank the person but say you were hoping for better. If the representative starts the cancellation process, say you need time to think about it before canceling. If you call back later, you may get a different customer service representative who can offer a better deal.

**Be prepared to cancel.** If that doesn't work, cancel your service and switch providers. After all, you can always come back as a new customer and take advantage of special introductory rates. But don't be surprised if your cable provider agrees to a better deal. People just like you have already saved hundreds this way, and you can read their stories on the Internet.

Once you have slashed your cable bill, move on to other bills, such as your Internet service, phone bill, and credit card bill. The same techniques that worked for your cable company can work well with other providers, too.

You are almost ready to get rid of cable television — or at least your premium channels — but you don't want to give up your favorite show. Unfortunately, that show is not available online or from Netflix, iTunes, or any other noncable subscription services.

Not surprisingly, you can drop cable and still enjoy your favorite show. Just buy the DVD for the current season when it's released. Of course, you won't be able to watch the show live each week, and you'll have to be careful to avoid episode spoilers on television and the Web. But a single season DVD or a box set of seasons will probably cost less than keeping cable or that premium channel for another year.

# Stream your favorite shows to TV

You can replace cable and the expensive cable bill and still enjoy TV programming. In fact, several new products and services can deliver TV shows and movies to your television – all without cable. The initial cost of switching to these new options can seem high, but your average yearly cost may still be cheaper than your annual cable bill. Pick a few options and run the numbers to see for yourself. Here are just a few examples of the choices you can try.

**Live network television.** The major networks, like ABC, NBC, and CBS, still broadcast their programming for free, so you can watch network television almost the same way you did before cable came along. However, to see today's programs, you not only need an antenna that picks up UHF and VHF, you also need a high-definition television (HDTV) with a DTV tuner. Check your HDTV manual to see if your set includes a DTV tuner. If not, just add a DTV converter.

**Netflix.** If network television is not enough, join Netflix. Depending on what you want to pay, you can either join the Netflix

DVD rental service or stream programming to your television. With the DVD rental service, you can rent movies or full seasons of your favorite shows — and they are delivered right to your door. If you have a wireless network, you can consider a Netflix plan that streams movies or TV shows through your computer to your television.

You may also stream programming to your television if you have a Wii, PlayStation 3, Xbox 360, Internet-enabled TV, or Internet-enabled Blu-ray player. If you plan to stream movies and TV programs to your television, be sure to ask whether you must first connect your television or another device to the Internet. Visit *www.netflix.com* to discover your options.

**Roku.** Visit *www.roku.com* for Roku digital players, set-top boxes that can connect your TV to subscription services like Netflix, Amazon Video on Demand, or sports options. The players may cost as little as $60.

**Apple TV.** Apple TV is a small, $99 box that hooks up to your television. Get one and you can purchase discounted movies and TV episodes from iTunes. Not all network shows are available from iTunes, but you may also be able to stream programs and movies through your Netflix subscription.

Other options that may replace cable include Google TV, Sezmi, and Boxee.

Put the wrong surge protector on your expensive, new television and your TV may still be at risk. Electric surges can travel along cable and satellite television lines and damage your TV.

Before you buy a surge protector, ask the salesperson to show you a model that not only protects the electrical lines leading into your television, but the cable lines that carry your cable signal. If you have digital satellite, ask about surge protection for your digital satellite line.

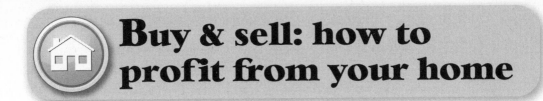

# Buy & sell: how to profit from your home

## Low-cost secrets that help houses sell

Cleaning, decluttering, and brightening a home can give you more bang for your buck at resale, according to a HomeGain survey of real estate agents. Try these simple, inexpensive steps to make rooms look bigger and brighter.

+ Remove extra or unused items from tables, stands, dressers, desks, shelves, counters, and floors.

+ Thin out the furniture in each room, especially anything that is bulky or rarely used.

+ When choosing furniture to keep in a room, pick pieces you can see through or see under such as glass tables, slatted chairs, or sofas with visible legs.

+ Open all the drapes, or replace them with translucent curtains.

+ Turn on all your lights and lamps. Every room should have at least three sources of light. To add more, borrow clean, attractive lamps, or buy them secondhand.

+ Remove doors that block off the kitchen from your den, dining room, or living room.

+ Repaint the walls a light color, and paint colored ceilings white.

And remember this bonus tip. If you are trying to sell your home, one thing you should never do is sign a listing agreement that lasts more than three months. You do not want to get stuck with an inexperienced or unsatisfactory agent, and you can always renew a three-month agreement if you are pleased with the agent.

Buying a house? Brave the winter cold in December or January to find the best bargains. The fall months of October and November may also bring you luck. Fewer homebuyers shop at these times so more homes are stuck on the market. Plus, sellers who keep their homes up for sale during autumn and winter may be more desperate to sell. Because the busy spring home-buying season is still months away, these sellers may be more willing to negotiate or take lower offers.

# Save thousands on mortgage payments

You may think you're getting a bargain with a 30-year mortgage because the monthly payments are lower than a 15- or 20-year mortgage. But remember, your payment not only includes the money you pay back but also interest on the money you borrow. And the longer you pay interest, the more it will cost you.

**TOP DOLLAR:** Homebuyers typically choose a 30-year mortgage, but the interest over the life of a 5-percent $100,000 loan can total $90,000 or more.

**VALUE:** A 20-year mortgage requires higher monthly payments, but you pay it off 10 years sooner. So a $100,000 20-year loan at 5 percent may cost up to $40,000 less in interest paid over the life of the loan. Sometimes, the 20-year loan may be offered at a lower interest rate than a 30-year mortgage.

**WHAT YOU GIVE UP:** The flexibility to put your earnings toward other expenses. The lower monthly payments of a 30-year mortgage leave more room in your budget for paying off debts, investing for retirement, building up an emergency fund, or paying unexpected expenses. And, unless your loan forbids prepayments, you still have the option to prepay whenever extra cash is available, shortening your loan term and trimming your overall interest expense.

But, if you stay in your home long enough, the higher monthly payments of a 20-year loan will save you money in the long run and leave you with a nice bit of extra cash after you pay off the loan.

# How to pay off your mortgage faster

Pay your mortgage biweekly and you may save thousands of dollars. You will also pay off your mortgage more quickly. Here is how – and why – this works.

Instead of making a mortgage payment every month, pay half your mortgage every two weeks. Because a year has 52 weeks, you will make 26 half-payments or 13 full payments. If you pay every month, you only make 12 full payments.

Since the entire thirteenth payment goes to principal instead of interest, it lowers the total interest you pay for the loan. A person with a $100,000 loan at between 6 and 6.5 percent interest could save up to $30,000 in interest over the life of the loan. If your interest rate or loan amount is higher, you can save even more.

But before you try this, check with your lender. Make sure that:

+ you will not pay a penalty for prepaying your mortgage.

+ your lender allows biweekly, partial payments.

+ your lender will credit the entire extra payment to principal.

+ you do not already have an automatic payment plan in place or can stop it if you do.

Be wary of automatic biweekly programs offered by your bank, lender, or anyone else. Free biweekly programs are rare. Most programs charge one-time or monthly transaction fees just to automatically debit your bank account every two weeks. If your lender will not allow biweekly payments, simply add 1/12 of your monthly payment to each month's check. Or make one extra payment each year, perhaps using your tax refund or a bonus from work.

**DEEP DISCOUNT**

You do not have to pay your real estate agent the standard 6 percent commission to sell your home. A *Consumer Reports* survey suggests you can still get good service even if you ask the agent to cut his commission to 3 percent.

The survey found that paying 3 percent has little effect on your final selling price or the quality of service you can expect from the realtor. People who paid 3 percent were nearly as likely to receive good advice and qualified buyers from their realtors. However, they were less likely to see their homes advertised in the local newspaper or have agent-driven open houses.

If you want to sweeten the deal, offer to hire him to both sell your current home and help you buy your new home if he will work for a lower commission.

# Refinancing: 3 steps to making an informed decision

Interest rates may have dipped below what you're paying on your current mortgage, but that does not mean refinancing will save you money. Follow this three-stage process to see whether refinancing is right for you.

**Determine if you can qualify.** Banks now require a higher credit score to qualify for good interest rates than they did during the housing boom. Before you apply for refinancing, you can visit *www.truecredit.com/mortgage*, pay a small fee, and discover the interest rate you are likely to get. Or use this process to determine how the credit score you need compares with the credit score you have.

Ask potential lenders what credit score they require for the interest rate you need. Then visit *www.annualcreditreport.com*, or call 877-322-8228 to order a free copy of your credit report and pay for your credit score. And remember, if you find and correct mistakes in your credit report, your credit score may rise.

Banks are unwilling to refinance a homeowner whose house is worth less than the outstanding balance of the current mortgage, a situation that may be caused by falling home values. Since a refinance requires an appraisal of your home, estimate your home value before you refinance. Use home valuation websites like *www.zillow.com*, or talk to a real estate agent. The more your home value exceeds your outstanding loan balance, the more equity you have and the better your odds of refinancing. But you also need a stable income and no overdue debts.

**Estimate when you will start saving.** Get an estimate of your closing costs and monthly payment. Subtract your new monthly payment from your old one to determine your monthly savings. Divide your total closing costs by your monthly savings to see how long you will spend "paying off" the closing costs. If this payback period is not too lengthy and you expect to live in your home for significantly longer than the payback period, refinancing may be worthwhile.

**Consider the cost of years.** Refinancing into a 30-year mortgage adds 30 more years to paying off your home. If you can afford your current payments and have paid off much of your existing loan, added interest payments from a new loan may cost more than keeping the old mortgage. Run the numbers to find out.

# Escape a last-minute refinancing trap

You are ready to refinance out of your expensive first mortgage for a lower interest rate, but be careful. If you have a "piggyback" loan, you could miss your chance to lock in the lowest rates.

A piggyback loan is a second loan you take out along with your first mortgage if you don't have the 20-percent down payment and want to avoid paying private mortgage insurance. But this may also mean you cannot refinance your first mortgage unless the lender for your piggyback loan agrees to subordinate that loan to the new first mortgage. In other words, the piggyback lender must agree that the first mortgage would be paid off before the piggyback loan if fore-closure occurs.

If the second lender refuses to subordinate, you can try to refinance the first mortgage for enough money to pay off both loans, but you may have to repeat the refinancing process to do it. By then, rates may have risen and you could end up paying more — if you can refinance at all.

So before you refinance, notify your second lender of your refinancing plans, and find out if that company will subordinate its piggyback loan to your new first mortgage.

## Stop paying for standard insurance you don't really need

Imagine cutting your mortgage payment by $16 to $50 each month for every $100,000 you borrowed. You can, if you qualify to drop private mortgage insurance (PMI).

Many lenders require you to pay for this insurance if your down payment is less than 20 percent and you do not have a piggyback mortgage. To see whether you pay PMI, check your HUD1 form from your loan closing papers, your monthly or annual mortgage statement, or contact your lender.

PMI can be painful because your yearly cost can be as much as 1 percent of your loan's value. Even worse, you are paying for insurance that does not protect you. Instead, PMI protects the lender from losses if you stop paying your mortgage.

Fortunately, if you bought your home after July 29, 1999, the Home-owner's Protection Act requires your lender to drop PMI when you pay down your mortgage to 78 percent of the loan value — or you can ask your lender to drop PMI once you owe 80 percent or less of your loan.

But different lenders use different numbers to determine when to drop PMI. Some only use your original loan value, while others use your current home value but may require an appraisal to determine that home value. Find out which number applies to you.

To calculate whether you have reached either 78 or 80 percent, divide the loan amount you still owe by either the total amount of the original loan or your current home value. If your result is 0.8 or smaller, contact your lender about dropping PMI.

But keep in mind the Homeowner's Protection Act does not apply to everyone. If you bought your home before it went into effect, you must contact your lender to learn how to drop PMI. Don't count on the bank to tell you it's no longer needed. Also, if you have a Department of Veterans Affairs (VA) or Federal Housing Administration (FHA) loan, you probably cannot drop PMI.

> **Time is Money**
>
> The first time you realize you cannot make a mortgage payment, contact your lender or a housing counselor immediately, so you can convince your lender that you are a trustworthy homeowner who wants to pay your debts. Lenders are more interested in working with someone who is not yet behind or only slightly behind on mortgage payments.

## 5 tips to avoid foreclosure

You can avoid foreclosure whether you have missed one payment or several. Even if lenders seem reluctant to work with you, knowing your options may help you find a solution they will accept. Start with these.

**Seek government help.** If you have a Federal Housing Administration (FHA) loan, ask your lender or the FHA if any special loan modifications are available. If you have a mortgage through the Veterans Administration (VA), contact the Department of Veterans Affairs for possible help.

The government plan "Making Home Affordable" may also help prevent foreclosure. See details in the story *Smart ways to save your home*.

**Find a housing counselor.** If you are uncomfortable talking to your lender or your lender will not budge, a housing counselor may help. To find someone legitimate, visit the Housing and Urban Development website at *www.hud.gov*, or call toll-free 800-569-4287. You can also contact the Homeownership Preservation Foundation (HPF) at *www.hopenow.com*, or call toll-free 888-995-4673. The non-profit HPF helps arrange loan modifications and prevent foreclosures.

**Offer a temporary plan.** For temporary setbacks, you can ask your lender to "reinstate" your loan if you make up your missed payments by a certain date. If you cannot, ask about a repayment plan where you pay part of your missed payments along with your regular payments until you catch up. Or ask for a forbearance plan where you have reduced or no mortgage payments for a few months before starting a repayment plan.

**Ask to modify your loan.** If you clearly cannot pay under your loan's current terms, provide documents that show how you could pay if your loan terms were modified. If you can pay a processing fee, your lender may agree to change the interest rate or number of years in your loan or switch from an adjustable loan to a fixed loan.

According to a 2008 law, lenders must modify loans and help homeowners avoid foreclosure as long as mortgage default has happened or is reasonably likely, the home is your primary residence, and the lender can recover more from modifying your loan than from foreclosing.

**Negotiate to sell your home.** If you cannot keep your home, your lender may allow you a limited time to sell the home as a way to pay off your mortgage. Some lenders may even let you sell to someone who can assume your loan. A lender that suggests a short sale will accept a buyer's offer for less than you owe and forgive the remaining debt, but this may have tax consequences.

## Smart ways to save your home

You may qualify for government help with paying your mortgage, preventing foreclosure, or even refinancing. Visit *www.makinghome affordable.gov*, or call toll-free 888-995-4673 for more details about programs like these.

**Unemployment Program.** If you cannot make your mortgage payments because you are unemployed, and your lender participates in the Making Home Affordable program, you may be allowed to pay no mortgage or a reduced mortgage for at least three months while you hunt for a new job.

**Home Affordable Modification Program (HAMP).** This program can modify your mortgage and reduce your monthly payment to 31 percent of your pre-tax income as long as you started your mortgage before January 2, 2009, and you meet other qualifications.

**Second Lien Modification Program (2MP).** If you have two mortgages and your first mortgage qualifies for HAMP, this program may help modify the second loan so you can make lower payments on it.

**Home Affordable Foreclosure Alternatives Program (HAFA).** Homeowners who cannot keep their homes but still want to avoid foreclosure should seek help through HAFA. You might be released from your debt through a short sale or deed-in-lieu of foreclosure. With the latter, the lender agrees to forgive your debt if you voluntarily transfer the property deed to the lender and move away. This is less damaging to your credit than a foreclosure, and HAFA may provide funds to help with your move.

**Home Affordable Refinance Program (HARP).** HARP helps homeowners who have trouble refinancing into more affordable mortgages. To qualify, you must be current on your mortgage payments, and your mortgage must be owned or guaranteed by Freddie Mac or Fannie Mae. If you're not sure who owns your mortgage, visit *FannieMae.com/loanlookup* and *FreddieMac.com/mymortgage*, or call toll-free 800-732-6643 and 800-373-3343.

**Safe & Secure**

Foreclosure scammers stand ready to take your home or your money the moment they know you are in trouble. So use tips like these to help you stay safe.

- Beware of anyone who asks you to transfer the deed to your house unless you are working directly with your lender to forgive your mortgage debt. Scammers often promise you can eventually buy back your home if you sign over the deed.

- Never give or send your mortgage payment to anyone but your mortgage company unless you confirm the mortgage company wants you to.

- Do not pay anyone that demands a fee for housing counseling services.

- Get all promises in writing, and keep copies of all your documentation.

- Never sign a document you do not understand or one that contains blanks or errors.

# Online shopping secrets

## Sniff out top deals with your computer

You've heard the hype about how you can save money shopping online. Now learn how other people are finding the deals. You have to do a bit of work to use the best online shopping secrets, but it's well worth your time.

**Dig up free shipping.** The high cost of shipping can sink your savings when shopping online. Start your online shopping search on *www.freeshipping.org*, and you'll get free shipping every time.

Just click on the type of product you want to buy from the choices at left, like shoes or books, and you'll get a list of online retailers offering free shipping. More than 800 online sellers are included.

**Click for coupons galore.** You can find current specials at your local stores without even having to buy a newspaper, possibly including some deals you may never have seen advertised. Certain websites gather coupons and coupon codes — to use for online shopping — from numerous stores. So plan ahead by finding coupons first, then shopping at your favorite store. You're likely to find coupons for free shipping, 20 percent or more off your purchase, or more specific offers or daily deals.

Try these coupon-gathering websites.

+ *www.retailmenot.com* — Find an up-to-date list of coupon codes and printable coupons from clothing stores, department stores, and more. You can help other shoppers by providing input at the website to whether the code or coupon worked for you.

+ *www.couponmom.com* — Click on the "online coupons" link to find current deals at retailers like Overstock.com, The Children's Place, and Lane Bryant.

+ *www.couponloco.com* — Look for your favorite store on a list, then see the current coupon codes.

+ *www.couponcabin.com* – See oodles of coupon codes from stores like Ann Taylor, Sears, and Kmart.

You can also do a quick search to find coupons at a single store by typing in "coupon" and the name of the store you want, like Target or Kohl's, in a search engine such as *www.google.com*.

# Top 20 shopping secrets

Shop like a pro, whether online or in person at the store. Learn these top 20 shopping secrets that can save you hundreds, and never pay anything close to full price.

+ Shop online outlets, such as *www.overstock.com*. You'll find lots of bargains, and merchandise is always changing.

+ Pick the "ship to store" option and avoid shipping costs.

+ Try on clothing or shoes, then buy online. This trick works for any store that has both online and store locations, like Talbot's or the Gap. You benefit from online outlets and discounts.

+ Don't assume online and real stores have the same prices. Call around to compare.

+ Pay attention to return policies if you have to ship something back. Stores may be different.

+ Avoid restocking fees, which are most common when buying electronics online.

+ Get feedback before you buy. Websites like *www.epinions.com* let customers rate their purchase and make comments about the product.

+ Leave the item in your online shopping cart. Sometimes if you navigate away from a site without buying, you have a good chance of getting an email offering you a good deal.

+ Know a bargain so you can pounce on it when you see it.

+ Get your rebate. Before you buy, check *www.ebates.com* to see if the store you're shopping at is linked. Sign up for free, and you can get a rebate on your purchases. More than 1,000 stores are included.

+ Check unfamiliar websites at *www.BBB.org*. The Better Business Bureau gathers information and complaints about websites that cause customers grief.

+ Look for a seal of approval. A symbol for VeriSign or TRUSTe can show that a website is legitimate and secure.

+ Spot website sloppiness. If you see lots of misspelled words or a Web address that ends in .CN, .RU, or .RO, it may be a fake.

+ Use a credit card rather than a check when shopping online. This gives you added recourse in case a deal goes bad.

+ Don't be afraid to ask for a better deal.

+ Shop when you're rested. Otherwise, you risk letting exhaustion lead you to a bad purchase.

+ Check your receipt for errors.

+ Think long and hard about buying scratch-and-dent items if you know you can't return them. The discount may not be worth it.

+ Shop before a sale, then put your items on hold until the price drops.

+ Be nice. You're more likely to get a discount if the salesperson is on your side.

## Find anything you want — for less

Don't pay full price for anything. Online shopping gives you access to thousands of people trying to sell exactly what you want to buy. From appliances to bicycles, afghans to blue jeans, you'll find just about anything you might want for sale at an online swap sale or auction site, like *www.craigslist.com* or *www.ebay.com*. Take advantage of what's out there.

**TOP DOLLAR:** Keurig single-cup pod coffee maker ($140 for the Special Edition model).

**VALUE:** Similar Keurig coffee maker for sale at *www.craigslist.com* ($65) or offered in an auction at *www.ebay.com* ($50).

**WHAT YOU GIVE UP:** Having a brand new coffee maker, and possibly getting the exact model you were shopping for. The savings may be well worth switching to a comparable model.

---

**Safe & Secure**

Check the safety of items you buy through online auction sites like Craigslist and eBay.

When an item is recalled for a safety issue, it's in the news. But unless you own that product, you probably don't pay attention to the recall. That's a problem when you decide to shop secondhand.

It's illegal to sell an item that's been recalled. That goes for everyone, including people selling in an online auction and even someone holding a garage sale.

Don't bet your own safety on the seller knowing about recalls. Protect yourself by checking two websites before you buy.

- *www.cpsc.gov* — Get information about product safety from the U.S. Consumer Product Safety Commission.
- *www.recalls.gov* — Find recalls by all federal agencies, including the Food and Drug Administration, Department of Agriculture, and the Consumer Product Safety Commission.

---

# 5 ways to save at Amazon

The online bookstore Amazon.com is not just for books anymore. You can find just about anything you're shopping for, from clothing and shoes to groceries and car parts. That makes it a great one-stop source — and don't forget the great prices. Here are the tools to help you save at this online megastore.

**Comparison shopping.** Many vendors sell through *www.amazon.com*, so you'll see a variety of prices on the same product. You may also have the option of buying used items, especially books. You can save big by checking all your options.

**Friday Sales.** Check the website every Friday for that week's Friday Sale item at up to 50 percent off. Click on the "Today's Deals" link at the top of the page. You never know what you'll find.

**Lightning Deals.** Each day, certain items are offered at deep discount — but only for a few hours and for a limited number of customers. When time or stock runs out, the deal is gone. See the "Lightning Deals" link under "Today's Deals."

**Warehouse Deals.** Find open-box products at low prices. Click on "Today's Deals" then "Warehouse Deals," and see what's available. Each item is checked for condition, so you deal directly with Amazon. You'll find great prices on high-tech items, like cameras and computers.

**Free super-saver shipping.** You'll get free shipping on most orders of $25 and up. If you don't quite have $25 worth of merchandise, use the Amazon Filler Item Finder, which you'll find at *www.filleritem.com*. Type in the amount you need to reach $25, and you'll get a list of small items, like a pocket Spanish phrase book or a boar-bristle pastry brush, you didn't know you needed.

**No-Sweat Solution**

You probably know exactly what type of printer paper or ink cartridge you need, unlike a pair of shoes you need to try on. Save time, money, and hassle by buying from home.

Office supply stores like Office Depot and online sellers such as *www.amazon.com* offer a huge variety of brands, so they probably carry what you need. It's easier to type in a product code at your computer than write it down, go to the store, and find it on the shelf. And who wants to carry home a 50-pound box of paper?

Even better, you'll get free shipping at *www.amazon.com* on most orders of $25 and up, while *www.staples.com* offers free shipping on orders over $50.

# Trade unwanted gift cards for cash

Your nephew gave you a generous gift card for your birthday. Trouble is, you don't shop at that store. Here's how you can turn unwanted gift cards into cash.

Online dealers will buy your gift card, then resell it to someone looking for a card from that store. You won't get the full value of credit on the card, since the dealer needs to make a profit. You'll probably get between 60 percent and 90 percent of the card's face value — certainly better than losing it entirely. It's best to compare offers from different websites to find the best deal for your particular card. Some dealers give you the choice of cash, credit at certain online stores, or a different gift card.

Typically, your gift card must have a balance between $25 and $200 to be traded. Pay attention to a card's expiration date, since dealers place limits on what they will accept. Happily, new laws mean gift cards will have looser restrictions and a longer shelf life before expiration.

Check out offers for your gift cards at one of these websites.

✦ *www.PlasticJungle.com*     ✦ *www.GiftCardRescue.com*

✦ *www.SwapAGift.com*     ✦ *www.GiftCards.com*

## DEEP DISCOUNT

Put your gray hair to good use with a free membership at *www.seniordiscounts.com*.

Simply enter your ZIP code to find local discounts for seniors from the site's 125,000 businesses listed. You can save around 10 to 25 percent on everything from hotel rooms to oil changes to salon services.

If you find the website is really helpful, splurge on a Gold Membership for $7.95 a year. You'll get greater savings, reviews of products, and more. That means for 67 cents a month, you can find hundreds of dollars a year in discounts, many of them unadvertised.

# Big deals at the big box

Walmart advertises itself as always having low prices. But you don't have to settle for the low price you find in the store. Try these tricks to pay even less at Walmart.

**Skip shipping charges.** Sometimes the item you want is not in your local store, but you find it online. Order online at *www.walmart.com*, then have your purchase shipped directly to your local Walmart store for pickup. The retailer says customers have saved millions in shipping costs this way. Best Buy, Sears, and others offer similar deals.

**Ask about price matching.** Many big-box retailers will happily match an advertised lower price on the same item. You may need to bring the ad to prove the other store's price.

**Haggle.** Yes, you can do it — even at big retailers like Walmart and others. Ask around, and you may find your friends are already negotiating with the big boys.

Frank B., for example, saved $280 off the price of a high-end washing machine at a big-box store. He simply asked for the price he wanted, then told the manager he'd go ahead and buy it the next day from a competitor. The manager was happy to keep Frank's business by giving him the discount he asked for.

**Root out coupons.** Find coupons online, then take them to the store to save. Search for your favorite stores at websites like these, and see what great current deals pop up.

+ *www.DealCatcher.com*

+ *www.GoGoShopper.com*

# Shop securely with online payment options

You may not want to use your credit card to make a purchase online. Now you don't have to. Check out the pros and cons of these alternative methods of paying online.

| Payment option | How it works | Details to consider |
|---|---|---|
| PayPal | Set up a PayPal account, attach your credit card and/or bank account, then pay for an item by authorizing payment from your PayPal account. | No need to share financial information with sellers. It's the most widely accepted form of online payment. |
| Google Checkout | Similar to PayPal, but you lack the option to attach to your bank account and withdraw money directly. You pay via bal–ance in your Google Checkout account or credit card. | Easy to buy from several online retailers without creating separate user accounts. |
| eBillme | You provide your email address and receive an ebill, then pay directly from your bank account. | Good if you don't have a credit card. |
| Bill Me Later | You provide your date of birth and part of your Social Security number. After a credit check, Bill Me Later pays for items you buy, then sends you a bill in 25 to 90 days. | You don't pay interest if you pay on time. Credit check may lower your credit score slightly. |

# Call up savings on your cellphone

Get high-tech help finding deals. Your cellphone becomes your personal shopping aid, tracking down deals and comparing prices. Here's how.

**Find electronic coupons.** When you don't have to remember to bring along a paper coupon, you're more likely to get the savings. Some stores offer digital coupons sent to your cellphone. The clerk then scans the coupons directly from your phone when you check out. You must opt in at a store's website to receive the coupons, which arrive to your phone through a text message. Target and J.C. Penney offer these, and you can find other store's phone coupons at *www.cellfire.com*.

**Comparison shop on your phone.** One simple phone number is the key to always getting the lowest price on everything you buy. When you're at the store considering a purchase, dial 888-DO-FRU CALL (888-363-7822) and input the bar code number of the item you're thinking about buying. You'll get a list of other stores that carry the item and their prices. You can also send a text message with the bar code to FRU11.

# 12 ways your computer can save you money

Your computer can help you save on everything from gasoline to taxes. Check out these great ideas for coming out ahead.

- ✦ Compare prices at *www.shopzilla.com.*
- ✦ Sign up to receive coupons at *www.coupons.net.*
- ✦ Save on groceries by checking Teri's List of great deals at *www.thegrocerygame.com.*
- ✦ Find the cheapest gas with the price comparison tool at *www.gasbuddy.com.*
- ✦ Save postage by sending emails rather than old-fashioned letters.
- ✦ Bank online and always know your account balance. You'll never bounce a check again.
- ✦ Send free electronic greeting cards from *www.123greetings.com.*
- ✦ Read the books you want for next to nothing when you swap at *www.paperbackswap.com.*
- ✦ Pay a flat monthly fee to make long-distance calls using a computer phone service like *www.voip.com.*
- ✦ Find cheap insurance at *www.bankrate.com.*
- ✦ Get the best rates on a CD by checking *www.bankrate.com.*
- ✦ Fire your tax man when you do your own taxes using software like TurboTax.

# Know your rights to avoid losing your shirt

You have certain rights as a customer, but the store probably won't tell you what they are. And you better not rely on a website or telephone sales rep to fill you in.

Remember these rights in case a purchase goes sour.

✦ You don't have to wait forever. Retailers must ship your online, mail, or phone order within 30 days if that's what they promised. If something happens and the store can't ship within that time, they have to get your approval for a delay. Say no, and you are entitled to a refund.

✦ You have the right to know a seller's return policy. Stores must make the policy clear, but it can be as strict as they want. Pay attention.

✦ You can use any repair service or parts vendor you want without voiding the manufacturer's warranty. That means you can use cheaper printer ink cartridges, and you can have your vacuum cleaner repaired by someone other than the manufacturer. Federal law says your warranty is still in effect.

**DEEP DISCOUNT**

Even after you drop a big chunk of cash on an expensive item, you can still save — without having to schlep back to the store to check prices.

Sign up online for free price-drop alerts from a service like *www.priceprotectr.com.* Type in the details of the item you bought, like brand, model, and so on. You'll get an email alert if the store offers the same item for a lower price. Then you may be able to get a price adjustment from the store where you made the purchase.

The service also has two useful features before you buy.

• Price target. Receive a notice when the price for the item drops below a specified target.

• Price watch. Get a notice whenever the price changes at all.

Check the store policy on price matching to find out how long you have to get a refund.

# Save with alternate living arrangements

## Enjoy family care without losing Medicaid benefits

Receive in-home family care without jeopardizing your Medicaid qualification. It's easy — pay a family member to care for you once you can no longer live alone.

As long as you pay them a reasonable salary, based on the duties they perform, Medicaid generally won't penalize you for it. Medicaid has become more suspicious of families trying to hide assets by giving money away as gifts. Pay for the care you receive, and Medicaid will be less likely to consider the money a gift.

Paying a relative not only compensates them for their time. It also helps reduce the size of your estate as you go, helping you qualify for Medicaid. In some cases, long-term care insurance will pay for a family member to care for you.

The key is to draw up a contract between you and your relative/caregiver. A contract makes the arrangement look more legitimate. Write one up before you need care, though. Don't pay your relative as an afterthought. Leaving them a lump sum of money after years of unpaid service will look suspiciously like a gift in Medicaid's eyes.

A caregiver contract, sometimes called a personal service or care agreement, should clearly spell out several things, such as:

+ exactly which duties the caregiver will perform, such as running errands, paying bills, cooking meals, cleaning house, giving medications, or bathing and dressing you.

+ how much they will be paid. You can pay your relative hourly, giving them a weekly or biweekly paycheck, or upfront with a lump sum of money. Hourly is less likely to make Medicaid or the IRS suspicious.

+ how many hours a week your relative will spend caring for you.

Call a few local home health agencies, and ask what they charge for the kinds of services your caregiver will be performing. Then pay your family member based on those rates. Don't be tempted to overpay just because they're family.

Spend a little money to have an elder-law attorney draw up the contract, so that it stands up to Medicaid scrutiny down the road. And be sure to discuss the details with the rest of your family to avoid hurt feelings and estate battles later.

**Freebie Frenzie**

Dozens of helpful senior programs are going to waste. The government can't wait to give them to you. It has even set up a special hotline. The Eldercare Locator connects people age 60 and older with help from a variety of agencies and organizations. Call the Eldercare Locator hotline at 800-677-1116, or visit the website *www.eldercare.gov*, and say "yes" to valuable free services, like these.

- transportation to errands and appointments
- basic housekeeping
- yard work
- meal preparation
- home meal delivery
- home repair and renovation
- legal aid
- energy assistance
- visits from home health care services
- adult day care
- exercise programs
- housing assistance
- help finding work
- home visits and support by telephone
- nutrition education
- crime prevention and victim assistance
- Medicare benefits counseling
- pension counseling

Uncover more programs through the website *www.benefits checkup.org*. Explore senior housing options, and get help paying for prescriptions, health care, and meals.

# Clever way to cut living expenses

Shared housing can cut your living expenses and offer companionship to ward off loneliness. It also gives you someone else to help with chores, cooking, cleaning, and repairs – all of which can keep you independent longer.

The idea behind shared housing is simple. Each person has a private bedroom, but areas like the kitchen, living room, and den are shared, public spaces. You can share your home with one or more people who pay rent and utilities, or you can take a room in someone else's home.

Screen potential roommates carefully, whether you're the homeowner or the one renting. Matching programs throughout the country can help you find suitable house-sharing candidates. Find matching programs in your state at *www.nationalsharedhousing.org*.

Figure out the financial split before agreeing to any arrangements. Decide how to divvy up utility bills and groceries. Consider giving your roommate a discount if they agree to help you with home repairs or drive you to doctor appointments and other errands.

# Great alternative to living alone

Be near your family, but still have your own place. ECHO homes offer an ideal way to enjoy your privacy without being totally alone, and they can save you the money you would otherwise spend on a nursing home.

Short for Elder Cottage Housing Opportunity, ECHO homes are manufactured homes placed in the backyard of an existing house – usually yours, a family member's, or a caregiver's. They're a perfect compromise between your desire for privacy and the need to be closer to friends and family who can help as you grow older.

+ The homes tend to be small, around 400 to 800 square feet, but they have everything you need, including a kitchen, bedroom, bath, and living room.

+ Expect to pay between $17,000 and $25,000 for a basic unit, more for a bigger, fancier one. That may sound like a lot of cash, but it's much cheaper than living in a nursing home.

+ ECHO homes are made to be movable, so you or your family can sell it once you no longer need it.

Check your local zoning laws before buying one of these units. Not all towns allow them. Rural areas where lots are large and zoning laws few are good candidates for ECHO homes. Bear in mind, you will likely have to pay extra to pour a foundation and hook up the utilities.

Your ECHO home could become a valuable source of income. You can place one on your property, move into it, and rent out your main home, perhaps even to your adult children. Still independent? Stay in your home and rent out the ECHO unit. Check your local zoning laws to learn the rules on rentals. Some states also offer "caregiver" tax credits that can help offset the cost of a unit.

You can buy or lease an ECHO, new or used. More companies are beginning to sell these homes, and in more styles, including these three companies.

+ MedCottage designs especially for seniors with medical problems. Call N2Care at 888-797-5818 for more information, or visit the website *www.medcottage.com.*

+ FabCab specializes in pref-fab and kit-built homes that are also environmentally friendly. Learn more at *http://fabcab.com* or by calling 425-243-4489.

+ Inspired In-law offers modular homes aimed at helping seniors live independently but close to family or caregivers. Call 800-683-5922, or visit *www.inspiredinlaw.com.*

## At-home answer for vets who need care

Veterans who can no longer live on their own but don't want to live in a nursing home now have another alternative. The U.S. Department of Veterans Affairs (VA) is broadening its Medical Foster Homes (MFH) program.

People who want to be caregivers apply to the VA. The VA then screens them and their homes, performing background checks as well as fire and safety inspections. Caregivers look after their foster vets full-time, providing personal care and home-cooked meals. The VA even trains them, all in an effort to help veterans age with dignity and comfort in a place that feels like home.

As a veteran, you – not the VA – are responsible for paying room and board, typically at a cost of $1,500 to $3,000 a month, depending on the type of care needed. The VA does, however, pay for primary health care and regularly sends health care professionals out to the home, including nurses, counselors, pharmacists, and dietitians. As a result, veterans in the MFH program tend to spend fewer days in the hospital.

You will also keep receiving your military pension and Social Security while living there, which can help pay your room and board. And you'll have a comfortable place to live long-term. If you're not happy in a particular foster home, simply ask the VA to move you elsewhere.

The Medical Foster Home program is growing but is not yet available in every state. Contact your local VA office to ask about foster homes in your area.

**No-Sweat Solution**

Continuing care retirement communities (CCRCs) take the stress out of deciding where to live as you age. They provide all levels of care. People who are still independent can start out living in a private home or apartment on the CCRC "campus." As you age and need more care, you can transition easily into assisted living or a nursing home on the same campus.

CCRCs aren't an option for everyone. They generally require a contract and hefty entry fee upfront, plus a monthly fee. If you're intrigued, though, look for one accredited by the Commission on Accreditation of Rehabilitation Facilities.

Read the contract carefully before signing it. Make certain the CCRC will refund your deposit to your family after your death. Visit *www.snapforseniors.com* for more advice on choosing a CCRC.

# Live on less by living abroad

Don't limit your retirement options to the United States. More and more retirees are stretching their dollars by living abroad. Popular retirement destinations include Mexico, Costa Rica, Guatemala, Panama, and Belize. Lately, other countries like Bolivia, Croatia, Thailand, Turkey, and Uruguay have also lured American retirees.

Temperate climates and low-cost housing, along with favorable income and property tax systems, make these countries attractive. Your money goes further there, which helps when you're on a fixed income. You can afford to live a more luxurious lifestyle. In most cases, you can still collect your Social Security benefits. Just do your research before you make the move.

**Rent first.** Visiting a place is not the same as living there. Rent for a few months in the country you want to retire in, before moving there permanently.

**Seek out ex-pats.** Look for a place with a large English-speaking community, unless you speak the local language. Otherwise, the language barrier may make you feel isolated.

**Keep separate bank accounts.** Consider keeping an American account in dollars for depositing your Social Security and pension checks and a local checking account in your host country's currency for paying local bills. You'll save a bundle in currency exchange fees over the long run.

**Check out the health coverage.** Medicare generally doesn't cover retirees living abroad. Health insurance in foreign countries, however, can be very affordable. Some countries, like Panama and Ecuador, even try to draw retirees with attractive pension programs.

**Think through tax burdens.** Panama, Malaysia, and some other countries offer tax perks to foreigners who retire there. And don't forget you still have to pay U.S. taxes. You may want to consult tax experts both in the United States and your new country.

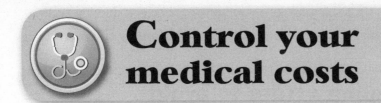

# Control your medical costs

## Bargain your way to lower health bills

It works at the flea market, so why not at the doctor's office? Asking for a better price can save money on just about everything – even medical and dental bills. Don't be afraid to try. The most direct and immediate way to lower your medical bills is to negotiate.

Doctors, hospitals, and medical labs are often willing to work out lower prices or extended payments. They would much rather get a portion of the full payment than be out the whole amount.

Ann H. found the courage to ask her dentist's office for a discount after her family lost their dental insurance coverage.

"We're not poor, but paying for dental cleanings and X-rays for a family of four can be a stretch when you're footing the entire bill," Ann says. "When I asked the billing manager if there was anything that could be done, she said they routinely reduce the bill by 10 percent for people with no dental insurance who pay in cash. We save around $60 every six months, so it helps."

Follow these steps to join the 60 percent of people who get the price break they ask for at the doctor's office.

+ Ask for a discount before you have a procedure done, if possible. But don't be afraid to negotiate afterwards.

+ At the hospital, ask the patient navigator or social worker for help. Get her on your side before you approach the billing department.

+ To negotiate with your doctor or dentist's office, ask in person and offer to pay in cash. This saves the office credit card fees.

+ Provide your financial or insurance information if asked, so the billing department knows you are telling the truth about your needs.

+ It's not unusual to get a break of up to 30 percent on hospital bills. Insurance companies routinely get a discount of 60 percent.

# 6 costly billing errors to avoid

Bills are no fun. Sorting through the fine details of a hospital bill is tedious and time-consuming. But if you don't do it, nobody will. You can save yourself thousands if you learn to identify the most common hospital billing errors.

+ Duplicate charges for the same test, procedure, or supplies.

+ Tests that never happened. Keep track of what procedures you have done so you don't get billed for those the doctor ordered, then canceled.

+ Unbundled fees. You may be charged for a certain service, like a room fee for a procedure, then also get stuck paying for items that should be included in that fee, such as gowns and gloves.

+ Operating room time. Compare the anesthesiologist's record of time in surgery with the hospital's billing of the procedure to be sure they match.

+ Upcoding. Don't pay for a name-brand drug if your doctor ordered a generic.

+ Number of days in the hospital. You'll probably be charged for the day of admission but not the day of discharge, or perhaps the other way around — but not both.

It's up to you to resolve the overcharge if you spot a problem. First, contact the billing department of the hospital or doctor's office and your insurance company to try to fix the error. Put your concerns in writing, and address them to a particular person. You'll probably get a better response, since the recipient is required by law to address the issue within a certain amount of time.

If that doesn't help, especially if the error would be quite costly to you, consider hiring a professional bill reviewer. These folks are experienced in dealing with such problems, and they typically work for a percentage of the money they save you. Find a local medical billing reviewer by checking the website of Medical Billing Advocates of America, *www.billadvocates.com*, then clicking on the "Find an advocate" link.

It's worth disputing false charges, even if your insurance provider would cover the extra cost. High charges can count toward your life-time spending cap, and you might need those funds later.

**No-Sweat Solution**

Don't go bargain hunting when you need to pick a hospital. A study by health care watchdog group HealthGrades found people admitted to the most highly rated hospitals have a risk of dying that is 52 percent lower than at low-rated hospitals. Consumer groups track hospital quality ratings, looking at factors like following best practices for cleanliness, readmission rates, and costs. These three organizations offer hospital comparison information.

- Hospital Compare, *www.hospitalcompare.hhs.gov*, is maintained jointly by the Centers for Medicare and Medicaid Services and other groups. You can search by hospital loca-tion or other factors to find information on all major hospitals in the country.

- The Leapfrog Group, *www.leapfroggroup.org*, provides ratings of 1,300 hospitals, focusing on practices such as hand-washing and staffing.

- Joint Commission, *www.qualitycheck.org*, is an independent nonprofit group that accredits U.S. hospitals. You can search by hospital location, hospital name, or service to find reports based on facility inspections.

# Get Uncle Sam to pay the bills

It's not too late to get help from your Uncle Sam. You may find forgive-ness for unpaid hospital bills – even if they've gone to debt collection. A little leg work may let you erase your debts.

Your first step is to seek help from your hospital's business office or patient service representative. Ask if the hospital gets federal funds. If so, they're required to give you an application for charitable aid. You may be eligible for federal assistance under the Hill-Burton program.

The Hill-Burton program is a federal plan that requires certain health facilities to give medical care for free or at reduced costs. In 1946 the government began giving money to some health care facilities. The hospitals, clinics, and nursing homes that get these funds must give something back in return — free or low-cost services to people in their communities.

Your eligibility is based on your income, but you don't have to be in the poorhouse to qualify. Hospitals, clinics, and other facilities may offer free or inexpensive services to people with an income up to twice the poverty level. And you may qualify for nursing home assistance even if your income is up to three times the poverty level. You can apply before or after you receive care, even if your bill has gone to a collection agency.

Call the Hill-Burton hotline at 800-638-0742 for more details and a list of hospitals, clinics, nursing homes, and other facilities in your area that participate in this special program. If you're at one of those facilities, contact someone in the business or patient accounts office about Hill-Burton assistance. They can tell you what services they offer and whether you qualify.

Other charitable organizations may also help.

+ Patient Access Network Foundation, *www.panfoundation.org*, or 866-316-7263. If you're a U.S. resident being treated for one of 21 specific diseases, including breast cancer, multiple sclerosis, and pancreatic cancer, you may get up to $8,500 a year to help pay for drugs.

+ HealthWell Foundation, *www.healthwellfoundation.org*, or 800-675-8416. You can get help paying for drugs, insurance premiums, and other out-of-pocket costs. Both you and your doctor need to fill out forms annually.

# Taking your medicine pays off

Don't skip taking your prescriptions, thinking you're saving money. Just the opposite is true.

A new study finds that taking your medicine can lead to lower medical bills. The savings come mostly from shorter stays in the hospital and fewer trips to the emergency room.

People in the study had one of four chronic conditions – congestive heart failure, high blood pressure, diabetes, and high cholesterol – so you might think they would be sure to take their prescribed drugs. That wasn't always the case.

Only about half of people in developed countries take their medicine like they're supposed to, according to the World Health Organization. Make sure you're one of them. You'll feel better while you save money.

# Simple tool saves on pricey care

Most older adults take several different drugs every day, but too many don't remember to take them correctly or at the right time. Many families keep a loved one safe by hiring a home health aide to be sure pills are taken correctly. But that's expensive, easily costing $12,000 to $21,000 a year.

Instead, consider buying a programmable electronic pill box for around $70 or less. These handy gadgets can keep you on track with medications and avoid the expense of a home health aide. Plus you get to keep your independence. Shop around to find the features you need.

+ Some pill boxes are divided into sections, so you can fill them ahead of time, then follow the routine through the day or week.

+ An alarm alerts you when it's time to take your medication. Alarms may be audible, visual, vibrating, or text, and some units can be programmed with up to 24 reminders per day.

+ Those with timers can't be opened until it's time for you to take the next dose.

+ High-end units even store information, like your health records or contact information for the doctor.

Ask your pharmacist to recommend a pill box that fits your needs based on the medicines you take. Every year 1.5 million people are victims of medication errors. This simple tool may keep you from being one of them.

**Freebie Frenzie**

Next time you come down with an ear infection or strep throat, you may be able to get generic antibiotics for free. Many drugstores and supermarket pharmacies, including Wegmans, Publix, and Giant, will fill your prescription at no charge. There is no catch, but the stores are hoping you'll stock up on other supplies while you're there. Be sure to follow your doctor's orders as you take the antibiotics.

**CASH SAVER**

Tired of spending money on painkillers for your arthritis? Try a natural remedy that is totally free.

Research shows the right kind of physical activity may help cut the pain of knee and hip osteoarthritis (OA). Seniors who followed an exercise program suffered less pain after six months. Those who also took classes in "activity strategy training," or lessons on how to go about their daily activities with OA, benefited even more.

Exercise has other benefits for people with arthritis:

- helps you lose weight, a factor for many with OA
- boosts joint flexibility
- improves strength in muscles and tissues supporting your joint

Good choices include classes in tai chi, gentle yoga, or water aerobics, or taking part in any other activity that will strengthen the tissues around your swollen, painful joint.

# Make a sound investment in your hearing

Heard the one about the woman who paid too much for hearing aids? It's no joke. Hearing aids can cost $2,500 or more per ear, and the cost is usually not covered by health insurance. Leave no stone unturned as you work to find a lower price.

**Check your insurance.** Medicare and most insurance plans don't cover hearing aids, but there are exceptions.

- ✦ You may get coverage for a visit to the doctor to determine your need for a hearing aid.

- ✦ You may get help paying for a cochlear implant to treat severe hearing loss or deafness.

- ✦ Some Veterans Affairs programs and federal employee insurance plans help pay.

**Find the right provider.** You have numerous choices about where to get tested and fitted for hearing aids, and many different types of hearing aids to pick from. Not all types will work well for every person.

Choose an audiologist or hearing aid center with a good reputation. Ask for references from friends, and contact the Better Business Bureau. Make sure you will be thoroughly tested so the right kind of hearing aid is ordered. It won't do any good if it doesn't work for your needs.

**No-Sweat Solution**

If you're having memory problems, a hearing aid may be all it takes to get your mind back on track.

Research shows seniors with hearing loss — who spend too much energy straining to understand what others are saying — have a harder time recalling the details of what they hear. The study compared people with good hearing to those with mild-to-moderate hearing loss. It seems that working too hard to translate conversation means you don't have enough brainpower left to remember and put it to use.

Untreated hearing loss is also tied to loneliness, safety risks, stress, and depression. So it's worth the effort to get it fixed.

**Sweat the small stuff.** Once you've made a choice, read your contract carefully. Pay attention to details on how long you can return hearing aids if they don't work — usually at least 30 days — and what the warranty covers. Then follow instructions about how to get used to your hearing aids, including returning for follow-up visits. Be sure the purchase price includes at least two or three visits after the initial fitting.

**Try haggling.** Hearing aids are typically priced with 120 percent markup. That gives some wriggle room on the price, so most people who ask for a better deal get one.

**Ask for help paying.** The Lions Club International's Affordable Hearing Aid Project (AHAP) offers financial assistance to people with limited means. You can apply through your local Lions Club for assistance in the form of new or refurbished hearing aids. Call 630-203-3837 for more information.

Similar help may be available from other charitable groups, including your local United Way, Kiwanis, or Optimist Club.

Finally, find out if your state has a program to help cover the cost of hearing aids if you need them to do your job. This assistance would be through a vocational rehabilitation program.

# Reap great deals on eyewear

Most health insurance plans and Medicare don't pay for much eye care. You're on your own. Here is how you can avoid paying outrageous prices for eyeglasses.

**Check out your free options.** These groups can help you get an eye exam and provide glasses free or at a greatly reduced price.

+ Vision USA. This program, run by the American Optometric Association (AOA), provides free eye care to uninsured and low-income workers and their family members who need it. Contact Vision USA at 800-766-4466 or see *www.aoa.org*.

+ Lions Club. The "Give the Gift of Sight" program can help you find free or discounted eye care. Call 800-747-4448 or see *www.lionsclubs.org* to get contact information for your local Lions Club office.

**Buy online.** Beat the high prices of expensive eye-care boutiques by shopping the discounters. You'll get a great pair of glasses at a fraction of the price, easily saving $200 or more. Here are a few online shops to try.

+ *www.zennioptical.com*. Prescription eyeglasses for just eight bucks? You bet – and you can get them no matter where you live. Bifocals start at $25, while progressive lenses are as low as

$37. Simply pick the frames and lenses you want, enter information about your prescription, and place your order. You'll pay $4.95 per order shipping and handling, and you may have to wait a few weeks before your glasses are delivered. But it's worth it when you can easily save 82 percent or more on eyeglasses compared to the local optical shop, where you would probably spend around $200 to $400.

+ *www.glassesusa.com.* Here you can save big and find great styles. Just select your frames and lenses, which are heavily discounted compared to eye-care boutiques. Then try the clever "virtual mirror" to try on your frames and see how they look. You may even get free shipping. Check the website's home page for current offers.

+ *www.39dollarglasses.com.* If you want cheap glasses but don't want to wait, try this website. You get frames, lenses, and even next-day delivery if you don't mind paying a bit more.

+ *www.eyebuydirect.com.* Again, glasses are inexpensive at this discount site, and you can do a virtual try-on. Plus you'll get a money-back guarantee.

## See your way to eye-care savings

Optometrist, optician, ophthalmologist — all these professionals help take care of your eyes. Your choice to make an appointment with one type of specialist should depend on what eye problems you have. But you may save money by staying out of the ophthalmologist's office if you don't need to be there.

**Know your eye doctors.** The three "O" specialists do different jobs because they have different training.

+ An optician is licensed to make, fit, and sell corrective lenses. He's not a doctor at all, but he works from the prescription you get from your eye doctor.

+ An optometrist is a doctor of optometry, or O.D., who has four years of graduate training from a college of optometry.

+ An ophthalmologist is a medical doctor – M.D. – with at least three years of specialty training beyond medical school. This is the kind of eye doctor you need if you're having eye surgery.

Both optometrists and ophthalmologists can screen for glaucoma, cataracts, and macular degeneration, and they both can prescribe medicine for eye diseases and write prescriptions for corrective lenses. You may need to see an ophthalmologist if you have a serious eye condition.

**Pay only for the care you need.** If you don't have a serious eye condition, you may be able to save money by getting your eyes checked and a prescription for corrective lenses from an optometrist at a retail store like Costco or Walmart.

Typically an exam costs between $50 and $100, depending on where it's done. You may pay around $50 to see an optometrist at a retail store or optical chain. But at a private doctor's office or medical clinic, you'll probably pay closer to $100 to see an optometrist or $150 to see an ophthalmologist. The price may go up further if you need extra services beyond the basics, such as pupil dilation or retinal photos.

# Smart savings on sunglasses

Cataracts, macular degeneration, skin cancer on your eyelids, benign growths in your eyes – all these conditions are risks of too much sun over the course of years. Even people who protect their skin with sunscreen don't always take care of their eyes while out in the sun. But sunglasses are more than a fashion statement. They can protect your eyes – if you wear those with the features that are really important. You don't need to spend a lot, either.

**TOP DOLLAR:** Oakley Radar Pitch sport sunglasses for men, made of plastic and available in three colors, $200 at *www.oakley.com*.

**VALUE:** Woodsman Pro Camouflage Sports Sunglasses are $25 at *www.amazon.com.* Or you can choose any other inexpensive pair that has a tag saying the lenses protect against 100 percent of UVA and UVB rays. That's really all you need to know you're buying good-quality sunglasses.

Other features you may want to look for include shatterproof lenses, a wraparound style to protect your eyes from sun at all angles, and an orange tint to cut reflection if you have macular degeneration. But you can find these features on both high- and low-end sunglasses.

**WHAT YOU GIVE UP:** Name brand. Since many sunglasses, from high-end designer brands to discount drugstore varieties, are made in the same Italian factories, you're truly throwing away money if you pay more just for the sake of a brand name.

---

**Freebie Frenzie**

Seniors can get free eye exams from volunteer ophthalmologists through EyeCare America.

To qualify you must be 65 years or older and have gone without an eye exam for three years. You can get a comprehensive eye exam and up to one year of treatment for any problem found in the exam. The exam includes glaucoma screening if you are at increased risk based on your age and family history.

You won't pay out-of-pocket costs. Doctors who work with the program waive copayments and don't charge anything beyond what Medicare or insurance pays.

Get a referral to a participating ophthalmologist near you by filling out the brief questionnaire at *www.eyecareamerica.org,* or calling 800-222-EYES (3937).

---

# Think twice about costly MRI

A standard MRI – magnetic resonance imaging – to diagnose back pain costs roughly $1,000. That's a lot to shell out if you don't need the test. Ordering an MRI has become common for some doctors treating low back pain, but experts say it may not be right for every back.

An MRI is a common test to order because it's noninvasive, although some people don't like feeling trapped in a small compartment for a long time. An MRI also produces clear pictures without exposing you to radiation, making it better than some other types of imaging.

But back pain can be caused by a number of different problems, not all treatable with surgery. An MRI may show changes that can appear to be fixable through surgery, such as spinal stenosis, or shrinking of space between disks. But the images may simply be showing abnormalities in your back that have nothing to do with your pain. An MRI that suggests you need invasive treatment may actually do more harm than good.

If your doctor sends you for an MRI for back pain, question the choice. Conservative guidelines say to wait one to two months to let nonspecific back pain improve on its own. That is unless you have other red flags, like weakness in your foot or leg, problems urinating, fever, or a history of cancer.

Your back pain may be resolved through exercise, over-the-counter painkillers, and time. All are much cheaper than that $1,000 MRI.

# Bypass pricey hospital readmission

Once was enough. You're home from the hospital, and you don't really want to go back. Unplanned hospital readmissions cost $15 billion annually in Medicare and Medicaid costs alone for people returning to the hospital within 30 days. Here's how you can stay home and save your money.

**Take it slowly.** Just because you were out of the hospital within hours or days of your procedure doesn't mean you'll be back at your regular activities quickly. Typical recovery time for an appendectomy or heart bypass surgery is four to six weeks, while even having a pacemaker implanted will slow you down for a month.

**Keep things clean.** Follow instructions for keeping your incision clean and dry to avoid infection, a major reason for readmission. Researchers found more than half of serious post-op infections happened after people had been discharged from the hospital.

**Raise your legs.** Be sure to elevate your legs as instructed to avoid a blood clot, another major reason for readmission. At home, watch for signs of a blood clot forming, like pain, swelling, and heat in one leg, and do the required activities to avoid it.

**Get your head on straight.** Research on people having heart bypass surgery found those who were either depressed before the surgery or full of anxiety afterwards were more likely to end up back in the hospital within six months. The most common reasons for readmission were arrhythmia, chest pains, and infection.

**Find help.** Discharge instructions can be complicated and confusing, and you don't want to skip taking your medicine or be unable to check your wound. Have a friend or relative help by writing down instructions at your discharge meeting and helping you through the routine once you get home.

**Stick with the plan.** Problems can arise if you don't follow your doctor's orders for rehabilitation and physical therapy, for example after joint surgery.

**Freebie Frenzie**

Take advantage of programs that can provide health screenings for free.

Check your local hospital to see if it offers free screenings for common problems, like depression, high blood pressure, or breast cancer. And be aware of health fairs at a local university or medical center, where you might also find free wellness checks.

Finally, see if your employer pays for flu shots or other preventive care. Help from these sources can be a lifesaver.

# Become a medical 'tourist' for big savings

Traveling to find cheaper medical care is all the rage. If you can't afford treatment in the United States, consider a country where costs are low and service and quality of care are high. You can't use Medicare benefits outside the United States except under extremely limited circumstances, but you may come out ahead anyway.

Thousands of Americans travel for more affordable treatment every year. The trip may be worth considering if you can save, say, $10,000 on a knee operation. Popular destinations include India, Thailand, Singapore, and Costa Rica.

**Find the silver lining.** Getting your treatment away from home offers these benefits.

+ Lower cost. Travel to a country where the cost of living is much lower than at home — but the quality of care is still high — and you can easily save 80 percent on treatment.

+ Great customer service. Certain destination hospitals are known for their fine accommodations tailored to Western patients.

+ Shorter waits. You'll spend time on a plane, it's true, but you should be able to schedule appointments more quickly.

+ Insurance perks. Some health insurance companies are including treatment overseas.

+ Vacation options. Depending on your condition, you may be able to add some sightseeing to your visit overseas.

**Read the fine print.** Just like at home, you'll need to ask some questions before you schedule a procedure overseas.

+ How much will you save by going abroad? Include the cost of a plane ticket and an extended stay while you recuperate overseas — not simply the cost of the procedure.

+ Is the hospital accredited by the Joint Commission International (JCI) – a nonprofit that certifies the safety of hospitals?

+ Are you physically able and willing to travel a great distance for treatment?

+ What doctor will treat you after you return home? Major procedures require follow-up care.

You can find help in planning your trip from companies like World Med Assist, Premier MedEscape, and Patients Without Borders – all members of the nonprofit group the Medical Tourism Association. Visit this organization's website at *www.medicaltourismassociation.com*, or call 561-791-2000.

# Deep discounts on overseas treatment

These sample prices show how much you can save by traveling across a border for medical treatment.

| Procedure | Price in U.S. hospital | Price in Costa Rica | Price in Thailand | Price in India |
|---|---|---|---|---|
| Angioplasty | $57,000 | $13,000 | $3,788 | $3,300 |
| Heart bypass | $144,000 | $25,000 | $15,121 | $5,200 |
| Hysterectomy | $15,000 | $5,700 | $2,727 | $2,500 |
| Knee replacement | $50,000 | $11,500 | $12,297 | $6,200 |
| Gastric bypass | $32,927 | $12,500 | $16,667 | $5,000 |

# Health insurance money-savers

## Earn rewards for healthy choices

Get extra cash, free coverage, and lower medical expenses, courtesy of your insurance company and your boss. In its 2010 Employer survey, the Kaiser Family Foundation found that three out of every four companies now offer at least one wellness program, including:

+ weight loss programs.

+ gym membership discounts.

+ smoking cessation programs.

+ nutrition classes.

+ personal health coaches.

+ on-site gyms.

Companies may offer financial benefits to get employees interested. Some promise gift cards, cash, travel rewards, and merchandise. They may even cut your health insurance premiums and deductibles or stash extra money in your Health Savings Account.

Your insurance company is getting in on the act, too. You can now get free preventive care through your health insurance, regardless of whether you have insurance through your employer or through an individual policy. That means free screenings for high blood pressure, diabetes, cholesterol, and cancer; counseling for weight loss; help quitting smoking; treatment for depression; and routine vaccinations, including flu and pneumonia shots.

# Wise up to insurance loopholes and limits

Insurance policies are full of loopholes and limits that can cost you when you need care the most. Watch for these hidden gotchas.

**No stop-loss amount.** Look for insurance that covers 100 percent of your care after you spend a certain amount of money out-of-pocket. A 20-percent copay may sound like a small amount, but without a stop-loss cap you could get stuck paying 20 percent of a $100,000 hospital bill. Beware of policies that don't count prescriptions or doctors' visits toward the limit.

**Caps on hospitalization.** Don't be fooled by policies that cover all of your hospital stay except the first day. Your first day in a hospital is usually the most expensive, thanks to tests, intensive care, and emergency surgeries. In fact, you may be better off with a policy that has a higher deductible and out-of-pocket limit, than one that puts a cap on services.

**Limited doctors' visits.** Some policies only cover a few doctors' visits a year once you meet the deductible. Others charge hefty copays for routine visits, or refuse to cover appointments unless they follow a hospital stay. Read the fine print, and know what you're getting.

**Fake health insurance.** Avoid policies labeled "limited benefit" or "not major medical" insurance. They won't come close to covering your medical expenses.

**Low premiums.** Bargain-priced plans probably don't cover much. Get sick, and you could end up in the poor house. Compare prices at websites like *www.ehealthinsurance.com*. The more expensive the policy, the more comprehensive it's likely to be.

**Unnamed illnesses.** Unless a plan specifically says it covers something – like chemotherapy or outpatient surgery – then it probably doesn't. Never assume otherwise.

An insurance broker can help you sort through policies, explain their limits, and choose the best one for your situation. Demand to see an Explanation of Benefits before buying anything, however. Insurers like to withhold it until after you have bought their policy, but you need it up front. A sales brochure or executive summary is not enough.

Call your state's insurance commissioner to check complaints against the insurers and policies you're considering.

## Sidestep hikes in Medicare costs

Consider signing up for Medicare even if you continue working past age 65. It's tempting to stay on your boss's plan, but financial advisors warn against it.

Delaying Medicare will raise your premiums for life. You could also end up with a big coverage gap when you finally do retire. You will have to wait until the next Medicare open enrollment period, which could be months after your employer's coverage runs out.

Keep in mind, you will be automatically enrolled in Medicare Parts A and B when you begin drawing Social Security, unless you specifically decline the coverage.

## Money-saving reason you need Part D

Medicare Part D, which covers prescription drugs, is not mandatory. Some people want to drop it if they aren't using it, but think twice before you do.

For every month you put off Part D, your premiums will go up by 1 percent for life. Just one year of delay will boost your premiums by 12 percent. People who postpone Part D because they still have drug coverage through their job or union generally don't get penalized, however.

You can only sign up for coverage once a year, from October 15 through December 7, with a few exceptions. Delay Part D or miss the deadline, and you won't be able to enroll until the next year — even if you get sick and desperately need drug coverage. That can be financially devastating. Diseases like cancer can strike without warning, and the life-saving medicines needed to treat them add up fast.

Instead of skipping Part D altogether, simply sign up for the plan with the lowest premium. That way, you still have a safety net. To shop for cheaper coverage, call Medicare at 800-633-4227 (800-MEDICARE), or visit the Medicare website at *www.medicare.gov*.

## DEEP DISCOUNT

The Medicare Part D coverage gap, or "donut hole," is slowly shrinking each year. It will close completely in 2020. Until then, people who end up in the gap can get help paying for their medicines.

- **Brand-name prescription drugs.** You'll get half off their cost while you're in the "hole." Your discount should ring up automatically at the pharmacy once you cross into the coverage gap.

- **Generic drugs.** Medicare pays 7 percent of the price of these drugs in 2011, while you're in the coverage gap. Medicare's share will grow each year until it pays 25 percent in 2020.

You must be enrolled in a Medicare Prescription Drug Plan or a Medicare Advantage Plan with prescription drug coverage to snag these discounts. People with Extra Help Medicare do not qualify.

## Maximize your money from Medicaid

Many people need help paying their medical bills but don't qualify for Medicaid because their income is too high. Medicaid spend-down may help. It lets you count your medical bills against your income, lowering it enough to qualify you for coverage.

Each state sets its own limits on how much income you can earn and still qualify for Medicaid. That means each state decides how much money you need to spend before Medicaid kicks in. Talk to a case worker to learn your spend-down amount and time frame to submit expenses. Then submit receipts and invoices for medical expenses, like:

+ doctor and dentist visits.

+ prescription drugs.

+ lab work.

+ health insurance or Medicare premiums.

+ transportation costs for getting to and from appointments.

These bills count, even if you can't afford to pay them. Keep in mind, though, you — not Medicaid — are responsible for paying any bills you use toward spend-down. Medicaid only covers costs you have after you meet the spend-down.

**Book early.** Schedule your doctor appointments and prescription refills for early in the spend-down period. The sooner you meet the threshold, the more time you'll have under Medicaid.

**Dig up old bills.** Old medical bills can count toward your spend-down amount, as long as you still owe on them. If you're still getting bills or collections notices, they most likely qualify.

You can only use an old debt once, but you can break that debt into parts and spread it over several periods. Say you have a lingering $10,000 hospital bill, and you must spend-down $2,000 each period to qualify for Medicaid. You can put $2,000 of that 10 grand toward one spend-down period, then spread the remaining $8,000 over future periods.

**Save them up.** Sometimes, you may not meet your spend-down until late in the period. That means you'll only get a few days or weeks of Medicaid coverage. Consider hanging on to those bills instead of putting them toward spend-down. Save them up, then use them to meet your spend-down earlier in the next period.

# Lower the premiums on long-term care

Your early 60s are the perfect time to buy long-term care insurance — you'll enjoy much lower premiums than in a few years. Still, coverage doesn't come cheap. Here is how to pick a good policy without breaking the bank.

**Don't choose the cheapest one.** A policy that costs much less than others should raise a red flag. It may start out a bargain, but its premiums are more likely to shoot up. Buy the best policy you can afford, without spending more than 7 percent of your income on premiums.

**Be willing to wait.** Choose a plan with a 90-day waiting period before benefits kick in. The premiums will be more affordable.

**Shorten the payout.** Most people don't need a lifetime payout. That is a good thing, because those policies are pricey. Cut premium costs by choosing a three- to five-year payout period.

**Share the benefits.** Consider a shared-benefit plan instead of a separate policy for each spouse. Individual plans offering five years of care may not be affordable. A flexible, shared-benefit policy, however, gives you a pool of years to split between you and your spouse.

For instance, a three-year shared-benefit policy gives you six total years of care. If one spouse uses two years, then the other will still have four. People typically need about three years of long-term care, unless they develop a lengthy illness like Alzheimer's disease.

**Beat back inflation.** What seems like a big payout now may not be enough down the road. Get a policy that keeps up with inflation, or one at least tied to the Consumer Price Index (CPI). A CPI-linked insurance policy is not as good a guarantee as an inflation-adjusted policy, but it could cost 40 percent less.

**Talk to the boss.** Consider buying long-term care insurance through your job. You will have access to group rates, which are usually lower.

**Find flexible care.** Look for a policy that covers home care and unlicensed caregivers. They cost much less than a licensed health care agency.

Get a second and third opinion before buying anything. Have competing insurance agents show you different long-term care policies. Then show them to a neutral third party, such as a financial planner or elder law attorney with long-term care experience, for an honest opinion.

Beef up your long-term care coverage with a Partnership qualified (PQ) policy. These policies are sold by private insurance companies but meet special state requirements. With them, you can apply for Medicaid if you use up all of your long-term care insurance, while keeping more assets than Medicaid normally allows.

With a Partnership qualified policy, available in more than half of all states, Medicaid will ignore assets totaling the amount of your policy's value. Call your state's department of insurance, and ask which agents and companies sell PQ policies in your state.

States with Partnership programs generally honor each others' policies. So if you move to another PQ state after buying yours, you may still qualify for asset disregard.

# Don't get duped by health care credit cards

Every day, people get scammed by the professionals they should be able to trust most — their health care providers. Unscrupulous dentists, chiropractors, doctors, and veterinarians push special health care credit cards as an easier way to pay for their services. In reality, these cards make lots of money for providers but rarely benefit you, the customer.

Providers like them because the card companies pay in full and up front, whether or not you have received any services. Card companies may also pay providers kickbacks, based on how much money you charge on your card. Some offices even push credit over cash payments.

In 2010, the Attorney General (AG) of New York began an investigation into the card companies and the health care providers who push them. Avoid getting duped with this advice from the New York AG office.

✦ Get a second opinion before agreeing to an expensive procedure. Make sure you actually need all the work a provider claims you do, especially if they urge you to pay with a health care credit card.

✦ Ask your provider about working out a payment plan that does not involve a credit card account.

✦ Look into a loan from your bank or credit union, if you must borrow. Their interest rates and terms may be better than any credit card's.

✦ Don't cave into pressure and sign up for a card. Ask the provider if they get financial incentives from the card company. And if you do feel pressured, find another health provider.

✦ Make sure you understand any financial documents the provider gives you before signing them. Some may try to sneak a credit card application past you without telling you what it is.

✦ Never let a provider charge you for future procedures in advance. If they go out of business or you change your mind, you may never get your money back.

✦ Be wary of cards that advertise a zero-interest introductory rate. That low rate will skyrocket down the road, and you may owe interest retroactively.

# Healthy living for less

## Save money by staying healthy

Living a healthy lifestyle does more than just keep you out of the hospital. It can also safeguard your retirement savings. Follow these three simple steps to avoid wasting your nest egg on health care.

**Get some exercise.** Staying physically fit can help you avoid high blood pressure and heart disease. These conditions can cost you $606 extra per year when you're 40 years old, according to Nationwide Better Health, a health-management company. If you instead invest that amount over 25 years, you could rake in $35,000 a year from the investment.

Aim for at least 30 minutes of moderate-intensity activity on most days.

**Watch your diet and lose weight.** Steer clear of diabetes — along with heart disease, stroke, and some cancers — by keeping to a healthy weight. Rand Health, a nonprofit research and policy group, says diabetes costs an average of $454 per year. That expense can soar to $12,000 annually if you don't carefully control the disease.

So between ages 40 and 65, you're talking about spending an extra $700,000 as a penalty for carrying extra weight. Factor in other costs, like having to replace clothing when you can't fit what you have in your closet, and you're really paying the price for added size.

**Don't smoke.** Skipping the cost of cigarettes can keep more than $150,000 in your pocket over 25 years. Avoid this unhealthy habit, and you may also steer clear of emphysema and cancer, thus saving the cost of medical treatments. The average cost of treating lung cancer for the first 10 years of survival, if you're that fortunate, is more than $107,000.

Close your eyes and imagine you're eating a big piece of cherry cheesecake. Think about each bite, enjoying every morsel slowly in your mind. It won't cost money or calories, and it may help you avoid overeating the real treat and sabotaging your diet.

Researchers found that people who imagined eating a certain food, either M&M candies or squares of cheese, ate less of that treat when they had the chance. It sounds backwards, but the experts think the act of imagining actually tricks your brain, fooling yourself into thinking you've already enjoyed the treat.

The trick seemed to work only with a specific food, so be sure to zero in on a treat you expect to be tempted with later. Enjoy it now, and eat less later.

## Shape up your body — and your bank account

When you're out of control in one area of your life, it may seep over into other areas. That's the weight-debt connection.

Financial expert Suze Orman noticed this link while doing research for a book. She found that women who were overweight also tended to be hiding their debt – mostly credit card bills – from their husbands. The correlation was about 2 pounds of excess weight for every $1,000 of hidden debt.

Orman believes the two are connected in that some people have trouble controlling their spending just as they have trouble controlling what they eat.

If you notice you have both problems, you may be able to use similar tricks to bring both spending and eating under control.

✦ Budget both calories and money on paper.

- Practice delayed gratification.

- Prioritize bills and foods. Spend your calories on the most nutritious foods, and pay the urgent bills first.

- Consider the changes to be lifelong rather than quick diets or spending cuts.

- Earn more. This might mean finding a side income to pay down your bills or exercising more to increase the number of calories you can eat.

As your checkbook gets back in balance, so will your scale.

# Lose weight without losing your shirt

Weight Watchers and other commercial programs offer weight-loss tips and support groups to help you make lifestyle changes. Some programs also sell prepackaged meals. These programs can be expensive, but they may help you reach your goal. To save money, choose a low-cost option like the nonprofit group Take Off Pounds Sensibly.

**Take Off Pounds Sensibly (TOPS).** This may be your best deal at just $26 a year plus a nominal chapter fee. You'll receive encouragement to stick with the food and exercise plans that you get from your own doctor through weekly chapter meetings and a newsletter. Buy and prepare your own food.

**Weight Watchers.** Pay $39.95 a month for help from this well-known group, or you can pay less for an online-only plan. You'll benefit from weekly meetings and instructions on eating to lose weight. Buy and prepare your own food.

**Jenny Craig.** Plans start at $6 a week plus the cost of Jenny Craig prepackaged food, which runs $11 to $15 per day. One-on-one counseling is available, either in person or by phone.

**Nutrisystem.** Pay only for Nutrisystem prepackaged food, around $360 a month, less if you use auto delivery. Counseling, classes, and a newsletter can help keep you on track.

Timing is everything. You can save money on a gym membership by signing up in June, July, or August. Summer is typically the slow season at health clubs, so you may find a deal during the hot months. Avoid buying a membership early in the year when gyms are crowded with new members trying to keep their New Year's resolutions.

Try these other money-saving tricks to keep more cash when you join a club.

- Look for a discounted membership if you exercise during off hours, like before 11 a.m. or after 8 p.m.
- Ask if you can have the membership fee waived.
- See if you can save money by paying for six months or a year in advance. Be sure you will actually use the gym once you've made the investment.

# Find free help getting fit

Getting in shape can be difficult. Sometimes it takes a village to stay on track. Find help getting fit — and paying for it.

**Hit up the boss.** Before you join a gym, see if your employer or health insurance company will help pay for membership. You might save on the gym membership or on your insurance cost, since insurers know healthy people are cheaper to cover.

**Find a group.** Organize a group fitness class with your coworkers. You might share exercise videos that you use together, or pick a time and place to meet and go on a fitness walk. Camaraderie will help you continue the program.

**Track your steps.** Try these free websites to help track your walking or running miles. You can map out the route before you go, or log in your route afterwards and find out how many miles you covered. Having a goal makes the activity more fun and meaningful.

+ *www.MapMyWalk.com*

+ *www.LogYourRun.com*

**Log your calories.** You can also find free online tools to help track calories in and calories out. Log in the food you eat and activities you perform, and the program will keep track of both and give advice on reaching your fitness goals.

• *www.MyPyramid.gov*

• *www.FitDay.com*

# Heel pain help for less

Custom shoe inserts to treat heel pain can easily run $500, including a doctor's exam and tests. But for most people suffering from the common heel pain plantar fasciitis, drugstore orthotics work just as well. For less than $50, they're a painless purchase to ease the pain.

Heel pain is often caused by inflammation of the soft tissue on the bottom of your foot that connects your heel bone to your toes. If the pain is sharp when you first get out of bed in the morning, it's likely caused by plantar fasciitis. This problem may get worse after you exercise on a hard surface or wear thin-soled shoes or high heels.

It can also come from being overweight or having flat feet, high arches, or tight calf muscles. People who overpronate, or roll their feet inward, may be at risk.

You may find relief from wearing an orthotic – a soft silicon heel cushion or heel cup – inside your shoe. Those you buy off the shelf at a drugstore work well for most people. But if you have a serious biomechanical problem, like overpronation or having one leg shorter than the other, you may want to ask your doctor about custom orthotics. Insurance may cover the cost.

If the pain persists, try these self-help remedies.

✦ Apply ice to your heel.

✦ Limit your activities – especially weight-bearing exercise – when the pain is worst.

✦ Lose excess weight.

✦ Use over-the-counter pain relievers when needed.

+ Stretch first thing in the morning. Sit on the edge of your bed, and cross your foot over your other knee. Grab your foot with the hand from the same side, fingers on the ball of your foot, and pull your toes back toward your shin until you feel a stretch in your arch. Hold while you count to 10, then repeat 10 times.

## Prevent pricey bedbug battle

Don't let the bedbugs bite — and don't pay $5,000 to rid your home of these pests. Take simple precautions to keep them out of your nest.

Bedbugs are small, flat, bloodsucking insects that hide during the day in cracks in furniture or tiny tears in mattresses. They come out at night and bite sleeping humans. You may not even notice the bite, and bedbugs don't usually transmit disease. But bedbugs do leave behind their saliva, which can cause a reaction, inflammation, and itching.

Bedbug infestations have become more common in the United States lately, likely because people travel overseas more than they used to, carrying bedbugs home in their luggage or clothing. Also, reduced pesticide use means bugs of all kinds can flourish.

Take steps to keep bedbugs out of your house.

+ Don't buy used mattresses, bedding, or furniture. Bedbugs can hitch a ride into your home on these.

+ Be cautious if you buy used clothing. Look for signs of the critters on the clothing. Be aware that they can hide in the lining of a jacket, for example, so you may not see them. Kill any hidden bugs by immediately sealing the clothing in a plastic bag and freezing for three days. Then have the clothes dry cleaned, just to be safe.

+ When you travel, even to a nice hotel, inspect the room carefully for signs of bedbugs. Tiny reddish-brown flecks left on the sheets or other surfaces may signal trouble. Don't place your luggage on the floor, where it's more likely to get infested. Put it on a dresser or other hard surface. When you return home, unpack your suitcases outdoors, then freeze your clothing in plastic. Put the empty suitcases in your car for several hours on a hot or cold day.

Don't waste money on mattress-sanitizing services.

Around 30 percent of people are allergic to the waste products of dust mites, microscopic arachnids that can live in mattresses and pillows. The problem comes from an enzyme that coats dust mite feces. Where there are lots of mites, even people not allergic can become sensitive.

You can hire a company to treat mattresses and other fabric items using specialized steam cleaning or UV light. The cost is as high as $80 to clean a single mattress. Mites will probably be killed, but they'll be back within a month. Save the cost by handling the problem yourself.

- Wash your sheets and pillowcases in hot water once a week.
- Declutter the bedroom.
- Vacuum often. You may even consider replacing carpets with hard-surface floors.
- Look into buying zippered covers for your mattress and pillows to limit your exposure to dust mite refuse.

# Save money on cholesterol control

A natural approach to cholesterol control is also the cheapest.

Research proves lowering your LDL cholesterol can also reduce your risk of heart disease complications. You can do that by taking statins like Crestor or Lipitor for around $3.45 a day. You can also take supplements like vitamin C and lycopene. These may help prevent plaque by protecting the inner layer of blood vessels, thus helping to lower cholesterol.

Rather than paying for drugs or supplements that you take every day, go the cheaper way. Eat foods high in these cholesterol-controlling nutrients — tomatoes and tomato products.

One study found that drinking about 17 ounces of clarified, or filtered, tomato juice a day for a month kept cholesterol from oxidizing and attaching to artery walls — a process that hardens and blocks your arteries. This amount of tomato juice nearly tripled people's levels of lycopene. Cost for this natural remedy? About $1.24 per day.

# Enjoy heart-healthy goodness for less

The health benefits of olive oil come from its healthy monounsaturated fatty acids (MUFAs), a big part of the Mediterranean diet. Trading the butter on your bread for olive oil to dip it in can lower your risk of dying of heart disease. Great things olive oil can do include raising your "good" HDL cholesterol, lowering triglycerides, bringing down high blood pressure, and protecting your arteries.

Food like this that is good for you often costs more. Not always. Shop carefully, and you can enjoy the benefits without paying the high prices of gourmet goodies. Be sure to pick extra-virgin olive oil, which has the most antioxidant polyphenols. It also has a delightfully distinct taste.

**TOP DOLLAR:** Pago Baldios San Carlos extra-virgin olive oil at the gourmet food store Dean & Deluca ($22 for a 17-ounce bottle, or $1.29 per ounce).

**VALUE:** Extra-virgin olive oil at Trader Joe's (about $3.49 for 17 ounces, or 21 cents per ounce). Trader Joe's is known as a discount grocer that stocks unusual and gourmet items.

**WHAT YOU GIVE UP:** If you have very sensitive taste buds, you may notice a slight difference in flavor. But all extra-virgin olive oils are unrefined and come from the first pressing of the fruit, so they retain lots of antioxidants. If you can do without the cachet of a well-known brand, just keep testing varieties until you find one you like.

# Don't be fooled by sunscreen hype

You can buy sunscreens that promise to provide a sun-protection factor (SPF) of 80, 90, even 100. That sounds like a lot of protection, but these claims may not hold up in the light of day. Paying more for a super-high SPF is often a waste of money.

**Know the numbers.** SPF measures protection from UVB rays. The number is supposed to tell how much longer you can stay in the sun compared to wearing no sunscreen. So if you could normally be in the sun without sunscreen for 10 minutes without getting burned, then applying an SPF 20 sunscreen should let you be out for 200 minutes without damage.

But tests show these numbers don't mean what you may think they mean, especially with higher-SPF products. You might think a sunscreen with SPF 60 is twice as good as an SPF 30, but that is not the case. SPF 30 sunscreen blocks 97 percent of rays, while SPF 45 blocks 98 percent of rays. You probably don't need much more than that.

Even more confusing, SPF refers only to protection against UVB rays, which cause sunburn — not the UVA rays that cause deeper skin damage. Both types are linked with skin cancer. That's why you should look for sunscreen that says it protects against both UVA and UVB rays.

**Don't overpay.** *Consumer Reports* tested 12 sunscreens and found four that worked best. These were not necessarily the pricey varieties, but included store brands like Walgreens Sport Continuous Spray SPF 50 at $1.33 per ounce and Target's Up & Up Sport Continuous Spray SPF 30 at 87 cents an ounce. Meanwhile, some brands costing $4 an ounce and more didn't score nearly as well.

**Follow best practices.** Your best bet is to use sunscreen properly.

+ Apply sunscreen one-half hour before you go into the sun.

+ Use plenty. It takes about 1 1/4 ounces — a shot glass full — to cover your entire body.

+ Reapply often, around every two to three hours.

+ Don't neglect high-risk areas, like the tops of ears, the part of your hair, and the bridge of your nose.

# Top choices for reliable health info

You don't need to trek to the library when you need health information, unless it's to use their computers. Every year, about 72 million people find health advice on the Internet. Check out these free and reliable websites that can help you figure out what is wrong with you and what treatment you may need.

+ WebMd at *www.webmd.com*. The big kahuna of online health information, this website now offers an interactive nutrition center.

+ MayoClinic at *www.mayoclinic.com*. This website offers easy-to-read, expert information on health conditions, symptoms, drugs and supplements, and even medical tests and procedures.

+ EverydayHealth at *www.everydayhealth.com*. This network of sites covering various health problems can connect you to a support group for your specific condition. You can also create your own home health page to track your exercise and weight-loss progress.

+ HealthCentral at *www.healthcentral.com*. A symptom-checker tool is included in this network of sites covering various conditions.

Of course, Internet research cannot replace a visit to your physician when you are sick or injured. In those cases, it's best to get checked by a professional.

# 4 ways to save on mobility aids

If pain or disability gets in the way of being active, you may need the help of a mobility device, whether a wheelchair, walker, or cane. But these important gadgets can be expensive, and you sure can't wait for your next birthday. Don't pay full freight for the equipment you need to keep going.

**Compare prices online.** It's nice to examine a wheelchair at a store, but you may find a better deal by shopping on the Internet. The major online mobility-device sellers will let you custom order exactly what you need, and you may even get it at 30 to 45 percent off retail. That's a lot of savings when you're looking at a $2,000 wheelchair. You can also take a low price you find online to a local merchant and ask for a price match.

**Look at used options.** Walkers, power wheelchairs, and so on are made to fit the specific needs of the individuals using them, so they can be hard to sell. That is good news for buyers, who can find great deals. Locate someone selling exactly the item and size you need by checking popular websites like *www.eBay.com* or *www.Craigslist.com*.

**Check out demos.** Like furniture floor samples, demonstration models of power chairs, lifts, and other items can go for up to 50 percent off. If you don't mind living with a certain color choice or a slight blemish, you may save a bundle.

**Don't forget your benefits.** Medicare part B may cover the cost of durable medical equipment – wheelchairs, walkers, and so on – when your doctor prescribes it for you to use at home. A Medicare Advantage Plan must cover the same equipment as regular Medicare, but you may have to foot part of the bill. Call your plan to find out.

For more about what is covered by Medicare, or to find a Medicare equipment supplier near you, go online to *www.medicare.gov* or call 800-MEDICARE (800-633-4227).

# 'Lighten' the cost of treatment

What would you rather do — take a pill or sit under a bright light for a while every day? Considering the costs and possible side effects of drugs, you might opt for light therapy to help banish depression.

Light boxes are already an accepted treatment for certain conditions, including seasonal affective disorder (SAD) and jet lag. Now, new research shows they may help with depression. A small study of seniors found that light therapy worked as well as antidepressants in boosting mood after just three weeks. It also helped the participants sleep better.

You can buy 10,000-lux light boxes on the Internet or in some drugstores for as low as $50. Some health insurance companies will cover the cost. Even if you opt for an expensive unit, the one-time cost may be cheaper than paying for antidepressants, which can easily run $25-$200 a month depending on whether you get a generic or brand-name drug.

Light therapy does come with some safety concerns. Possible side effects include headache, eyestrain, nausea, and agitation. Make sure you talk to your doctor before buying a light box and trying the therapy on your own.

# Stop wasting money at the pharmacy

## Free Rx for people in need

Prescription Assistance Programs can help you get free or nearly free prescriptions, even costly "tier 3" drugs. Also known as Patient Assistance Programs (PAPs), they typically help cash-strapped people with no insurance or too little coverage get the medicines they need. Some PAPs will help with drug costs even if you have Medicare Part D coverage.

The first step is finding a PAP that covers your medicines, then learning if you qualify. Different PAPs have different eligibility rules, but most set income limits. Once you find a program, you and your doctor will need to fill out paperwork. These organizations can help you find the right PAP for your situation, for free.

**Partnership for Prescription Assistance (PPA).** Tell the people at PPA which medications you take, your income, and what, if any, drug coverage you have. They will tell you which PAPs you may qualify for. You can answer these questions through their website at *www.pparx.org,* or call 888-477-2669.

**RxHope.** This organization claims it can help you get your medications faster than other programs. Find your medicine from a list on its website at *www.rxhope.org,* and RxHope will link you with PAPs that can help. You can even begin filling out some of the aid applications online, but your doctor will have to complete them before sending them in. For help by phone, call RxHope at 877-267-0517.

**NeedyMeds.** This group keeps a list of current prescription assistance programs. NeedyMeds does not have a telephone help line, but you can get plenty of information on their website at *www.needymeds.org.* Search for your medicine, then click on the drug's name for details about the PAPs that cover it, who qualifies for each program, how to apply, and phone numbers to call for more information.

Unfortunately, if you can't find a program through one of these websites, there's probably no PAP for that medication. It still helps to call the company that makes your medicine and ask. Sometimes, a drug company will help needy people, even if it doesn't have a formal assistance program.

**No-Sweat Solution**

Bring a copy of your health insurance formulary to every doctor's visit. The formulary lists the prescription drugs your insurance covers and may give you an idea of how much each costs, based on its tier. This list can help your doctor prescribe only medicines that are covered, plus choose less-expensive options.

You may have received a copy of your formulary when you first signed up for coverage. If not, call the phone number on the back of your insurance card to request a new one.

# 5 ways to trim pill bills

Become a savvy saver, and you won't need to skip medicine to make medical ends meet.

**Ask for samples.** Ask your doctor for samples when he first puts you on a new medicine. This saves you from spending money on a prescription only to find out it doesn't work or has too many side effects.

**Call around.** Drug prices can vary from one pharmacy to another. Phone several stores to find the best price for your prescriptions.

**Hit the club.** Even if you don't have a membership at Costco or Sam's Club, these warehouse stores could help you save up to 75 percent on prescription drugs. That's because you don't have to be a member of either club to fill your prescriptions at their remarkably low-priced pharmacies.

**Shop the sales.** Yes, even medicine goes on sale. Stock up on over-the-counter drugs when you find a great deal — but check the expiration dates first. Look for coupons, too, in store ads and weekly coupon circulars.

**Remember your age.** Another discount could be staring you in the face. Ask the pharmacy if they honor senior discounts on over-the-counter or prescription drugs and medical supplies.

# Get more for your money with older drugs

New drugs don't necessarily work better than old ones. They may simply cost more. New drugs are protected by patents for as many as 20 years. Cheaper, generic versions don't become available until the patent runs out. Until then, you pay top dollar.

It's not always a bad tradeoff. Some groundbreaking medications may well be worth their high price. But all too often, you're simply paying for a new name.

Drug makers can get a new patent on a medicine by making slight changes to it. Then they give it a new name and start charging a whole lot more for the "new and improved" version. In reality, the new version may not work any better than the old one – but it's guaranteed to cost more. Drug companies often do this right before the patent runs out on a huge moneymaking medication.

Beat them at their own game. The next time you hear about a fancy new drug, or your doctor suggests trying one, ask instead if there's an older, generic version. Melanie Sanders did. When her insurance changed a few years ago, it stopped covering a brand-name medication she couldn't do without. "It wasn't cheap, even with an insurance copay. But then it became impossible to afford."

So she mentioned the problem to her doctor. He explained that the brand-name drug was a reformulation of an older, generic drug. Together, they decided to try her on the older medicine. She went from paying more than $100 a month to paying $4. "We had to bump up the dosage, but it seems to work just as well as the expensive version."

The active ingredients in a generic drug must be exactly the same as in the name-brand. However, the inactive ingredients may differ. This shouldn't affect how the medicine works, but in rare cases, some people may be allergic to certain inactive ingredients. Pay attention to how you feel when you switch medicines, particularly if you suffer from diabetes, food intolerances, celiac disease, or allergies.

Be particularly careful when changing to the generic version of Coumadin (warfarin) or Synthroid (levothyroxine). These and certain other drugs have a narrow therapeutic index. Take just the right dosage, and they effectively treat an illness. A little too much, and they become toxic. Your doctor may want to monitor you more closely when switching these medications.

## Serious savings on OTC drugs

Store-brand medicines, just like store-brand groceries, offer serious savings. Cut the cost of getting well by forgoing name-brand drugs in favor of their store-brand equivalents. Compare these recognized remedies to their no-name counterparts.

| Name-brand medicine | Price ($) | Store-brand medicine | Price ($) | Savings (%) |
|---|---|---|---|---|
| Advil, 100 tablets | 10.99 | Ibuprofen, 100 tablets | 7.99 | 27 |
| Nicorette gum, 170 pieces | 79.99 | Nicotine gum, 170 pieces | 56.99 | 29 |
| Tums, extra strength, 96 tablets | 5.49 | Chewable antacid, extra strength, 96 tablets | 4.99 | 9 |
| Robitussin CF, 12 oz. | 9.99 | Tussin CF, 12 oz. | 8.99 | 10 |

## Halve the cost of high-priced medicine

Get two pills for the price of one when you split them. Many medicines can be safely split for big savings. Ask your doctor or pharmacist if yours can be. Your doctor will need to write your prescription for twice the regular dose. Then simply cut each pill down the middle.

Not all drugs are safe to split. These pills, in particular, should never be cut.

- capsules containing powder or gel

- extended release or long-acting drugs

- medicines with a narrow range of effectiveness, like warfarin (Coumadin)

- pills that contain more than one drug, such as Avandaryl for diabetes and Lopressor HCT for high blood pressure

- enteric-coated pills designed to dissolve in the small intestine

Don't try to divide medications with a kitchen knife or razor blade. Invest $5 to $10 in an inexpensive pill splitter made just for this purpose. Anything else will cut unevenly and could cause the pill to crumble, dangerously skewing your dose.

## Go big for greater savings

Toilet paper and sodas aren't the only things you can buy in bulk for less. People who bought three months of medicine at a time, instead of one month, spent 29 percent less out of pocket, say researchers at the University of Chicago.

Ask your insurance company if they will cover a three-month supply of medication for chronic health conditions. Then find out if your pharmacy offers a discount when you buy prescriptions in bulk. You may snag an even better deal ordering them by mail directly from your insurance company. Call your insurer and ask.

## Little cards, big deals

Drug discount cards can shave 10 to 70 percent off the price of your prescriptions, depending on the card and the medicine. State, county, and city governments; drug companies; nonprofit organizations; membership groups like AARP; and for-profit businesses all offer discount cards. Some are free but others may charge an enrollment fee, or annual or monthly fees.

It's easy to feel overwhelmed with so many choices. Start narrowing the field with these easy steps.

**Ask about coverage.** Make sure any card you consider will actually cover the medicines you take, especially if it charges a fee. Call the group issuing the card and ask what drugs it covers. If one card doesn't cover your medications, another one probably will.

**Talk to your pharmacist.** Call your local pharmacy and make certain they accept the cards you are considering. Ask your pharmacist which one will save the most money on your medications.

People who have no insurance coverage and don't qualify for Medicare should look into these options. All are free, but you may have to meet eligibility requirements, including income limits.

+ The Pfizer Pfriends card covers drugs made by Pfizer. Your annual income will determine how much you save. You can request an application by calling 866-706-2400 or print one from the website *www.pfizerhelpfulanswers.com*.

+ The Together Rx Access Card can cut 25 to 40 percent off the cost of brand-name drugs from a variety of companies. Apply through the website *www.togetherrxaccess.com* or call 800-444-4106.

+ The NeedyMeds Drug Discount Card shaves 20 to 60 percent off a range of medications. You can only get it through the Internet at *www.needymeds.org/drugcard*.

If you have Medicare Part D coverage, try the AstraZeneca card AZ&Me for discounts on drugs made by this company. Apply online at *www.azandmeapp.com* or by calling 800-292-6363. You can also apply for the GlaxoSmithKline card, GSK Access. People who qualify can pick up their GlaxoSmithKline medications for free at any retail pharmacy. Enroll in the program online at *www.gsk-access.com*, or call 866-518-4357.

# The truth about Canadian pharmacies

Buying your prescriptions from a Canadian pharmacy can actually cost more money than filling them in the United States.

In 2004, U.S. Customs and Border Patrol stopped 807 prescription drugs being shipped from a Canadian pharmacy to its American customers, via the Bahamas. Nearly half were simply generic versions of foreign drugs or drugs that were generically available in the United States. Shockingly, some people were being charged three times more than what they would have paid for the same medicines in the United States, plus another $15 to $30 for shipping and handling.

Don't fall for the lure of cheap, foreign drugs. Talk to your doctor and pharmacist if you have trouble affording your medications. Ask if any of your prescriptions has a generic version, or if there's a similar, less-expensive drug available.

# Free help managing your medicines

Get free, expert help managing your medications and avoiding side effects. Under Medicare Part D, insurance providers must offer free Medication Therapy Management (MTM) if you:

+ have three or more chronic conditions, such as diabetes, high cholesterol, high blood pressure, or arthritis.

+ take eight or more medications covered by your Part D insurance. Some insurers offer MTM if you take as few as two medicines.

+ are likely to spend at least $3,000 each year out of pocket on your Part D medications, or have already spent more than $750 on them in the last three months, or more than $250 in the last month.

Meet these criteria, and your insurer will automatically enroll you in Medication Therapy Management. Make sure you take advantage of this valuable service. It entitles you to a Comprehensive Medication Review at least once a year, where an expert – usually a pharmacist – will go over all the medicines, herbal therapies, and supplements you take; any side effects they're causing; and untreated health problems you may have.

The expert will contact your doctor to make recommendations like changing drug dosages or stopping medicines you don't need. On top of that, you'll get a followup review of your medications at least every three months.

This kind of expert help matters more than you might think. Thanks to this one-on-one attention, the person managing your medicines can catch dangerous errors, like a family doctor and a specialist prescribing two different blood thinners. They may also spot potentially dangerous interactions between your medications and supplements.

The service is free. If you think you qualify for Medication Therapy Management but have not heard from your Part D insurer about it, call your insurance agent and ask.

# Pamper yourself for pennies

## Sample your way to free stuff

It's a match made in free-stuff heaven. Companies need customers to test their products, and you'd love to try new beauty and hair-care products without paying for them. Here's how you can get in on the goods and get free samples of exactly what you want.

**Start with centralized sampling.** If you have a computer, you're in luck. Websites that collect offers for free samples can let you request a variety of products from a single location.

- ✦ Start sampling at *www.startsampling.com*. Type in some basic personal information, including your home address, and you'll get free samples sent to you. Along with lots of grocery store freebies, you'll find offers for personal items like Aveeno shampoo, Hugo Boss men's fragrance, and Dove conditioner. You can also print out coupons for savings on similar items.

- ✦ Get goodies at *www.heyitsfree.net*. This website is updated regularly with offers of free samples and coupons for all kinds of products. Click on the "Body products" link to see offers for free shampoo, hairstyling products, deodorant, and more.

**Head to your favorite store.** Macy's, Belk, Dillard's, Nieman Marcus — your favorite department store has a deal for you. Look for free gifts with purchase of brands like Clinique and Estee Lauder. The gift typically includes five or six products, and you may get to choose between shades for warm or cool skin tones.

Kiehl's, an old-fashioned store selling natural products, hands out free samples — some 10 million giveaways a year. You can choose your three free samples at a Kiehl's store, where the selection is usually largest, or at the Kiehl's counter in a department store. You can also pick three free samples with an online purchase at *www.kiehls.com*. Call Kiehl's at 800-543-4572 to find a location near you.

Sephora stores offer generous samples when you make a purchase. Just ask and a salesperson will hand you a sample of the product you want to try. You can also request three free samples when you place an order online at *www.sephora.com*. Sephora carries its own brand, along with more than 150 other brands, including Lancome and Ralph Lauren.

**DEEP DISCOUNT** Don't be fooled by "discount" websites that claim to sell beauty products for less. Compare prices, and you may find they actually charge more than you'd pay at a department store or drugstore.

But certain websites really do offer deals.

- *www.beautyticket.com*. You'll find great prices, like certain shades of Estee Lauder eye shadow for just $9.99. Selection is limited.

- *www.fragrancenet.com*. You can easily save 50 percent off a variety of fragrances. Find deals on Elizabeth Arden, Calvin Klein, Bill Blass, and oodles more.

- *www.strawberrynet.com*. Sale items at this website offer serious savings. But shop carefully for deals among the site's selections from more than 250 brands.

# Top values in mineral makeup

You've seen the new mineral makeups – powder foundation, eye shadows, and blushes made from natural minerals like zinc oxide, ultramarine, and titanium dioxide. Women pay high prices for them because they're supposed to be pure, yet they cover and camouflage flaws like broken capillaries, rosacea, and scars.

But the high-end mineral makeup brands are pricey, and they may not be available in your area. Check your drugstore for a great substitute.

**TOP DOLLAR:** Bare Escentuals foundation ($25 to $28, plus $20 or more for a brush). Prices are in line with luxury brands like Dior or

Chanel. You may even feel pressured to buy the Bare Escentuals starter kit – foundation, brushes, and other accessories – for around $60.

**VALUE:** Neutrogena Mineral Sheers loose powder foundation ($11.99).

**WHAT YOU GIVE UP:** Top mineral makeup brands are free of dyes, fragrances, preservatives, and mineral oil, so they won't cause a skin reaction. You may not get all those benefits in a cheaper brand. Be sure to read the label.

## Easy tricks to hair-color savings

When you were younger, you changed your hair color for fun. Now that you need to cover the gray, it seems harder to color and make it last. Try these tricks to stretch the weeks between hair coloring.

+ Pick a color that lasts, like blond or brunette, but not red.

+ Use a clarifying shampoo the day before you color.

+ Protect your hair from the sun with a hat or protective conditioner.

+ Don't wash your hair daily after coloring, and try a highlight-activating shampoo.

+ Try a homemade rinse to camouflage gray. If you're brunette, brew some black coffee or black tea, and use it after shampooing. Blondes can rinse with a mixture of 1 tablespoon lemon juice in a gallon of water. Redheads – try a batch of strong red hibiscus tea.

## Shave dollars with sharp ideas

It's as regular as death and taxes – shaving. You have to do it, but you don't have to break the bank keeping control of unwanted hair.

**Sharpen up.** Keep your blades sharp by storing them outside of the humid bathroom, perhaps just sealed in a plastic bag. Water droplets can lead to rusting and jagged blades, so dry them off after you use them.

**Think outside the can.** Rather than buying pricey shaving cream, lather up with products you probably have around the house.

- ✦ olive oil
- ✦ hair conditioner
- ✦ hand lotion
- ✦ bar of soap
- ✦ baby oil
- ✦ dishwashing liquid

**Go electric.** Invest in an electric razor, and you can stop spending on blades, shaving cream, even the water that runs down the drain.

## Save a bundle in the men's aisle

Do you really need pink disposable razors, or would black razors work just as well? You can save money by buying men's versions of body-care products rather than items meant for women.

Research by *Consumer Reports* found that products marketed to women, including pain relievers, shaving cream, skin lotion, and body wash, are often priced up to 50 percent higher than those for men. This is true even when the items being compared are very similar, like replacement blades for your razor.

If your favorite brand offers both a men's and women's version, try the men's to see if it will work for you.

## Get the most bang from your deodorant buck

Got a bottle of milk of magnesia in your cabinet? Then you have a ready supply of underarm deodorant.

In a pinch, you can apply a bit of milk of magnesia under your arms with your fingertips or a cotton swab. Let it dry for a few minutes, and it will work all day to keep you smelling fresh. Magnesium in the liquid is thought to do the trick.

If you'd rather stick to a traditional antiperspirant, apply it at night for the best results. The active ingredient in antiperspirants needs to enter your pores to stop perspiration. It will keep working for 24 hours – even after you shower in the morning.

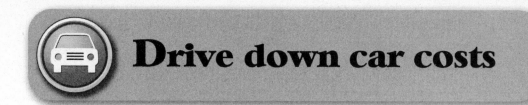

# Drive down car costs

## Avoid new-car rip-off tricks

Don't walk into a new-car dealership feeling powerless. You're the customer, and you are in control of whether there's a sale. Know the top salesmen's secrets, and you can pay bottom dollar for your next car.

First, pay attention to the warranty offer. Consumer expert Clark Howard advises that you should only consider buying an extended warranty from the car manufacturer or from your own car insurance company. He says not to buy a third-party warranty. But don't let yourself be bullied into buying an extended warranty at all. You can always buy it later – even if the salesman is pressuring you to say "yes" right away.

Watch out for these other dealer tricks that can leave you feeling like you've been cheated.

+ Do not hand over your driver's license. Some dealers will hold your license hostage as a way to keep you at the dealership longer. Make photocopies instead.

+ Say "no" to unnecessary add-ons. You have better things to spend your money on than gimmicks like rust proofing, fabric protectant, lifetime wax protection, or VIN etching.

+ Look at the big picture. When it comes to financing, consider the total cost of the vehicle, not just the monthly payment. Longer loans mean more interest charges.

+ Divide and conquer. Don't let dealers group your trade-in and financing in with the price of the car. Negotiate a fair price for each separately.

The new year rolls around, and you see shiny, new cars everywhere. Makes you want to trade in your jalopy for something new and fresh. Don't give in to temptation.

When it comes to price, the best time to buy a new car is in the fall. That's because dealers are eager to get rid of the current year's cars to make space for new models. To get the best selection, shop in September or October. By December the pickings will be slim.

But never shop for cars on Monday. Instead, wait until the end of the week — preferably near month's end, when salespeople need to meet a quota. Even better, shop Friday before a holiday weekend. Salespeople will be eager to wrap things up by making you a happy customer.

## Pick reliable brand over glitz for long-term savings

You don't have to pay a lot to get a great, new car. In fact, the most reliable car on the road today is also one of the least expensive.

According to *Consumer Reports*, cars made by Toyota, Honda, and — believe it or not — Scion, an offshoot of Toyota, get top marks in reliability. Meanwhile, certain higher-priced luxury cars, including some models of BMW and Mercedes-Benz, are on *Consumer Reports'* list of least-reliable cars.

**TOP DOLLAR:** Audi A3 ($27,270 for a four-door hatchback with a 2.0-liter engine).

**VALUE:** Scion xD, another attractive small car ($15,845 for a sporty 2011 four-door hatchback with manual transmission).

**WHAT YOU GIVE UP:** The cachet of a fancy name brand, and perhaps some features like an expensive stereo or titanium-finish wheels. But who cares? You need your car for transportation, not to impress your neighbors.

## Get the facts to avoid fraud

Before you buy that used car, find out if it's been in a collision, fire, or flood — or whether it's stolen.

First, you need to write down the VIN — Vehicle Identification Number — of the car you are considering buying. You'll find it engraved on a plate in several locations on the car. Then, check the VIN with one or more of these services that track car collisions and title problems to find out the car's history.

+ *www.nicb.org.* The website of the National Insurance Crime Bureau offers a free VINCheck service. Type in the VIN, and find out the car's history.

+ *www.nmvtis.gov.* The U.S. Department of Justice gathers information at the website of the National Motor Vehicle Title Information System. For $2.50 you can check a car's history based on the VIN.

+ *www.carfax.com.* This private service gathers information about auto histories. A CARFAX report is free from a used-car dealer, but costs $35 to $55 if you buy it on your own.

+ *www.autocheck.com.* An AutoCheck report costs about $15.

When it comes to vehicle history reports, duplication is a good thing. Don't count on any single database for complete information on wrecked or stolen cars. Run checks using more than one of these services, and get the car inspected by a mechanic before you buy.

## Don't lose your shirt on a used car

The value of a new car drops like a rock the minute you buy one and drive off the lot. That's why used cars can be so appealing — great prices. Learn how to tell a gem from a lemon, and you can drive away from high car prices.

**Look at owner history.** Check out the car's title. In most states, it will list how many previous owners the car has had. Divide the age of the car by the number of owners to get the average number of years held by each. If this number is lower than two, walk away from the purchase. The car likely has problems you don't want to deal with.

**Play it safe with certified.** Certified preowned vehicles cost slightly more than regular used cars but give you peace of mind. You may also score better financing and lower interest rates. The certification usually guarantees that a vehicle:

+ has no history of major damage.

+ has undergone strict mechanical and cosmetic inspections.

+ comes with an extra warranty on top of the original factory warranty.

**Buy demos.** Demo cars are nearly new, late-model vehicles that dealerships use for test drives or demonstrations. They are still covered by a factory warranty, and they must have logged fewer than 10,000 miles. Otherwise, they're considered used. While they aren't as cheap as used cars, demos still cost less than new.

**Call in the fleet.** A fleet department is the bulk-buying arm of a car dealership. Fleet sales typically go to companies, but individuals can also buy a new car. Simply follow these steps.

+ Decide which make, model, and color of car you want before you approach the fleet department.

+ Go for test drives at the regular dealership, since you can't test drive through the fleet department.

+ Check prices online at *www.kbb.com*, *www.edmunds.com*, or *www.cars.com*.

+ Call the dealership and ask for the fleet manager. Make sure they route you to the fleet manager and not a regular sales manager.

- Ask the fleet manager what the invoice price is on the car you want, and negotiate the price.

## Buy the car of your dreams for thousands less

No matter which car model has you drooling with desire, you can have it in your garage without picking up a hefty car payment. Here's how.

**TOP DOLLAR:** Toyota Camry LE ($24,890 for 2011 model with 3.5-liter engine, V-6, automatic).

**VALUE:** The same make and model car, but three years old ($17,115 for 2008 Toyota Camry LE). This tactic stretches your money farther, while still netting you modern safety and convenience features. A three-year-old car in good condition with low mileage can sell for half the price of a new one. Used cars have already seen their biggest drop in value. On average, cars lose nearly a third of their value in the first two years, hence the three-year rule.

**WHAT YOU GIVE UP:** That big car payment. You also forgo the ease and convenience of buying new rather than the additional work of searching for a used car that fits your needs and budget.

## Get free help pumping gas

Severe arthritis, trouble walking, weakness in your hands – if you have a disability that makes it difficult for you to pump gas for your car, you can get help. That's according to the Americans with Disabilities Act.

If you have proof that you have been medically declared "disabled," like displaying a blue handicapped-parking tag on your car, you don't have to knock yourself out pumping gas or bring along a friend every time you need fuel. Even better, you will still pay the lower self-service price rather than the higher full-service price at a station that offers both.

Stations that are solely self-service and are being run remotely by a single employee are not required by law to offer assistance. But these stations are encouraged to find ways to help customers.

Look on the pump for a call button, perhaps with the blue handicapped logo, which you can use to let the attendant know you need help.

**No-Sweat Solution**

Car manufacturers have come up with a great tool to help you cut fuel use. Many new cars now come with fuel economy gauges — devices that tell you when you're driving efficiently and using less gas. These gadgets are common on gas-electric vehicles, and now they're being added to regular gas-burning cars.

Certain models of Ford, General Motors, Chrysler, Honda, Nissan, and Toyota autos include some type of indicator light or dashboard message to let you know how you're doing. Some look like the signal bars on cellphones, while others give a message when you're driving at peak gas-saving mode. Ask about this helpful money-saving feature next time you shop for a car.

# Pump up your fuel savings with good timing

Deciding when to fill up your tank with gas can be as important as where you stop. Pay attention to timing, and you can save dough on every single tank.

**Think Thursdays.** Gas station operators benefit by raising the price of gas when demand is highest. That's typically on the weekends. So prices tend to rise late in the week, usually starting on Thursdays. Fuel up before 10 a.m. on Thursday to take advantage of pre-rush savings.

**Beat the holiday rush.** You're not imagining it. Gas prices really do spike on holidays and holiday weekends, for the same reasons they go up on regular weekends. Fill your tank at least three days before a holiday, and you won't pay the holiday surcharge.

**Don't get too close to "E."** Start watching for low gas prices when your tank gets below half full. This leaves you time to find a good deal so you're not stuck paying too much at the last minute.

Along with price, consider these technical reasons to avoid waiting until your tank is nearly empty. When the fuel level is low, your car's fuel pump is not submerged in gasoline. That makes it run at a higher temperature, which means it's working harder and may fail sooner. In addition, empty space in your gas tank allows moisture to condense on the tank walls, possibly leading to rust.

**DEEP DISCOUNT**

Don't be fooled by these four, big, gas-saving myths.

**Myth:** You should press the gas pedal gingerly to start slowly and save gas.

**Truth:** This approach is no better than pounding the pedal to the floor for a jackrabbit start. Aim for moderation.

**Myth:** It's worth driving out of your way to save on cheap gas.

**Truth:** Not really, since you waste gas driving across town just to save a penny. Find the cheapest station that's on your regular driving routes.

**Myth:** Buying a fuel-saving device will help you get more miles per gallon.

**Truth:** Most of these gadgets don't work, say experts at the Environmental Protection Agency and the Federal Trade Commission, who tested various types.

**Myth:** Leaving the tailgate of your truck down makes it more aerodynamic.

**Truth:** This is false. Leave the tailgate up to improve how your truck cuts through the wind.

# Drive your way to lower gas costs

Face it — the days of paying less than a dollar for a gallon of gas are over. These days you might be thrilled to see a price closer to two bucks. The best way to fight rising fuel costs is to practice good driving habits. Change how you drive, and you can change how much you spend at the pump.

**Plan your route.** Make a point of avoiding left turns so you can keep from sitting at traffic lights, burning fuel. Idling your car for just two minutes uses as much gas as driving for one mile.

UPS delivery drivers follow this habit, even using a computer program that helps plan their routes to skip left turns. The company saved 3 million gallons of fuel the first year just by avoiding left turns.

**Avoid aggressive driving.** Jackrabbit starts, speeding, and quick stops can increase your car's fuel use by one-third when you're driving at highway speeds. To put it another way, your car loses about 5 mpg of fuel efficiency for every 10-mph speed increase above 55 mph. Slow down, enjoy the ride, and save gas.

**Cruise to savings.** Use your cruise control on the highway if the road is fairly level. If it's hilly, however, cruise control may actually use more gas as the car tries to speed up and slow down on steep inclines.

**Clean out your trunk.** Carrying more weight in your car makes the engine work harder. In fact, the U.S. Environmental Protection Agency reports that reducing your vehicle's weight by 100 pounds can boost its fuel economy by as much as 2 percent.

**Cut down on drag.** A roof rack that's not being used creates wind resistance. Take it down until you need it. In the same way, it's best to roll up the windows and use your car's air conditioning when you drive on the highway. But when you drive around town, you'll save fuel by opening the windows and turning off the air conditioner.

# Calculate your gas savings

Seems like everyone you know is replacing their gas-guzzler with a more fuel-efficient car to save money. How much do they really save? Plug your numbers into the fuel-savings calculator at *www.fueleconomy.gov* to find out.

These examples assume you'll pay about $2.73 per gallon for gas, drive 15,000 miles a year, and keep your car for eight years.

|  | Midsize car trade | SUV/minivan trade | Large-for-small trade |
|---|---|---|---|
| Old car average mpg | 2008 Ford Taurus 20 mpg | 2008 Ford Explorer 17 mpg | 2001 Chevy Suburban 14 mpg |
| New car average mpg | 2011 Toyota Camry 28 mpg | 2011 Honda Odyssey 24 mpg | 2011 Volkswagen Jetta 36 mpg |
| Annual fuel savings | $586 | $703 | $1,787 |
| Savings over life of car | $4,680 | $5,621 | $14,300 |

# 6 auto-care tasks to keep your car young

Make your car last by treating it like a baby. Ensuring the long life of your automobile is the best way to save money on transportation costs.

Today's new cars are so well built you can expect them to last a long time. In fact, the average car on the road is more than 9 years old. Take good care of your car, and you can hope to have it around for 200,000 or even 300,000 miles without high repair bills. But be sure you don't skip these six important auto-care tasks — unless you want to end up paying $4,000 for a new engine.

**Change the oil on time.** Doing this keeps sludge from building up in your engine, shortening its life span. Your owner's manual will tell you how often to do this. Don't wait longer than 300 miles beyond the schedule in the manual.

**Take care of your tires.** Keep them properly inflated and rotate them regularly, about every 6,000 miles.

**Keep the battery charged up.** Allowing the charge to run down, then recharging it, shortens the life of your car's battery. So don't let it get drained, either by running the radio or lights when the car is off or by leaving the car sitting for weeks at a time.

**Replace filters.** Clogged air, fuel, and oil filters can allow dirt to get where you don't want it. The few dollars you spend on these little items can help you avoid bigger problems later on.

**Inspect hoses and belts.** Otherwise you may find out these important parts are damaged only when you're left stranded.

**Keep it clean.** The process of washing your car lets you find rust and other damage to the body of the car before the problem can become too extensive.

## DIY tool ends dashboard light woes

Surveyors found some 10 percent of people with cars newer than 1981 are driving around with the "check-engine" light on. If that includes you, diagnose it yourself and save.

When the check-engine light comes on, it could indicate anything from a minor hiccup, like the gas cap being loose, to a critical issue, like an emission problem caused by a malfunctioning oxygen sensor. You need to find out what the problem is, perhaps by taking your car to a mechanic to get it diagnosed. That might set you back as much as $75 just to have a technician read the code to find out what the problem is.

Instead, buy yourself a handheld diagnostic tool to read the code so you can find out what the light means. You'll find these nifty code-reading machines for around $30 to $300. Although you can pay $800 or more for one that lets you record and analyze the codes, most DIY mechanics wouldn't know what to do with all that information. Look for a model in the $100 range, like the CarMD diagnostic tool, available for $99 from *www.carmd.com*.

Just plug the diagnostic tool into your car's on-board diagnostic system, typically with a small plug under the dashboard. The tool will tell you what the code means. Some models include software and a USB connection. You can then plug it into your computer and find out what is needed to fix the problem and maybe even what you'll pay for repairs. Buying a simpler, cheaper model still lets you take your car to a mechanic armed with information about the likely problem.

The gadgets don't reset your car's warning light, so it will probably stay on even if you fix the problem yourself. It is possible the car's computer may reset itself — you'll have to wait and see.

Whatever solution you choose, don't ignore the problem and continue driving with the warning light on. When you don't fix the issue, an improperly functioning oxygen sensor or other problem can make your engine use up to 40 percent more fuel.

## Stop being overcharged on car repairs

Check the bill after your car is repaired at the shop. In most states, you should not be charged sales tax on the labor portion of the bill — only the parts. But sometimes the shop may not list the labor charge as a separate item, or sometimes the billing clerk gets lazy and figures tax on the entire bill. That extra 5 percent or so shouldn't come out of your pocket. Request an itemized bill, and ask about tax on labor charges.

## Save by breaking the 3,000-mile rule

You babied your '57 Chevy, washing it once a week and changing the oil every 3,000 miles. Times have changed, and so have cars.

You probably don't need to change your car's oil every 3,000 miles. Thanks to improved technology, engines and motor oils can easily go longer between changes, letting you save your hard-earned money.

Experts at auto website *www.edmonds.com* say most car manufacturers today recommend an oil and filter change every 7,500 or even 10,000 miles — not the old rule of 3,000 miles. Check your vehicle owner's manual to be sure. It's especially important to follow the manufacturer's recommendations while your car is in its warranty period.

Along with saving money, fewer oil changes mean you put less used oil into the environment. Consider these other motor oil rules of the road.

+ Go ahead and change the "break-in" oil on your new car after the first 1,000 to 1,500 miles of driving. Doing this helps remove bits of metal and grit from your new engine.

+ Upgrade to a high-performance oil. Modern synthetic high-performance oils, although they cost a bit more, save you money in two ways. First, they reduce engine wear and let you extend the time between oil changes. Second, they can improve your car's fuel efficiency by up to 5 percent. That means you spend less on gas.

+ Ask your mechanic to use the largest size oil filter that will fit your car. This can help keep the oil cleaner longer between changes.

**DEEP DISCOUNT**

Don't worry about voiding your new car's warranty by having it serviced away from the dealer. An independent repair shop will probably charge less than a car dealership for regular maintenance. As long as you go to a properly licensed repair shop that uses parts supplied by the car's manufacturer or parts that meet the manufacturer's specifications, you won't void the warranty.

Be sure to maintain a record of exactly when you have recommended service items done, and keep the receipts. That way you'll have proof in case you ever need to show the work was done.

# By-the-book maintenance plan saves you money

The owner's manual for your new car includes a timetable for regular maintenance, but the dealership suggests a different plan. Which schedule should you follow?

Dealerships make money by keeping their crew of trained mechanics busy. That means they get more business if they can bring customers back sooner to have lots of scheduled maintenance done in the shop.

Common tasks on the list of regular maintenance include oil changes, tire rotation, and system checks. But the dealer's list may include additional services like cleaning the fuel-injection system or flushing the power-steering mechanism. You don't need to agree to this longer list of services.

Typically the best and cheapest path to follow is to ignore the dealer's advice. Instead, use the manufacturer's schedule as you find it in your owner's manual. This might mean waiting until your car has logged 10,000 miles before you do basic service rather than taking it in at just 7,500 miles. You can wait longer before you spend money on these maintenance tasks. Most importantly, you won't void your car's warranty if you follow the owner's manual instructions.

**No-Sweat Solution**

No need to track down multiple estimates for car repairs. Find out how much you can expect to pay using information at *www.repairpal.com*.

This free website contains information for cars made since 1990. Just select your car's make and click on "Get an Estimate," then type in the year, model, type of work you need done, and your ZIP code. You'll get price estimates based on surveys of thousands of repair shops across the country. That way you will know if the price quote you've been given is fair, or whether you should keep looking. The website also offers information about the car repair you're considering, like typical symptoms and possible causes.

You can also access this service on your iPhone or Android smart phone using the free RepairPal application. Look up the expected price right from the repair shop, and use it to negotiate a better deal.

# 5 checks to prevent a road-trip nightmare

You like your mechanic, but he won't be with you when you travel. Avoid paying extra for car repairs away from home by getting your car in top shape before you leave on a trip. Check these five key items to steer clear of problems.

+ Fluids. Check levels of oil, coolant, transmission fluid, power-steering fluid, and brake fluid. If levels are low, find out why and fix the problem.

+ Belts and hoses. Look for dry-rotting or cracking, and replace these parts when they're worn. If your car has 50,000 miles or more and still has the original hoses, they may be overdue for a change.

+ Windshield wiper blades and fluid. Poor visibility can lead to an accident, but you may not realize you're low on fluid or your wiper blades aren't up to snuff until you really need them. Check before that happens.

+ Tires. Inspect the sidewalls for bulges or cracks, and be sure your tires — including the spare — are properly inflated.

+ Lights. Don't get stuck paying the price of a ticket because you're driving with a burned-out headlight.

**Safe & Secure**

Don't skimp on safety. You can shop for the best deal on an oil change or air filter, but the air bag is the one item on your car you should only have replaced by a reputable dealer, no matter how cheap you may find it.

Air bags can cost $1,000 each, so they're ripe for crooks who may remove a good bag and replace it with trash and paper. Unscrupulous mechanics may also fix a damaged car whose air bag has deployed using the wrong air bag. Then when you need your air bag to save your life in a collision, it won't be there.

If you're worried your car may be the victim of this kind of fraud, call the hotline of the National Insurance Crime Bureau at 800-835-6422. Experts say you should have a used car checked for air bag safety before you buy it.

# 3 steps to quality car repair

Don't go blindly into the car repair shop. If you do, you're asking to get ripped off. Follow these three cardinal rules and you'll earn yourself a lower repair bill.

**Be nice.** Avoid paying too much by treating your mechanic with respect. Addressing a problem in a confrontational manner is a sure way to alienate a mechanic. You don't want him to dislike you when he has your car's health in your hands.

Instead, be friendly, don't complain in front of other customers, and show your appreciation. Say thank you by sending a note or even baking brownies for the shop staff after the work is done. Your mechanic will remember you and want to give you great service and a good deal next time.

**Be prepared.** Pay attention to your car's symptoms so you can describe them clearly and in detail. Giving the best information can help your mechanic get right to the problem without having to spend time – and your money – figuring out what's wrong.

Don't forget this dime-store item you should carry in your glove box. Keep a small notebook in your car's glove compartment so when you hear a weird sound or feel something funny going on in your car, you can write it down. Include details like when it happened, how fast you were driving, and what the weather conditions were. Having a record of a problem rather than a vague report can save you hundreds in unnecessary repairs.

**Be smart.** Never sign a blank form authorizing repairs. If you do, the bill could increase greatly without your approval. Instead, ask for a list of specific repairs and expected costs, then sign that detailed authorization.

And look for a Motorist Assurance Program (MAP) sign on the wall of your car repair shop. MAP accreditation shows the shop meets a set of minimum guidelines for diagnosing your car's problems. It's no guarantee of quality service, but it's a start.

# Pick performance over brand for best-bet tires

Tire manufacturers etch their names in bold letters on the side of tires, hoping this will function as free advertising. That's harmless, as long as you don't let brand name determine which tires you buy.

When you need tires that are not specifically for winter conditions, you can choose between standard, high-performance, and ultra-high-performance all-season tires. Standard models work fine for most drivers, but high-performance tires give you a little better grip and handling. That may make you feel safer in poor weather, and you don't even need to spend a lot for peace of mind.

**TOP DOLLAR:** Michelin Primacy MXV4 high-performance, all-season tires ($158 to $237 per tire at Kauffman Tire, depending on what size your vehicle needs). These come with a 60,000-mile warranty.

**VALUE:** Continental ExtremeContact DWS high-performance, all-season tires ($117 each at Sears). These tires have a 50,000-mile tread-wear warranty, and they provide best-in-class traction on winter roads. Experts say they're great tires for winter driving if you don't want to put on snow tires.

**WHAT YOU GIVE UP:** A few miles on the warranty, plus the familiar Michelin brand name. But if you need to buy all four tires, that little sacrifice may be well worth the $400 you'll save.

## Tire-care trio saves time and money

Where the rubber meets the road – that's an important place to take care of your car. Pay attention to these three areas of tire care, and you won't have to spend money later fixing avoidable problems.

**Take care of treads.** Trade the penny test for a quarter test. Experts now say to check the tread of your tires by inserting a quarter upside down into the grooves. If you can see the top of Washington's head, then your tires are nearing the end of their life. That means tread has worn away and you have less traction on the road. Many states have a legal minimum limit of one-sixteenth inch of tread, but it's better to keep it at one-eighth inch for safety.

**Keep up with inflation.** Driving on underinflated tires can cause tire failure, waste gas, reduce handling, and decrease lifesaving traction.

To help your tires perform well for a long time, follow these simple guidelines from the National Highway Traffic Safety Administration.

✦ Invest in a good gauge. It will cost less than the gas you'll waste by driving on underinflated tires.

✦ Check tire pressure often – at least once a month, before going on trips, and when there are big temperature swings. And don't forget to check the spare.

✦ Measure pressure when your tires are cold. Driving warms up the tires, so the pressure reading won't be accurate. Look for the correct "Cold Tire Pressure" for your car in your glove box, on the door, or in your owner's manual. Don't use the figure embossed on the sidewall of your tires. It will be too high.

✦ Make sure your tire valves have caps.

✦ Don't overload your vehicle with excess weight.

**Get them rotated.** Having your tires rotated every 6,000 miles or so helps them wear evenly and last longer. Tire rotation is well worth the $20 you'll spend.

But if you've spent extra to buy locking lug nuts, you may be in for trouble. These devices, intended to keep thieves from stealing your wheels, are the $4 car part that can cause $150 in damage during your next tire rotation.

That's because if the lug nuts have been stripped, mechanics may have to resort to extreme measures to remove them, perhaps chiseling at the nut to loosen it with force or even burning through the lug nut with a torch. That can easily damage the wheel, as well. Skip this extra expense.

**CASH SAVER**

You can fill your tires with free air, or you can pay around $10 per tire to fill them with nitrogen. Don't waste $40.

Filling tires with nitrogen is a bit of a trend with some benefits. Nitrogen may not leak out so quickly, since its molecules are larger, and it won't erode your tires. But no research has shown using nitrogen really makes a difference in the performance of average tires on an average car driving around town, as opposed to tires on a race car or airplane.

A better way to treat your tires and stay safe is to check the tire pressure regularly and fill them to the specified level. Many people don't stay on top of this job. Low tire pressure makes your car use more fuel, which costs more money.

# Don't waste money on spray wax

Next time you take your car through an automatic carwash, don't bother with the wax step. These machines spray a mixture of water and wax on the car's paint — but also on the windows, wheels, and other parts of your car that don't need waxing. Even worse than this waste, spray waxes are not strong enough to give your car's paint job any real protection. It's a waste of money.

Instead, buy a can of good, old-fashioned car wax and do the job by hand. You'll save money, protect your car's finish, and get a bit of a workout at the same time.

## Sell your car for a higher price

Appearance matters when it comes to selling a used car. Keep your vehicle looking new inside and out, and you'll earn a higher price when it comes time to let it go. Here's how.

**Clean out the inside.** Before you wash the outside of your car, clean the interior. You'll probably need to do this only about once a month, so take the time to do it right.

The basic rule is to treat your car's upholstery, carpet, and glass like you would similar surfaces inside your home. You don't need to buy specialty cleaning products for your car.

**Wash away the grime.** Unless you live and drive in extreme conditions, washing your car once a month is plenty. But rinse off salt or sand from winter highways or beaches as soon as possible.

Key here is being gentle so you don't harm the paint job or the clear-coat finish — the clear layer on top of the paint that makes a new car shiny.

+ If you want to use a drive-through carwash, pick one that is "brushless," uses felt cloths only, or simply sprays detergent and water.

+ Washing your car by hand is a great choice, and it'll save you the $9 or so you would spend at an automatic carwash. Be sure you work in the shade so you can dry the paint before water spots form.

**Get busy under the hood.** This step is not just for the sake of vanity. It's important to remove a buildup of grease, oil, fuel, and dirt from around your car's engine. Otherwise this gunk can cause deterioration of the nonmetal parts of the engine, like wires, rubber hoses, and gaskets.

When you see the engine starting to look grimy, find some rags and wipe down surfaces as well as you can without knocking loose hoses or other parts. But don't spray the engine with water. If you can't get the engine reasonably clean by wiping it down, get it professionally cleaned.

**No-Sweat Solution**

You don't have to spend a lot to make your car safer. For less than $10, you can pick up a glass treatment that will keep your windshield crystal clear and easy to see through in the rain and snow.

Good brands include Rain-X and PPG Aquapel. Just spray your clean windshield with one, and it'll make winter precipitation roll off without freezing onto your windshield. You won't have to squint through a slushy mess for the next six months.

Stop by your local auto supply store to pick up a windshield treatment, or contact the company.

- PPG Aquapel. Visit the company website at *www.aquapel.com* or call 800-861-4999.
- Rain-X. Navigate to the website at *www.rainx.com* or call 800-237-8645.

# Cheap ways to keep your car's cool

It's summer, so you crank up the air conditioning every time you get into your car. That little cardboard sun shield you bought for the windshield doesn't seem to do much good. Besides, you keep forgetting to put it up. Spend a little money and you can do a much better job of keeping your car cool, saving fuel costs in the process.

**Invest in a tint.** Most cars have tinting that blocks ultraviolet rays from the sun on the windshield only. For around $150, you can also have side and rear windows tinted.

Adding the extra tint keeps the sun off your skin while you drive on long car trips. It also keeps the interior of your car cooler so your air conditioning doesn't work so hard. Even better, there's less strain on your air conditioner as you drive on a hot day. Tests show you'll get 3 percent better fuel efficiency with tinted windows. But avoid a dark tint. Federal law requires that any tint on car windows still lets in 70 percent of visible light.

**Keep a lid on it.** A one-size-fits-all car cover can run as low as $50, and it can help save fuel. If you live in a sunbelt state, especially if you drive a dark-colored car and don't park in a garage, this little investment can help keep your car cooler. That means the engine doesn't have to work so hard to cool it off. Experts say you may get a 2 percent fuel mileage gain, depending on the conditions.

In colder parts of the country, a car cover can keep snow off your car and ice off the windshield. That way the engine has an easier time warming up the car without having to melt off snow and ice.

## DEEP DISCOUNT

You can save big with a waterless car wash. It takes about 116 gallons of water to wash your car at home. That's too much water, especially during a drought. A drive-through automatic car wash can easily cost $10, $15, or more. Save water and money — and whittle your waist with the exercise — by trying a waterless car-wash solution.

Waterless car-wash solutions let you do the job without pulling out the hose. Simply spray on the solution, then scrub away dirt with a microfiber cloth. The solution contains one ingredient to break down the dirt and another to capture it into a gel so it doesn't scratch your car. Buff your car with a second microfiber cloth, and you're done.

You'll pay about 50 cents an ounce for brands like Lucky Earth and Eco Touch. That comes to roughly $2 per wash.

# Ride your way to big savings

Many older people dread the day they can no longer drive. Don't. You'll find giving up car ownership can be freeing and is a great way to save money.

The average annual cost of owning a car is more than $8,000, including insurance, repairs, financing, taxes, and fuel. That would pay for a lot of cab, bus, or subway rides — and free you from the hassles of license and insurance renewal.

Of course, you also must consider safety as you age. Drivers age 75 and older have higher crash rates than any other group of drivers except for the notoriously risky drivers ages 16 to 25 years, according to the Insurance Institute for Highway Safety.

When you're ready to take the plunge, consider one of these options for car-free living.

**Volunteer driver programs.** Churches and nonprofit groups may have volunteer drivers who are happy to take seniors shopping, to doctor appointments, or wherever you need to go. You may find a local program that's free or requires a small donation.

**Taxicabs.** They're not just for people who live in big cities, although you'll need to schedule your trip with a dispatcher if you don't live where taxis routinely pick up passengers. Some taxis are wheelchair accessible and meet Americans with Disabilities Act standards.

**Senior vans.** Public transit and private agencies offer door-to-door service to seniors using vans or small buses. You may find that seniors and people with disabilities pay a reduced fare.

**Free or discounted bus or train passes.** Some cities offer these to senior passengers.

Contact one of these services to see what's available near you.

+ National Center on Senior Transportation. Located online at *www.seniortransportation.net* or call 866-528-6278.

+ Eldercare Locator. Navigate to the website *www.eldercare.gov* or call 800-677-1116.

# Find the key to secure locks

Everyone has done it — lock the keys in the car. When that happens, you're likely to spend time and money getting back into your vehicle. But you can avoid calling a locksmith and parting with $100 next time it happens.

If you lose your car key or lock it in your car, ask a friend to drive you to the car dealer. Be sure to bring the VIN number and proof of car ownership with you. They can make a new key to your car in just a few minutes, saving you the expensive locksmith charge.

Remember that a key can wear out over time. If that happens, it can damage the lock and cause an expensive problem. You can avoid lock troubles altogether by learning these simple secrets from a master locksmith.

+ Keep an unused master copy of each key you own in a secure place. Mark or tag each key so you'll remember what lock it fits. Don't put your master keys in a dresser drawer or other place where thieves may find them. Instead, keep them in a combination safe or safe deposit box.

+ When a key begins to look worn, have a new key made from its master. Then bend or break the worn key and throw it away. Put the new key on your ring to use, and return the master to your secure storage place.

+ Every six months — when you change clocks for daylight savings time — spray a little WD-40 into your locks to keep them running smoothly. You can also spray the key and use it in the lock to lubricate and clean the mechanism.

# Best-kept computer secrets that save

## Give your computer back its youth

Do you really need a new computer? You can get more life from your old system if you treat it right. Keep your computer running fast and glitch-free for 10 years or more with five simple rules.

**Rule #1: Defragment your hard drive regularly.** Like organizing your pantry, defragmenting helps your computer run smoothly by sorting through files and putting them in order. You should run the Disk Defragmenter at least every three months, including every time you install new software, remove software, or delete a batch of files.

**Rule #2: Toss out unneeded programs.** Cleaning up your computer's guest registry amounts to removing software you don't use anymore. That way, your computer won't have to sort through it when looking for important programs or information. Over time, holding on to excess software makes your computer run more slowly.

Be sure you remove programs by following the proper uninstall procedure — not simply by deleting program icons. Otherwise, you'll have trouble later.

**Rule #3: Check your security.** Viruses and spyware can slow down your computer, so keep it clean with software that also protects. You'll need programs to take care of the major threats against your computer — viruses, spyware, and spam. Keep your security software updated, or it won't do much good.

**Rule #4: Boost your memory.** If your computer is running slowly, but you can get it to speed up by closing all programs except the one you are currently using, it might need more random access memory, or RAM. Adding RAM to an older computer is a pretty cheap upgrade, running about $20 to $100 for most computers. It's also fairly easy to do yourself if you enjoy mucking around in your computer's innards.

**Rule #5: Consider expanding.** Adding an external hard drive can allow you to store photos, videos, music files, or other large files that are taking up space on the hard drive. Then you can delete those files from your main hard drive to help it run better.

An external hard drive may cost around $100. It's fairly small, maybe the size of a deck of playing cards, and it attaches easily to your computer with a cable that fits either a USB or FireWire port. If you ever have a system crash, you'll be happy to have important files stashed away safely.

**Freebie Frenzie**

Don't pay for virus and spyware protection when you can get it for free.

Microsoft's free Security Essentials combines both types of programs for Windows in a single package. You can download it at *www.microsoft.com/security_essentials/*. Click on the "Download Now" link.

## Weigh the costs of a budget printer

Pick a new printer that won't cost extra in the long run. You can buy a really cheap printer, then spend too much on ink.

No single printer is the best bet for everyone. The choice depends on factors like how often you print in color, how much you print, and whether you need features like photo or two-sided printing.

Find your best-bet printer at *www.printer.com*. Answer a few questions about your printing habits, and you'll get a list of recommended models including initial cost and expected five-year cost including supplies and maintenance.

## Pay less to print

You shopped carefully and found a great printer at a low price. You're not done yet. Like the manufacturers of razors, printer companies know they have you on the hook for replacement ink and toner cartridges. Don't let this continuing cost sabotage your printing savings.

**Change your printing behavior.** Practice these habits and get more life out of the ink cartridges in your printer.

+ Don't select "best" quality for your documents if you don't need it. Pick "draft' mode instead, and you'll save ink.

+ Skip the color. Save your tricolor ink cartridges by printing in black ink only — unless you really need to print in color.

+ Ignore the warnings. Your printer probably alerts you about "low ink in cartridge" even when 60 percent of the ink is still there. Don't toss the cartridge. Instead, shake it, put it back in, and get weeks more printing.

+ Pick an ink-sparing font. Download fonts from the Dutch company Ecofont at *www.ecofont.com*. Believe it or not, you'll save by using 15 percent less ink with a font that basically leaves small holes in letters. You won't notice the difference — just the savings. Choose ink-sparing versions of favorites like Times New Roman.

**Sink the high cost of ink.** You don't have to pay full price for printer ink cartridges. It's possible to save up to 80 percent on ink by shopping online. Just visit these money-saving websites.

+ 123Inkjets — *www.123inkjets.com*

+ ABCco — *www.abcco.net*

+ InkSell — *www.inksell.com*

+ Pacific Ink — *www.pacificink.com*

+ PrintPal — *www.printpal.com*

# Save big on a tiny computer

Consider an alternative to the favorite, user friendly tablet computer. You can spend less but still get many of the great features of the Apple iPad.

**TOP DOLLAR:** Apple iPad ($500 to $830, depending on your choice of memory and wireless features). Small tablets like the iPad let you do word processing, organize your calendar, play games, watch videos, check email, surf the Web – all on a tiny, portable computer.

**VALUE:** Archos 10.1 Android tablet ($300 to $350, depending on memory). This tablet's 10.1-inch screen makes it about the same size as the iPad, and it actually weighs a bit less. The Archos 10.1 has more than 5,000 apps written for it.

**WHAT YOU GIVE UP:** Running Apple's 140,000 apps, many written for the iPad, iPod, and iPhone. Unless you're already a die-hard fan, you may never miss features like the ease of reading books on the iPad or the ability to get help from experts at Apple Retail Stores.

---

**No-Sweat Solution**

Avoid the hassle of unplugging your computer and toting it to a repair shop. You can get help from trained technicians through the Internet with an online diagnostic and repair service.

Online computer services can do things like remove viruses, speed up your computer, back up files, and perform regular computer maintenance. Service may cost between $20 and $125, depending on how extensive the problem is and how long the fix takes. You'd easily pay that much if you took your computer to a shop.

These reputable companies provide online service.

- Ask Dr. Tech — *www.askdrtech.com*
- Ask PC Experts — *www.askpcexperts.com*
- Box Aid — *www.boxaid.com*
- Computer Geeks Online — *www.computergeeksonline.net*
- Geek Squad — *www.geeksquad.com*

To get online help, your computer must be functioning and able to access the Internet.

# Curb costs with a refurbished computer

Instead of paying big bucks for a brand new, state-of-the-art computer system, look for a refurbished model. You could save an average of 10 to 25 percent off the retail price.

These not-quite-new or used computers have been restored to like-new working condition. Your best bet is to get them directly from manufacturers. In many cases, these are computers returned by customers, previously leased systems, or those used as store models. Here's where to find refurbished computers online. Search on the word "refurbished" or "used," and you should be able to locate the manufacturer's outlet store.

+ Dell – *www.dell.com*

+ HP – *www.hp.com*

+ IBM – *www.ibm.com*

You can also find good deals on refurbished computers from independent resellers, like TigerDirect at *www.tigerdirect.com* – called recertified – and Newegg at *www.newegg.com* – open box items. Of course, you can also find them at eBay and other online auction sites. But be careful.

When shopping for a refurbished computer, make sure it has enough memory and processing speed to fit your needs. Is there warranty coverage or an option to return it? If you buy from an individual seller, make sure the seller deleted all files, spyware, browser history, cookies, and other programs. You should also insist on receiving the original software and license keys.

# Don't pay a cent for software

Freeware and shareware are two alternatives to commercial software that can save you money. Freeware is software you can download, pass around, and distribute without payment. In other words, it's free. Shareware is often free for a trial period, but you must register the software and eventually pay a small fee.

Besides the cheap price, these low-cost options are usually problem-free, well-designed programs. They're easy to install and update and simple to find on the Internet. And because they boast so many users, any bugs get spotted and fixed quickly. Even if you're not satisfied with the program, all you have to do is uninstall it. No need to haggle for a refund for something you didn't pay for in the first place.

Of course, you should use some caution whenever you download anything from the Internet. Only download from sites you trust, and make sure you have a good anti-virus program installed, updated, and running.

Before you buy that expensive software, look at these websites. You just might be able to get the same thing for free.

+ Download.com – *www.download.cnet.com*

+ Freeware Files – *www.freewarefiles.com*

+ SuperFiles.com – *www.superfiles.com*

+ Shareware.com – *www.shareware.com*

+ Tucows – *www.tucows.com*

At these sites you can learn more about applications and developers, read reviews, and download what you want. Whatever your interests – health, games, money, education, video, music, and more – you can find free software for it.

## Store digital photos safely — for free

Digital photography releases you from the problem of storing negatives and prints. Instead, you need to keep track of digital files. You can do that safely and cheaply with cloud storage.

Computing "in the cloud" simply refers to working off a server you access through the Internet rather than the hard drive of your computer.

You can store and work with your digital photos using one of several free websites. On most sites you can store photos for free, share them with friends, and buy prints or even gifts made from them. That's how you can have your vacation photos printed on a calendar, or your grandson's baseball photo stamped on a coffee mug.

Storing photos online means they don't take up space on your hard drive, and you can easily share them with friends. Another benefit is the security of off-site storage in case of a disaster that destroys your computer. And many photo sites offer free prints when you sign up.

Read the fine print, since some websites require you to make a purchase every so often to keep your membership active. Miss a deadline, and you could lose your photos.

Try one of these popular photo websites.

- ✦ Snapfish — *www.snapfish.com*

- ✦ Flickr — *www.flickr.com*

- ✦ Kodak Gallery — *www.kodakgallery.com*

- ✦ Shutterfly — *www.shutterfly.com*

- ✦ Adorama — *www.adoramapix.com*

- ✦ Dotphoto — *www.dotphoto.com*

You may also feel secure if you copy your photos to a CD for long-term storage.

**Freebie Frenzie**

No matter where you store your digital photos, you can edit them for free at *www.picnik.com*. With this easy-to-use software, you can crop photos, fix brightness or red eyes, make photo collages, and more.

# Get schooled for less

Your computer can help you stay organized, keep up with the news, and stay in touch with family. But first you have to know how to use it. Don't spend hundreds on expensive computer classes when you can get just the training you need for next to nothing.

Computer School for Seniors is an online school started by 66-year-old Mimi Witcher to help her fellow seniors get comfortable in the high-tech world. Log on to *www.cs4seniors.com* and you can pick what you want to learn about from courses designed just for you. Select from three main categories:

+ Get connected. Learn to use Facebook and Skype to stay close to family.

+ Explore the world. Use the Internet to make your life easier, edit your photos, plan your next trip, manage your finances — and more.

+ Learn about your computer. Pick lessons on your computer's software, like MS Word, Photoshop, or PowerPoint.

For just $36 you can take all the classes you want for a six-month semester, or pay $58 for a year.

**No-Sweat Solution**

You don't have a secretary, but you can still get help with your schedule.

Memo to Me, *www.memotome.com*, is a website that lets you set reminders for upcoming events. You can sign up for free with just some basic information, including your name and email address.

Then input events, and you'll receive email reminders at the times you pick. Events could be daily — like time to take your medication — weekly, monthly, annually, or just one-time occurrences. You'll get an automatic email reminder so you never forget a birthday or appointment again.

Basic membership is free, but you can also purchase a Platinum membership for $19 a year. Added Platinum benefits include getting additional reminder messages sent to your cell phone and automatic forwarding of email messages to a second account.

# Cut your phone spending in half

## Bundle up to save a bunch

Combining your home phone, cable television, and Internet services into a single package can simplify your life. You'll pay one bill for the entire package — likely a smaller bill than buying each service separately. It's called bundling, and it has never been simpler.

Typically you can find a triple-play package, which includes TV, Internet, and home phone, through your local cable TV company or satellite provider. But you may also find a quad package, which adds cellphone service.

Along with saving money, bundling offers additional benefits, like seeing caller identity on your TV screen and having a single phone number for customer service. The right bundle can save you hundreds of dollars a year. Here is how to get it.

+ Notice what is included. Weigh options that mean the most to you, like whether your favorite sports channel is available on the TV package. Different users have different needs, and you don't want to pay for technology you won't use — or not have an option you were counting on.

+ Try to get your services without having to sign a long contract. That way you can change your mind later.

+ When it's time to renew your service, don't accept a higher rate. Insist that you continue to get whatever special introductory rate you first paid, and threaten to drop the service otherwise.

## Cut the cord for home-phone savings

Cut the cord — that's what it's called when you stop paying for your landline home phone, instead using a cellphone or other option to place and receive calls. The idea may sound radical, but more than 20 percent of U.S. households have cut the cord so far, saving around $600 each a year. Here is how to make the transition.

- ✦ Pick a cellphone plan that has everything you'll need. Are most of your calls local or long distance? How many minutes per month will you use? Will you only use the phone to talk, or do you want to send text messages? The answers to these questions can help you find a plan that saves money.

- ✦ Investigate local 911 service. Nowadays cellphone services are supposed to have 911 capability, but it varies. Check service in your area to be sure emergency personnel will know your location if you call on a cellphone.

- ✦ Look into long-distance choices. Voice over Internet Protocol (VoIP), which uses your computer, can be a good backup for long-distance service. See the story *Banish high phone bills forever* for more information.

## DEEP DISCOUNT

Don't pay $1, $2 or up to $3.49 every time you dial 411 for directory assistance on your cellphone. Call 800-FREE-411 (800-373-3411) and get your personal or commercial numbers for free. Just listen to a brief advertisement, then give your location, speak a name or business category, pick your choice, and the number will be read back to you. You also have the option of receiving the number in a text message.

## Banish high phone bills forever

Have you checked your home phone bill lately? You may be paying too much for services you don't need.

**Get rid of the extras.** You can easily get along without these add-ons. If you don't use them much, you'll save by paying for them on a per-use basis.

- Call waiting may add between $4 and $8 to your monthly bill.

- Caller ID is convenient, but is it worth $5 per month?

- Call forwarding is another splurge of around $5 every month.

- A second phone line was useful when you had a teenager living at home. It may be time to stop paying that extra $20 a month.

**Shop for a long-distance deal.** If you're paying your local phone company every month just for the ability to call long distance, you may be paying too much. Instead, shop around for a budget service that will let you call relatives in another state for a lot less. Companies like GTC Telecom offer long-distance service at around 5 cents a minute.

Another option is to use a calling card with prepaid long-distance minutes. You'll have to key in a PIN every time you make a call, but you may pay as little as 3 cents a minute.

**Go high-tech.** Finally, you can switch your phone to Voice over Internet Protocol (VoIP) and pay as little as $50 a year. With this service, your phone line comes through your computer, so you need high-speed Internet access for VoIP to work. Researchers found VoIP service is top quality – as good as the best phone providers. You may want to invest around $100 in a battery backup in case your electricity goes out.

Consider one of these providers:

- Vonage costs as little as $16 per month. It has been a lifesaver when natural disasters like Hurricane Katrina interrupted cell-phone service.

- Skype is free when you contact another person who also has Skype software. If you both have webcams – cameras attached to your computers – you can do two-way video chatting, just like on that old cartoon "The Jetsons." You can also make calls to non-Skype phone numbers. Find a good plan, and you'll pay around 2 cents a minute.

- Magic Jack involves a little $40 gadget that plugs into your computer, then connects directly to your telephone. You'll probably pay around $20 a year for service.

# Pay less for senior-friendly phone

You see ads everywhere for the Jitterbug, an easy-to-use cellphone designed for seniors. You can also find others — maybe cheaper versions — with the features you really want.

A cellphone designed for seniors offers benefits like a large, easy-to-read display screen. These phones typically have fewer buttons, and functions are easier to manage. For example, some have a single button to call 911, while others let you navigate through the menu by answering "yes" and "no" questions.

Some phones include a single button that accesses the three to five numbers you call most often. Basically, you want to skip the complicated gadgets that you'll never use, like cameras and full keyboards.

The Jitterbug phone costs $150, plus you'll pay around $10 per month for service. Consider one of these other senior-friendly phones.

+ Coupe — $40 with a two-year contract from Verizon Wireless.

+ LG UX280 — $40 with contract. The LG phone is compatible with hearing aids. It's also a good phone if you want to send text messages.

+ Pantech Breeze — $50 with a two-year contract and rebate.

+ ClarityLife — $270 with no contract from specialty retailers. This phone is even bigger than Jitterbug, so it's easier to hold if you have arthritis.

# Cellphone secret saves you big bucks

Pay-per-minute to talk, extra charges for each text message, higher rates for international calls — all these fees add up when you use your cellphone. Don't be surprised at month's end by a big bill from your cellphone company. Consider a deal that will keep you talking while you save more than $500 a year on phone service.

A typical traditional contract including cellphone and service might cost you $99 a month. That comes to $1,188 per year. People who use a cellphone for less than 400 minutes every month can easily save money using a prepaid phone. Simply buy a phone, then load it with prepaid minutes and avoid a contract. You can find phones at discount stores like Walmart for less than $10 each. Then spend $20 for up to 565 minutes of talking, and you're paying around 7 cents a minute.

You can reverse the shopping order by first finding a really great unlimited prepaid plan, then buying your phone from the service provider. Boost Mobile offers unlimited talk, texting, and Internet use for just $50 a month. Sign up for its Shrinkage plan, and you'll pay $5 less for every six months you pay your bill on time, down to a low point of $35 per month.

Other inexpensive services include:

✦ Virgin Mobile — *www.virginmobile.com*

✦ Metro PCS — *www.metropcs.com*

✦ TracFone — *www.tracfone.com*

## Safe & Secure

Spyware on your cellphone can track your calls and send the information to a third party. It can also spy on text messages and even take control, running up your bill by sending dozens of premium messages. In a worst case, the software can get your personal information and disable your phone.

Such evil software is more of a problem on a touch phone with Internet access than a regular calls-only phone. If your battery stays warm when you're not using the phone, it lights up unexpectedly, or you hear a click or buzz while talking, the phone may be targeted.

Take security steps just like you do with your computer.

• Load anti-virus and anti-spyware programs on your phone.
• Don't open text messages from people you don't know.
• Lock your phone using a security password.
• Install only programs from trusted sources.

# Best bet for budget 'smart' phone

You really want an iPhone, with its beautiful touch screen, easy-to-use camera, and fabulous applications (apps). But it's hard to justify the high price for a gizmo that is part communication device and part high-tech toy. Consider a smart-phone alternative.

**TOP DOLLAR:** An iPhone will cost you $299 for the iPhone 4, plus $36 activation fee, plus $69.99 per month unlimited-minutes plan through AT&T. Or you can buy just the phone – iPhone 3G for $499 to $699 with no contract.

**VALUE:** Samsung i9000 Galaxy S, a smart 1GHz-processor phone running the Android operating system with a touch screen, camera, and Bluetooth wireless connection (as low as $99 when you buy from AT&T Wireless). This very smart phone can run Android apps.

**WHAT YOU GIVE UP:** That attractive Apple logo, plus the ability to run iPhone apps. You can find tons of apps written for Android phones in the Android marketplace, but so far the selection of games is a bit sparse. Decide what is important to you.

# Raise your dumb phone's IQ

So-called "smart" phones are fancy cellphones that do more than just make telephone calls. Some come equipped with Internet access, a video camera, and software that can do everything but read your latest dental X-ray. But not everyone wants to pay for that kind of pricey gizmo. Turn your dumb phone into a smart phone, and skip paying for an upgrade.

A "dumb" phone refers to a simple cellphone that is free of applications, web browsing, email, and so on. But if your cellphone can send and receive text messages, you can enjoy most of the fun and convenience of an expensive smart phone.

**Find a restaurant.** Send a text message to Google (466453) from anywhere in the country. Just type in your query, starting with "local" and a key term for what you're looking for, like pizza. You'll get a message in return with restaurant options.

**Get driving directions.** There is no need to buy a separate navigational gadget when you can send a text message to Google for directions. Begin the message with "directions," then enter your start and end locations with "to" in between. You can request ZIP to ZIP or street address to street address.

**Check your calendar.** If you have set up an electronic calendar using Google calendars, you can check your calendar for upcoming events so you won't miss an appointment. Text "next" to see your next scheduled event, or "day" to see your daily schedule, to GVENT (48368).

**Access sports scores.** Keep up with that football or baseball game score, even if you have to attend your niece's wedding on a key Saturday afternoon. A free service called 4Info lets you send a text to 44636 with key words, like "Redskins Steelers news," and see the latest headlines. You can also get news and weather.

**Find answers to all your questions.** Since your dumb phone can't do an Internet search, you need a middleman. Get help from the trained guides at *www.ChaCha.com.* Send a message to 242242 with your question, like "what will be the date of Easter in 2015?" You'll get your answer back, along with a brief ad. The service is free.

But be aware that these tricks may eat up your texting limits, so you may want to upgrade to an unlimited plan.

## Stop 'cramming' from fattening your bill

Surprise! Your monthly phone bill may contain charges for items other than phone services. Third-party billing means other services — music downloads, cellphone ring tones, charitable contributions – can all appear on your landline or cellphone bill. That's fine if you actually ordered the service, but fraudsters have figured out you may not pay close attention. Hence the practice of "cramming" – stuffing your bill with bogus charges.

Catch false third-party charges by checking your bill carefully every month. Then dispute the charges with your phone company. You may enlist the help of the Federal Trade Commission (FTC). Call 877-382-4357 or navigate to *www.ftccomplaintassistant.gov*.

Your best bet is to stop the problem before it starts. Call your phone carrier, and ask to block all third-party charges.

Save your calling minutes when you bypass lengthy recorded instructions next time you leave a message on a friend's cellphone.

- Press * when calling someone with a Verizon phone.
- Press 1 for Sprint.
- Press # for AT&T or T-Mobile.

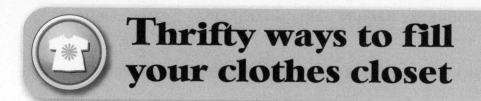
# Thrifty ways to fill your clothes closet

## Look like a million for pennies

Only fools pay retail. That's the mantra of serious shoppers, who know how to find great deals. You can get designer outfits for pennies on the dollar if you learn the tricks of these well-dressed bargain hunters. The first step is to get out of that high-priced boutique and do some research.

**Explore consignment shopping.** Unlike thrift stores, where people tend to donate clothing they don't want, consignment stores take in better-quality used clothing, with the owner receiving a portion of the sale price. That means you have a greater chance of finding newer items from your favorite designer, often at 50 to 90 percent savings.

Try shops in nice neighborhoods, where better-quality clothing tends to hang out. You'll find the best variety if you shop on Mondays, since many people drop off clothing on the weekend. Find a good local consignment shop at *www.consignmentshops.com*. If you don't find a store near you, click on the "Web shops" link to access consignment store websites.

**Pick the best of budget-friendly stores.** You may not think "fashion" when you make a run to Target for laundry detergent. But Target works with current designers to create affordable lines of women's clothing and accessories. You may find a dress by Isaac Mizrahi, a jacket by Gaby Basora, or a Mulberry handbag created especially for Target and priced at $15 to $50.

Other stores are getting into the action, with Kohl's department store featuring a line by Vera Wang.

**Go online for sample sales.** You can snap up great deals from websites that offer short-term savings on high-end clothing and accessories. You may first need to register at each site to see the current deals. Many items are around half price, but because they're top quality, they're still not cheap.

+ *www.SheFinds.com*

+ *www.HauteLook.com*

+ *www.Gilt.com*

+ *www.TheTopSecret.com*

If you like a particular designer, you may find a great new piece by searching the online auction site *www.eBay.com*. First shop in a local store to find the item and size you want, writing down information about the brand and style number. Then type these details into the eBay search engine. You may find a great deal on just what you've been looking for.

## DEEP DISCOUNT

Save on sales tax by shopping online — sometimes.

You can avoid paying sales tax if you buy from an online store that has no physical presence in your state. That means no store, warehouse, or factory. It's perfectly legal, and it can save you up to 10 percent on your purchase.

But you must pay sales tax for online purchases from a store with a location in your state. For example, you'll pay tax on your online purchase from Macy's if there's a Macy's store across town.

Multiply your savings by shopping at an online store that offers free shipping, like the shoe and clothing store *www.zappos.com*. You pay no shipping or tax in most states when you buy from this website. You don't even pay for return shipping if you decide you don't like your purchase.

# Time your shopping for greatest deals

Never buy a great outfit when you first see it. The price is at its highest when the season starts, and retailers are betting you can't resist. Instead, wait a month or so. If you still love the item then, it should be on sale. You can save a bundle on clothing purchases if you follow some simple rules about shopping at the right time. Here is what the experts say.

**Buy winter clothes in January.** These four weeks of the year are the best time to buy winter clothes. Cold-weather items are typically marked down by about 30 percent in January, when spring collections start to hit the stores.

**Get summer clothes in July.** Again, you'll save on warm-weather pieces just when you need them most, but when the stores are gearing up for the next season. Wait a little longer for a new bathing suit, and you'll find great deals in early fall.

**Make a run for athletic shoes.** Sales on these must-haves are often timed to the schedule of charity races, often held in April. November is also a great time to buy, since stores want to move out athletic shoes to make room for boots and other winter footwear.

**Harvest denim in the fall.** Don't be tempted by back-to-school sales in August and September. By October the stores slash prices on items like blue jeans, so you'll find even bigger discounts. But beware — selection shrinks along with the prices. If you are hard to fit, you may not be able to wait so long.

**Scout out store schedules.** These vary depending on the type of store.

+ Thrift stores. Make friends with an employee, and find out if the store receives donations from dry cleaners. Shop soon after that to find deals on high-end — and clean — clothing.

+ Department stores. Pounce on Saturday evening deals. New markdowns are typically advertised in Sunday circulars, and the sales officially start Sunday. But managers often put up sale signs late Saturday, so you can take advantage of the best selection.

# Simplify your wardrobe to save money

Forget the trendy sweaters and must-have jackets. Filling your closet with items that will soon go out of style means you'll need to shop again next season. Instead, pare down and simplify your wardrobe with classics. All you need to put together more than 100 outfits are 21 basic items.

The key to creating a great-looking wardrobe of pieces that will last is careful planning. Pick your favorite neutral — navy, black, or brown — so you can mix and match items within that color family. It's best to avoid the lighter neutrals, like white or cream, since they tend to look drab or dirty more quickly. You'll want suits that can be worn either together or as separates. Also find a dress that looks great either alone or with a jacket or cardigan. Finally, avoid definite trends that will soon look outdated. Instead, go with more utilitarian classic pieces that will look fresh for years.

Use this shopping list for your new wardrobe. Remember, you don't need to buy everything at once.

+ Suits to wear as separates. You'll want two pairs of pants, two skirts, and two jackets. Be sure to dry clean the entire suit together, even if you don't always wear the pieces together.

+ Pick out another two pairs of pants that flatter your body and look good with your new jackets. You'll get lots of use from khakis and a nice pair of jeans or denim slacks.

+ Find two sweaters that look great on you and work with your lifestyle. Cardigans are great choices, since you can dress them up or down.

+ Look for about 10 tops that you can wear with the cardigans, under the jackets, or by themselves.

+ Buy a sheath dress that goes with the blazers and at least one cardigan. Make sure it's comfortable and good quality, since you may be wearing it often.

Select each item carefully, and you should be able to wear the six bottoms with all 10 tops, with or without a cardigan or jacket. That gives you more than 100 different outfits to keep your look fresh.

**No-Sweat Solution**

Look but don't touch. That's a great trick to help you save money.

Research shows you're more likely to buy something if you hold it in your hands, especially for 30 seconds or longer. Apparently just looking at a cute coat or dress doesn't have the same effect as touching the fabric and holding the item. Experts believe it's because your mind assumes a kind of ownership of an object you have held, even for less than a minute.

So stick to window shopping outside your favorite store if you really want to avoid spending money.

## Clothing TLC makes investment last

The best way to save on clothing costs is to hang on to what you already own. Keep every item in your closet looking new and fresh by following these basic tips for storage and care.

+ Wash clothing in cold water, and skip the heat of the dryer. Hanging items to dry saves energy, plus it lets you avoid shrinkage and damage from the heat.

+ Foam on hangers can discolor your shirts, so use hangers made of wood, plastic, or fabric padding instead.

+ Freeze your cashmere and wool sweaters in a sealed plastic bag for 72 hours to kill bug larvae. Then remove them from the plastic and store in breathable cotton pillowcases. Moths don't eat cotton, so your favorite sweater will be safe from these critters.

- You can also make your own moth-repelling sachets from rosemary, vetiver, rose petals, and lavender.

- Stuff your empty leather bag with tissue paper — just like at the store — so it holds its shape and doesn't develop creases.

- Wash athletic shoes by hand with a toothbrush and soapy water. They can be damaged if you toss them into the washing machine and dryer.

- Store leather shoes in the off-season with cedar shoe trees inside to keep their shape and absorb odors.

## Turn old shoes into new treasures

Buying a new pair of shoes or boots can be a mixed blessing. Although it's exciting to find something new, you have to endure the discomfort of breaking in the new pair. On top of that, you're out the cost of the shoes. Here is a way to get your old shoes in tip-top shape without splurging for a new pair.

**TOP DOLLAR:** New Kenneth Cole leather boots at a cost of $150 or more.

**VALUE:** Reconditioning your old boots at a shoe repair shop. You can do whatever you need, from fixing a tear or replacing worn parts to restoring the leather's color and finish. Complete reconditioning might cost $100, but it's still cheaper than a new pair. Because top-quality materials are used in the repair process, your boots may be even better after the repair job than they were new.

For even less you can:

- replace heels on shoes — $20.

- stretch leather shoes in the area where they rub a bunion so the shoes are more comfortable — $12.

- add textured strips to the slippery soles of a pair of shoes to prevent a fall — $8.

+ lower the heel on a pair of high-heel shoes by up to one-half inch — $8 to $15. Imagine how much more comfortable your old favorites will be.

**WHAT YOU GIVE UP:** The fun of wearing this year's style. Of course, today's must-haves will be out of fashion soon, so you may be better off with your classic style.

**No-Sweat Solution**

Don't buy just one pair of socks. A single sock does you no good, so when you lose one in the wash, you're out the whole pair. That's frustrating and costly.

Many styles of socks are sold by the bagful, so you save money at the start with a bulk discount. You also scoop up savings in the long run because all the socks match each other. Lose one, or get a hole in it, and you still have pairs left.

# Join the club for savings

The person in front of you is getting a great deal at checkout. You can get the same savings by joining rewards clubs from the stores you love most.

Membership is usually free. Some experts even suggest you sign up for every rewards card or savers' club that is offered to you. Even if you don't shop at that store often, you should eventually earn some kind of discount or receive a coupon.

You may start earning rewards as soon as you join. Chico's clothing store, for example, lets you join its Passport program for free. Scan your membership card with every purchase, and you earn points toward discounts. Once you've spent $500 total, you save 5 percent on every purchase. You also receive information about special sales and offers.

Check your favorite store to see if it has a similar club. Talbots offers its Classic Awards program, while Coldwater Creek has the OneCreek program. Just be aware that some clubs require you to sign up for a store credit card as part of membership.

If you need to provide an email address as part of membership, first open a free Internet email account, like Gmail or Hotmail. Then your main email box won't be filled with junk mail.

## 4 super tips for garage sale shopping

Find treasures at yard sales on new-to-you clothing. Here is how to get the best deals.

**Go late in the day.** Sellers are eager to unload items near closing time, so you have a better chance of negotiating a great price.

**Be picky.** Check items carefully for stains, tears, missing buttons, and working zippers. If you're not sure whether a stain will wash out, better not make the purchase.

**Negotiate without fear.** It's expected, so don't feel bad asking for a lower price. Start by offering about two-thirds less than the asking price. You'll probably end up saving at least 20 percent.

**Take small bills.** It's easier to negotiate a lower price if you don't have to hand over a $20 bill for that $2 blouse.

# Powerful energy & water savings

## Cut your summer cooling bill this year

Ease the load on your air conditioner and keep more money in your bank account with these tips.

+ Install blinds with a highly reflective coating. They can reduce the heat buildup from a sunny window by about 45 percent. Keep these blinds closed and lowered to help cut your cooling bill. Sunlight is the main source of heat buildup in your home.

+ Add awnings to west-facing or south-facing windows and reduce heat buildup by up to 65 percent.

+ Use heat-producing appliances during the cooler part of the day so your air conditioner will not have to work as hard.

+ Install window air conditioners in shaded windows that face east or north, whenever possible. Placing these units in south- or west-facing windows exposes them to more sunlight and heat and may reduce their efficiency up to 10 percent.

+ Plant deciduous trees on the northeast, southeast, northwest, and southwest sides of your home.

+ Use window fans at night and large oscillating fans anytime.

+ Plant trees and shrubs close enough to shade the outside air conditioning unit, but no closer than 2 feet away.

## Get more value from your ceiling fans

You can save more than $15 a year on utility bills. Just replace your old ceiling-fan-and-light units with new ones that have the Energy Star label. The Energy Star units are 50 percent more efficient to keep expenses down.

If your ceiling fan came without a light, light kits are available to help you add one. Be sure to choose a kit with the Energy Star label so the new light does not add excessive costs to your power bill.

**CASH SAVER**

Your air conditioner stopped working. Don't call the repairman yet. Instead, let the unit cool down for a few minutes, then check the fuses or circuit breakers and, if needed, reset them.

If the compressor for your central air conditioner stops working on a hot day, check your owner's manual to find the high-pressure limit switch and learn how to reset it. It may be as simple as pressing a button on the compressor's access panel.

## Slash utility bills

The average annual energy bill for an American family is now over $2,000. But many government agencies and energy providers have programs that offer relief. Try these household tips and government giveaways to help you slash your utility bills.

**Chill out.** Wash clothes in cold water, whenever possible. More than 90 percent of the cost of doing laundry comes from heating the water.

**Try medium hot.** Turn your water heater down from 140 degrees to 120 degrees and you will likely save at least $436 a year in utility costs.

**Trim heating and cooling bills.** Lower your thermostat 1 degree in the winter to cut heating costs by up to 3 percent. In summer, raise the thermostat 6 degrees and use ceiling fans to keep cool for up to 10 percent less.

**Think senior discount.** If you are age 60 or older, you may be eligible for state energy assistance programs through the Area Agencies on Aging (AAA). Call the AAA's Eldercare Locator toll-free at 800-677-1116, or visit their website at *www.eldercare.gov*. They can put you in touch with the services in your community that may help you with home energy costs. If your city has a Department of Senior Affairs, check with them as well. Keep in mind that some programs may have an income requirement.

**Get free upgrades.** You can have energy-saving improvements made to your house for free through the Weatherization Assistance Program (WAP) – regardless of whether you rent or own. This program reduces household energy bills by an average of $437 every year. WAP helps make the homes of low-income families more energy-efficient.

If you qualify, you get a home-energy analysis and solutions, such as insulating the attic and walls. The National Energy Assistance Referral (NEAR) project can help you reach the WAPs in your area. Call NEAR toll-free at 866-674-6327.

If you don't qualify for weatherization help, you may still qualify for the Low Income Home Energy Assistance Program (LIHEAP). It offers short-term help paying utility bills and may provide some free weatherization. Contact NEAR for LIHEAP information, too.

**Save extra.** Check these websites for tax incentives, loans, and rebates that may help you save even more.

+ *www.dsireusa.org*

+ *www.energystar.gov*

+ *www.ase.org/taxcredits*

+ *www.energytaxincentives.org*

+ *www.energysavers.gov*

**Call the utility company.** Ask your electric and gas companies if they offer rebates, credits, assistance, or discounts. You may be pleasantly surprised.

# Unbelievably easy ways to cut heating and cooling costs

Heating and cooling costs may be a big part of your power bill, but that does not mean you have to buy a new furnace or air conditioner.

**Lower winter energy costs 30 percent.** Install a programmable thermostat and set it lower at night or when no one is home. Experts say you may save up to 20 percent on your heating costs that way. But don't stop there. Close the heating vents or radiators in rooms that rarely get used and you can save up to 10 percent more on heating.

**Save another $20 a month.** A dirty filter can hamper your furnace or air conditioner so badly that you pay up to $20 a month extra on your power bill. So don't scrimp on those $1 heating and air conditioning filters. Change them every month.

**CASH SAVER**

Strangely enough, replacing your old PC with a new one would not save enough electricity to justify a new computer's price tag. But you can still slash your electric bill using your existing computer.

Just switch off its hidden energy hog, the screen saver, and set the hibernation or sleep options to start when the screen saver would have appeared. According to SmallBiz, this one change could save you up to $100 a year.

# Pinch power pennies while you sleep

You can cut a $100 heating bill by $10 a month if you lower your thermostat 10 degrees at night and use an electric blanket or mattress pad, claims the Electric Blanket Institute (EBI). This may sound like sales hype, but calculations by *Consumer Reports* experts suggest those figures are probably accurate.

Yet, an electric mattress pad may be better than an electric blanket for two reasons, the EBI suggests. Some of the heat from the electric blanket escapes into the room, but heated mattress pads keep more of the heat between the blankets and the mattress — where you are. Even better, heated mattress pads cost less to run each night than electric blankets.

If you decide to try a heated mattress pad, be sure to choose one carefully. Good features to look for include automatic shutoff after 10 hours, overheat protection, machine washability, and quiet controls and operation.

**Freebie Frenzie** Get several cords of firewood for a cheaper price. If you live near a national forest, contact the national forest staff or the nearest office of the National Forest Service, and ask if they offer firewood and how to get it if they do. It's illegal to collect firewood in a national forest without a permit.

In addition, some parks require you to cut or haul the firewood yourself. Timing may be important, too. You may be less likely to need a chain saw if a recent weather event has felled trees in the forest.

# Discover 13 surprising cash drains

Tiny air leaks in your home may be stealing your money. In fact, experts say you may save 10 percent or more on your energy bill just by reducing your home's air leaks.

Check with your utility company to learn whether they offer a free energy audit. If they don't, here is how you can do your own. On a windy, cool day, turn off your furnace, shut all your windows and doors, and switch on any exhaust fan that blows air outside, such as bathroom fans. Light a stick of incense and pass it close to possible leak sites. Anywhere incense smoke is blown away or sucked outside, you may have a leak.

"Some leaks around windows and doors may be obvious, but be sure to also inspect for cracks and gaps around places like electrical outlets, plumbing pipes, dryer vents and phone jacks," says Michael Sites, a Product Specialist for Touch 'n Seal insulating foam sealants.

To make certain you find all your leaks, use this list and be sure to check areas in your basement and attic.

+ windows

+ doors

+ electrical outlets

+ dryer vent opening

+ outside water faucets

+ recessed can lights

+ whole house fans

+ house entry and exit points for electrical wiring, gas pipes, cable TV, and phone lines

+ house entry and exit points for plumbing

+ house entry and exit points for ductwork

+ mail chute

+ attic hatch or door

+ phone jacks

Make a list of your leaks and visit the local hardware or home improvement store. Ask what kinds of materials you need to seal each kind of leak. In general, you need caulk, weather stripping, spray foam, outlet sealers, and foam board. You may also opt for a whole house fan shutter seal, a little attic insulation, and some Velcro.

Seal and caulk air leaks around windows, doors, electrical outlets, plumbing fixtures, dryer vents, outside water faucets, recessed can lights, whole house fans, phone jacks, and anywhere plumbing, ducting, or electrical wiring penetrates through walls, floors, or ceilings. Use weather stripping around windows, doors, attic hatches, and mail chutes. Install outlet sealers, inexpensive foam gaskets that fit behind outlet covers, and look for similar covers for phone jacks.

# Save more money with a home energy audit

You love your old house but hate the high energy bills that come with it. Fortunately, a home energy audit can help you find and fix the problems that are crippling your home's energy efficiency and raising your bills.

**TOP DOLLAR:** A professional audit by a certified auditor costs $300 to $800.

**VALUE:** A do-it-yourself (DIY) audit or an audit by your utility company may be free or cheap. Your utility company or the Internet may provide instructions to help you do your own audit or you can use the leak-finding instructions in this chapter. If you have a computer, try the free Home Energy Yardstick at *www.energystar.gov/yardstick* or the free Home Energy Saver at *hes.lbl.gov*.

**WHAT YOU GIVE UP:** The best energy auditors provide high-tech equipment, such as blower doors and infrared cameras. The blower door test ferrets out gaps and drafts, while infrared scanning spots temperature differences that indicate air leaks and either poor or no insulation. The auditor may also review your energy bills. Although both auditors and online audit tools offer recommendations on how to fix energy efficiency problems, the auditor may also:

+ assess the efficiency of your appliances.

+ help you calculate your return on investment from switching to high-efficiency appliances and equipment.

+ check for carbon monoxide hazards.

If you want an auditor, look for professionals who are certified by the Building Performance Institute or the Residential Energy Services Network. Visit *www.energystar.gov* for a list of their Home Energy Raters.

But remember, a professional energy audit is just one way to keep more of your dollars. A DIY audit may have lower upfront costs, but it can still help you save money every month.

# Insulate yourself from leaking dollars

Poor attic insulation and leaks in your heating and cooling ducts may be costing you up to $600 a year. Start taking that money back.

Your attic may already have insulation, but many older homes don't have enough insulation. If you have less than 11 inches of fiberglass or rock wool or 8 inches of cellulose, adding or improving insulation will probably help. Estimates vary, but you may save $300 or more every year.

According to GreenAndSave.com, a company that measures the annual savings of energy efficient changes, sealing those leaky ducts may save as much as $400 a year, too.

# A 'light switch' that pays you $24

Switching to compact fluorescent light bulbs (CFLs) could lower your lighting energy costs 66 percent in just three years. See for yourself.

| Details | Incandescent | CFL |
|---|---|---|
| watts | 100 | 23 |
| life | 750 hours | 12,000 hours |
| price | $0.31 | $2.50 |
| bulbs needed | six for three years | one for about eight years |
| cost of bulbs | $1.86 | $2.50 (for three years) |
| cost of electricity | $35.04 | $8.06 |
| total three-year cost | $36.90 | $10.55 |
| total savings from switching to CFL | | $24.40 |

# How turning off lights steals your money

Turning off lights when you leave a room is not always a good idea. In fact, sometimes you should leave the lights on to save money. Here's why.

According to the experts at *Energystar.gov*, compact fluorescent light bulbs (CFLs) should only be used in places where the lights stay on for at least 15 minutes at a time. Why? Turning a CFL on and off many times each day can actually shorten the life of the bulb enough to counteract the savings from turning the bulb off.

So if you have only been in a room two minutes and expect to return in one minute, leave the light on, especially if you will be in and out of this room frequently. In addition, don't install CFLs in attic storage areas, closets, or other places where lights are typically on for less than 15 minutes at a time.

Make sure you know the right way to clean up a compact fluorescent light bulb (CFL) if you break it. These bulbs contain a small amount of hazardous mercury, so remember these cleanup steps from the Environmental Protection Agency.

- Clear the room of people and pets, open a window, and leave the room for 15 minutes.
- Shut off the central heat or air conditioning system.
- Use stiff paper or cardboard to scoop up the glass and powder, and drop it into a sealed plastic bag or into a glass jar with a metal lid.
- Use duct tape to pick up any leftover glass or powder.
- Wipe up the remaining mess with a damp paper towel and drop the towel into the jar or bag.
- Wash your hands.
- Visit *www.epa.gov* for more details and be sure to check your local ordinances for any special CFL disposal rules that may apply in your area.

# Check light bulb labels to save cash

Now you can find out how much money a light bulb will add to your electricity bill every year, just by looking at the light bulb package. The Federal Trade Commission now requires more informative labels for light bulbs. On the front of the package, the new labels must show the yearly cost of using the light bulb for three hours a day. Check the back to find out how many years the bulb should last if used three hours a day.

Put those two together and you get a good idea of whether a particular light bulb is worth its price tag. These label numbers can also help you compare one bulb with another. Just remember to adjust your calculations to match the bulb's daily average use. A heavily used bulb will cost more to use each year and will probably burn out long before its estimated life ends.

The new labels also provide extra information to help you avoid buying the wrong bulb for your needs. Just a few years ago, you could get brighter light simply by replacing a 60-watt bulb with a 75-watt or 100-watt bulb. But now a 23-watt compact fluorescent light (CFL) can be brighter than a 60-watt incandescent. The new labels not only tell you how many watts a bulb uses, but also how bright the bulb is. Check the front of the package for the bulb's brightness in lumens. More lumens mean a brighter bulb. On the back of the light bulb package, you will find other decision-helping details including:

+ the bulb's wattage.

+ mercury content, if any.

+ whether the light is warm – more soft, yellow glow like older incandescent bulbs – or cool, whiter like daylight.

Use this new label to get the bulb you want, the energy savings you need, and more value for the price.

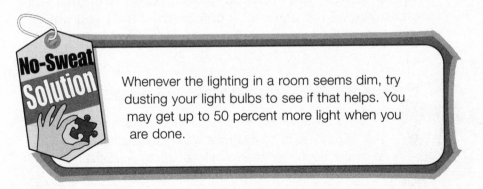

Whenever the lighting in a room seems dim, try dusting your light bulbs to see if that helps. You may get up to 50 percent more light when you are done.

## Painless trick trims your electric bill

You are probably paying for more electricity than you actually use – possibly up to 10 percent of your electric bill. This happens because many appliances and electronics keep using electricity, even when you are not using them. Experts call this phantom power, vampire power, or standby power, but you can just call it expensive.

Fortunately, this is easy to fix. First, identify which items are causing the problem. Common offenders include computers, DVD players, televisions, stereos, electronics chargers, and kitchen appliances like your microwave. A glowing standby light or a display that stays lit after you have shut off or stopped using an appliance or device is a good clue that it's drawing standby power. Items that have a remote control are also prime suspects.

Next, decide which solution to use for each item. Here are your choices.

+ Simply unplug the product when you are not using it and plug it in when you need it. Your savings could range from around $3 a year for unplugging your microwave to more than $150 a year for unplugging a plasma television. Be aware that unplugging or switching off digital video recorders (DVRs) may prevent them from recording programs and may force you to reset the scheduling every time you turn them on.

+ To manage whole groups of electronics at once, plug them into a power strip with a surge protector. A flick of a switch can turn off power or restore it, plus each device is protected against power spikes. You can even find "smart" power strips that will power down all the items on a power strip when you power down one particular "trigger" item, such as your computer.

**No-Sweat Solution**

Imagine how much money you would save if you could set your appliances to do their jobs when your electricity rate is lowest, no matter when that time occurs. A research team at Michigan Technological University may have created a smart electricity meter that will do that for you.

"Say it has been determined that the price of power is lowest at 2:00 a.m.," says John Lukowski, leader of the research team and associate professor of electrical and computer engineering. "The meter can be set to automatically start the dishwasher at that time each day."

Until this meter is available to the public, take advantage of off-peak rates. Contact your electric company and find out when their off-peak rates are available. Whenever possible, arrange to use your dishwasher, clothes dryer, and other appliances during these times.

## Shrink your clothes-drying costs

Slash your clothes-drying time, plus save wear and tear and power, with something you already own and can use over and over. Just add a dry towel to the load. It helps soak up the moisture more quickly, so clothes need less time to dry. That means less wear and tear on your clothes from tumbling in a dryer and less wear and tear on your wallet from high energy bills. To cut drying time even more:

+ Put the next load in while the dryer is still hot. This eliminates the time clothes tumble while the dryer is heating up.

+ Use the moisture sensor option if your dryer has one, so it will only run for as long as your clothes take to dry.

+ Set the washer for an extended spin or high-speed spin or simply run an extra spin cycle to wring out more moisture before transferring clothes to the dryer.

## Cut drying time and prevent dryer fires

Speed up your clothes drying time and save big bucks on electricity. If you have a ribbed plastic or vinyl vent duct on the back of your dryer, lint is more likely to collect inside it. This creates a fire hazard and gums up the works, so your dryer runs longer. To fix these problems, just replace the old duct with a 4-inch, rigid, metal duct.

# Easiest ways to slash your water bill

Small changes that make a big impact are the best way to reduce your water bill — and these are two of the best ones.

**Shorten your shower.** You may be surprised at how five minutes can lower your water bill. You can save approximately 2,000 gallons of water every year, just by making your shower one minute shorter. If you can reduce your shower time by four-and-a-half to five minutes, you can save 9,000 gallons of water each year.

**Use your head to pay less.** If shorter showers are not for you, shave your water bill with one small device instead, a new low-flow showerhead. Unlike showerheads with water restrictors, a low-flow showerhead is designed to let you shower more comfortably with up to 50 percent less water. If used to replace an older, water-hogging showerhead, a low-flow showerhead pays for itself in under six months.

To test whether you can get these savings, fill a bucket with a gallon of water and mark the depth. Use up that gallon of water and place the empty bucket in your shower where the water falls. Turn the shower on so it flows as fast and hard as it does when you shower. Time how long the water takes to reach the gallon mark. If it takes less than 20 seconds, a low-flow showerhead will save you money.

# Give new life to your hot water heater

One hour with your water heater could help trim your energy bill for months to come. That is because your water heater may already be performing more poorly than it should — and may even be storing less hot water.

Mineral deposits and dirt naturally build up inside the water heater tank over time. This gunk can make your water heater's heating element less efficient, and it takes up space your water heater would normally use for water. Fortunately, fixing the problem is simple. You can flush your tank with these easy steps. Just remember to check the manufacturer's instructions before you begin.

+ Grab a bucket, turn off the water heater circuit breaker or gas valve, and shut off the incoming water.

+ Find the drain valve near the bottom of the tank, place the bucket beneath it, and open the valve. If it has been awhile since the tank was flushed, attach a garden hose to the drain valve and run the hose outside.

+ Let the water drain into the bucket until it runs clear. If the water is still dirty when the tank empties, allow the tank to refill with a few gallons of water before draining it again.

+ When you are done, turn off the valve, restore the incoming water, and turn on the water heater circuit breaker or gas valve.

For best results, flush your tank at least once a year. You may need to flush it more often if you have hard water.

# Toilet shopping: how to flush out the best deal

Your old toilet is on its last legs, and you are fed up with paying high water bills. You want a new toilet that saves money.

**TOP DOLLAR:** High-efficiency toilets (HETs) that need 1.3 gallons of water or less cost between $300 and $510.

**VALUE:** The current standard, 1.6-gallon, low-flow toilets, range from $80 to $440.

**WHAT YOU GIVE UP:** You may give up long-term cost savings if you choose the cheaper 1.6-gallon toilet, but a two-person household only saves an extra $9.76 a year with an HET, compared to a standard low-flow toilet. If you have a two-person household and pay the median price of $405 for an HET, it may take 14 years to make up the price difference in water savings.

Yet, the HET may make up the price difference earlier if you live in a larger household or pay less than $405. You may also find rebates for HETs available from your utility company or from local, state, or federal government agencies. If circumstances like these make an HET worthwhile, keep in mind that HETs with the Environmental Protection Agency's WaterSense label have been tested to make sure they can clear waste from the toilet bowl.

But the standard 1.6-gallon toilet is lower-priced without rebates — and it still slashes your water costs. Not only can it save you around $140 on the purchase price, it also saves you roughly $48 a year in water costs compared with older, 3.5-gallon toilets. Even better, these savings pay for a $265 toilet in less than six years.

**Time is Money**

Get your laundry done faster and save energy, too. Use shorter six- to eight-minute cycles for clothes that are not stained and have only been worn a time or two, recommends the Whirlpool Institute of Fabric Science.

According to *Energysavers.gov*, even if your clothes are stained, you can probably stick with the warm or cold water settings on your washer as long as your stains are not the oily kind. This change may help you wash your clothes with as little as half the electricity you normally use, an improvement that can trim your power bill. Just be sure to check that all the stains are gone before you put your clothes in the dryer.

# Clear stubborn clogs without a plumber

Slow or clogged sink? Don't call a plumber — try these ingenious tricks first.

✦ Stuff a soaked rag in the overflow holes near the top of the sink or in the second drain of a double sink. Coat the rim of the plunger with petroleum jelly for a better seal. Fill up the sink halfway with water, press the plunger over the drain, and rapidly pump up and down. This creates extra air pressure to push against the clog.

✦ Mix one cup of baking soda and one cup of salt, and pour down the clogged drain. Add a half cup of white vinegar. Wait 15 to 20 minutes, then pour a big pot of boiling water down the drain. Don't use this method if you have tried a commercial drain opener that is still standing in the drain.

✦ Thread a flexible metal snake or plumber's auger down the drain and try to clear the clog. If you don't own a snake or auger, you can rent one, but the rental cost will be added to the cost of a plumber if you can't budge the clog.

# Freeze alert: prevent an expensive winter disaster

Water pipes that freeze and burst can take a deluge of dollars out of your wallet. But a $3 fix can help you avoid the costly damage — and high water bill — from burst water pipes.

Visit your local hardware or home improvement store and ask about self-sealing, polyethylene sleeves for pipes. These usually cost around $3 or less for 6 feet. The Institute for Business and Home Safety suggests you wrap these around all the pipes you can get to. Do not forget pipes in unheated or uninsulated areas inside your house. Your wallet will thank you.

Graywater is a clever way to cut your water bill by reusing water collected from showers, bathroom sinks, leftover drinking water, and washing machines, but it can be dangerous if used or collected incorrectly.

Popular ways to collect graywater include keeping a bucket in the shower and collecting leftover drinking water from people and pets. But don't collect water from kitchen sinks, dishwashers, toilets, or from laundry loads that include diapers or clothes exposed to pesticides or other toxic chemicals.

Never touch or spray graywater and be sure to avoid using it to irrigate any edible plant. Instead, use recently collected graywater as drip or flood irrigation for your lawn, flowers, and other inedible plants — and then enjoy watching your water bill dwindle.

# Do the math before you go 'tankless'

The average household spends up to $600 a year on water heating alone, but according to *Energystar.gov*, switching to a new Energy Star tankless water heater may save you $115 every year. Other estimates suggest you will save even more.

Unlike regular tank water heaters, tankless heaters don't heat water 24 hours a day. Instead, they only heat water when you need it. This speedy, on-demand heating costs a lot less than all-day water heating, so you should save money. Unfortunately, you may have to wait a long time.

According to *Consumer Reports*, gas-powered tankless water heaters do save money on energy costs every year you own them, but the savings may be as little as $70 a year. Gas tankless heaters also save more money and produce more hot water faster than electric tankless water heaters, particularly where groundwater is cold.

Unfortunately, the combined cost of the tankless heater and its installation is so expensive that those savings may take 15 to 22 years to pay for the unit – even longer if your old water heater was Energy Star certified. Tankless heaters not only cost more than regular water heaters, you may have to pay extra installation costs for changes like upgrading your gas pipes to accommodate the heater's demands.

But government and utilities often offer rebates and incentives that can significantly lower the cost of a tankless water heater. What's more, the efficiency of Energy Star tankless gas water heaters may be higher now than when *Consumer Reports* did their tests – plus prices may have dropped. So contact your gas company and local and state government about incentives and rebates.

Get estimates of the cost, including installation costs, of a regular tank gas water heater and a tankless gas heater. Don't wait until your old water heater fails because you won't have time to shop for the best price.

To figure the cost of the tankless heater, subtract your rebates and incentives from the installed cost of the tankless heater. Then subtract the installed cost of the regular water heater. Divide the result by your expected annual savings to find out how many years the tankless water heater will take to pay for itself.

# 5 ways to trim repair bills

You usually save money on repairs by doing them yourself, but sometimes you absolutely have to call a repairman. Remember these money-saving tips when you do.

+ Call a repairman as soon as possible if you decide you can't do a repair quickly by yourself. Some repairs, like water leaks, become more expensive the longer you wait.

+ Learn as much as possible about the problem and the repair before you call the repairman. If you have a computer, the

Internet may help with this research. You can also find books that offer guidelines for common home and appliance repairs. Knowing more may help you better describe the problem to the repairman, so he needs less time to diagnose the problem. Your new knowledge may even help you tell which parts of a repair you truly need.

✦ Arrange for the repairman to fix other problems at the same time. Some repairers charge separately for each visit, even if they can't do the repair during the first visit.

✦ Make sure the repairman won't have to spend extra time cleaning up or clearing a way to reach the repair site. How much time it takes the repairman to fix the problem determines most of your cost.

✦ Watch the repairman carefully during the repair. You may learn something that will help you diagnose or fix a future problem.

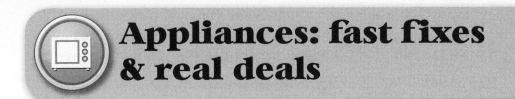
## Easy way to keep clothes dryer costs down

Extend the life of your dryer and cut your utility bills with a five-minute trick twice a year. If you ever use dryer sheets, you definitely need to know this secret.

Your dryer blows hot air over clothes as they tumble. This hot air removes moisture from clothes and carries it through the lint filter and out of the dryer. If your lint filter gets clogged, moisture stays in your dryer, making it work harder and longer to dry your clothes. But lint is not the only thing that can block your lint filter. Chemical deposits from fabric softener sheets can gradually gum up the filter, too.

To avoid this, remove the lint filter, wash with soapy water, and scrub off the residue with an old toothbrush. While you are at it, use your dryer manual to find your moisture sensor and wipe the sensor with a cotton ball and rubbing alcohol. Fabric softener film can affect it, too.

Do this at least twice a year, limit your use of dryer sheets, and clean lint from the lint filter after every load. This helps your dryer operate more efficiently, so you are less likely to face high utility bills or a dryer that fails before its time.

## Win the appliance rebate game

Are you owed some money? Nearly 50 percent of rebates are never claimed, the Federal Trade Commission (FTC) reports. These money-makers are famous for being difficult to redeem — even for appliances. But you can claim yours with ease once you know the right tricks.

+ Check the rebate information before you buy. Carefully read the instructions, including the fine print, to be sure you qualify for the rebate and can meet the deadlines. If you do not have a computer, make sure you can get your rebate form without visiting a website.

+ Keep all your purchase paperwork and the papers and packaging that come with the product. You may be surprised at what you need to get the rebate.

+ Mail your rebate well before the deadline. Allow enough time to mail something else if the company claims your rebate materials are incomplete.

+ Never skip steps or questions on the rebate form. For example, if the form asks for an email address and you don't have one, write "no email" in the space.

+ Keep copies of everything you must send in for the rebate — including the rebate form, your store receipt, the item's bar code, forms, product containers, serial numbers, and the mailing envelope.

+ Staple all the rebate items together before mailing.

+ If you want to be doubly sure, use certified mail and ask for a receipt.

+ Call before the rebate deadline to make sure they received your rebate claim and that no further documents are needed.

+ Check your junk mail. Rebate checks sometimes arrive in envelopes that look like junk mail.

+ Contact the company if your rebate has not arrived by the time the company promised. If no date or time frame was given, the FTC says you should receive your rebate within 30 days.

+ If the rebate never arrives, file a complaint with your state's Attorney General or the FTC at *www.ftc.gov* or 877-382-4357.

You might think you can't recycle old appliances, but you can recycle just about anything. In fact, a free service tells you who recycles it near your home.

Call 800-CLEANUP (800-253-2687) or visit *www.earth911.com* and indicate your ZIP code and what you want to recycle. Whether it is a washing machine, batteries, or something more unusual, you will discover the places nearest you that recycle the item.

Your options for recycling appliances may include retailers who pick up and recycle your old appliance when you buy a new one, scrap metal recyclers, or your local trash company's "heavy pick up and recycling" program.

# Get the maximum discount on your new refrigerator

Upgrade your refrigerator and other appliances and you can get little-known discounts on top of the ones advertised at the store.

**Add a monthly discount.** Every appliance has two price tags — the store price tag and the monthly operating costs. A new, energy-efficient refrigerator automatically cuts your electric bill, because older appliances use far more energy than newer ones. But you can save even more than that by picking the right refrigerator features.

+ Choose a model without an automatic ice maker or through-the-door ice and water dispenser. You will not only save electricity, but money off the purchase price, too.

+ A manual defrost refrigerator uses less energy if you remember to defrost it regularly.

+ Pick a refrigerator with the freezer at the top instead of a side-by-side model and you will pay lower power bills every month.

**Get paid for your purchase.** The government and some utility companies are often willing to pay you for replacing your old energy-hogging refrigerator with a new, energy-efficient version. You may also get money for buying other energy-efficient appliances. Check these sites to see if you qualify for a rebate or tax incentive for a recently purchased appliance.

+ *www.dsireusa.org*

+ *www.energystar.gov*

+ *www.ase.org/taxcredits*

+ *www.energytaxincentives.org*

+ *www.energysavers.gov*

Also, ask your electric and gas companies if they offer rebates. You may be pleasantly surprised.

# Never pay the sticker price

Try haggling to save money. It's easy and takes just seconds. Yet, many people don't know they can do it.

You might be surprised to learn that many retailers expect you to negotiate. Just make sure you take steps to do it well.

+ Research prices before you shop. Read local ads and call a few stores to get a price for the appliance you want. If you have a computer, check price comparison sites like the website *www.pricegrabber.com*. Use this information to bargain.

+ Find the best stores for negotiating a better price. Independent appliance stores and regional chains may be more willing to negotiate than large, famous, national chain stores. But while national chains may not give you a price break, you can still try asking for concessions on delivery or installation.

+ Start your negotiations at a lower price than the one you are willing to accept.

+ Always ask, "Is that your best offer?"

+ Be polite, patient, reasonable, and a little assertive.

+ Don't be afraid to walk away. You can come back another day. In fact, getting your price may be easier later if the salesperson needs to meet a sales quota by the end of the month.

Your dryer is taking longer and longer to dry your clothes, but you hate to spend money on repairs.

Try this first. Unplug your dryer, and ease it away from the wall so you can reach the big vent hose. Disconnect the vent hose from the dryer, but leave the other end attached to the wall. Suction lint out of the vent hose with your vacuum cleaner hose attachment.

When you're done, reattach the vent hose to the dryer and plug it in. Find where your dryer vents to the outside world and clean off lint at that end, too.

Run a load through your dryer. If the clothes still take a long time to dry, call a repairman. If your clothes dry quickly, you have fixed the problem and saved money.

# 3 ways to get extended warranties for free

Don't pay for an extended warranty. Get it for free instead. In fact, you have three possible ways to gain longer warranty coverage without paying a penny.

+ Pay with your credit card. A number of credit cards extend a standard warranty by up to one year. Contact your credit card company to see if they offer this service and, if they do, ask to register your new purchase for the warranty extension.

+ Any product that has earned the Good Housekeeping Seal is under a two-year limited warranty from *Good Housekeeping* magazine. If the product proves defective within two years of the date when you bought it from a retailer, *Good Housekeeping* will refund your money or replace the product. If you need to claim this warranty, write to Consumer Services & Seal Coordinator, Good Housekeeping Magazine, 300 W. 57th Street, New York, NY 10019.

✦ Chances are, the real warranty on that TV, washer, or just about anything else is months, even years longer than the fine print says it is. All states legally require an implied warranty of merchantability. This warranty may apply after a regular warranty expires and may last up to four years after the purchase date.

The warranty means the seller promises the item will do what it was made to do. So if you buy a refrigerator, the seller promises it will preserve foods at a constant cold temperature.

Unless the seller or manufacturer either sells the item as-is or includes a written policy that no warranty is given, all products are covered by this warranty. Contact your state consumer protection agency to find out the details and length of this warranty in your state.

## Deep discounts on dinged dishwashers and more

You could save hundreds on a washing machine that got scratched when it was unloaded or a refrigerator that got dented in the retailer's warehouse. These imperfections mean the retailer can no longer charge full price for the item even if it works perfectly and has a full warranty. The appliance becomes a "scratch and dent" item — and a huge bargain.

**TOP DOLLAR:** That Amana side-by-side refrigerator normally costs $1,499 and the Maytag stainless steel dishwasher sells for $800.

**VALUE:** The same Amana side-by-side refrigerator with a small ding sells for $830 and an imperfect Maytag stainless steel dishwasher goes for $400, a combined savings of $1,069.

**WHAT YOU GIVE UP:** You may or may not get the delivery, installation service, manuals, installation hardware, and accessories that usually come with an appliance. You must also ask about warranties and return policies, and insist on being shown all the product's defects, because some items are sold as-is.

What's more, finding "scratch and dent" items takes a little work. Call retailers in your area to see what they do with scratched-and-dented appliances. Some, like Sears, have outlet stores, while others have in-store departments. Also, check appliance rental stores and thrift stores.

## Get more for your money

Don't be fooled by brand names when buying appliances. Take two models from the same brand and one may be a top-rated performer while another ranks near the bottom. Similarly, one electric range from a top brand may be repair prone while the same brand's dishwasher runs perfectly for years. In fact, that is exactly what research from *Consumer Reports* has found. So what should you look for instead?

Rather than focusing on a brand, find the top models and their brands by visiting the library. Read *Consumer Reports* and other product reviews. Find out the features to look for and avoid, as well as which models perform best and reliably.

If you have a computer, check *www.consumersearch.com* and search for other product reviews by experts. You can also read reviews by product owners at sites like *www.amazon.com* or the websites of major appliance chains.

Before you buy, find out if you can get your appliance serviced and repaired locally. Some appliances from lesser-known brand names may require an out-of-town repair firm.

## Tame your kitchen energy hog

Your refrigerator uses more power than any other kitchen appliance. Try these four ways to keep your refrigerator from eating up expensive electricity.

+ Your refrigerator and freezer consume less energy when packed full. Rinse plastic quart or gallon jugs, fill with water, and use them to fill in the gaps. To fill smaller gaps, keep peanut butter, nuts, and other high-fat foods in your refrigerator instead of the pantry.

✦ Make your refrigerator use less power instantly with a one-time, no cost quick fix. If your refrigerator is too cold, it can use up to 25 percent more power. Check the temperature of each compartment by leaving a refrigerator or outdoor thermometer inside your refrigerator overnight. Keep your refrigerator compartment between 35 and 38 degrees and your freezer at 0 degrees.

✦ Let warm or hot foods cool before putting them in the refrigerator, and cover all foods with lids. This reduces the heat and moisture your refrigerator removes.

✦ Stop using the top of your refrigerator as storage space. Your refrigerator needs plenty of open space around it so it can easily get rid of hot air.

## Score discounts after the sale

Just because you bought your new appliance doesn't mean you are done saving money. You can get a discount after you leave the store — days or even weeks later.

Many stores have a price protection policy or price adjustment policy. Here is what that means for you. If you can show that the same appliance you just bought is selling at a cheaper price just a few days or weeks later, the store will refund the difference. Keep in mind store policies vary. Some stores only refund the difference if their price dropped, while others will refund for cheaper prices at another store.

When you shop, ask each seller whether they have this guarantee, how to claim it, and when the guarantee would not apply. Contact your credit card company and ask the same questions. Some credit cards offer price protection guarantees on items you purchase. Just remember to keep watching prices after you buy your appliance so you will not miss your chance for extra cash.

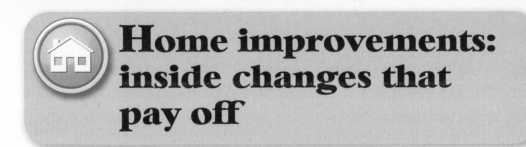

# Home improvements: inside changes that pay off

## Indoor remodeling that repays

Remodeling your home's exterior can improve your curb appeal and help you sell your home. But changing your interior living space is important, too. According to *Remodeling* magazine, these are the indoor renovations that give you the highest percentage of your money back.

**Minor kitchen remodel.** Replace your cabinet knobs, drawer pulls, cabinet doors, and drawer fronts. Also, update the wall oven, cooktop, flooring, counters, sink, and faucet.

**Attic bedroom.** Convert bare attic space to a bedroom, full bathroom, and closet with carpeting, heating, and air conditioning.

**Basement remodel.** Convert bare basement to den and full bath.

**Major kitchen remodel.** Switch to semi-custom cabinets. Add a kitchen island, custom lighting, and garbage disposal. Change out the countertops, wall oven, dishwasher, sink, faucet, and flooring.

**Bathroom remodel.** Upgrade to a ceramic tile floor and solid surface countertop. Replace the tub, toilet, sink, medicine cabinet, floor, and wallpaper.

To find out which project may be the best choice for your area, talk to a local real estate agent.

## 5 home features to think twice about

Some wildly popular home features and additions may no longer be good investments. According to a survey by the National Association of Home Builders, these are becoming less popular.

- ✦ fireplaces
- ✦ wall-to-wall carpet
- ✦ living rooms
- ✦ kitchen desks
- ✦ skylights

Before you add, upgrade, or update one of these, consider whether other projects would be a better investment for your hard-earned money.

**DEEP DISCOUNT** Give yourself brand new flooring and carpeting for Christmas, but at bargain prices. With a little planning, you can save plenty by shopping between Thanksgiving and Groundhog Day. Most people are too busy to shop during the holiday season and too broke to shop afterward, so stores are more likely to offer bargains then.

## 4 ways to save on new carpet

You have just developed a bad case of sticker shock after seeing the installation price for your new carpet. But do not worry. You can bring the cost down with these tips.

- ✦ Insist on a separate estimate for each extra service like moving your furniture or disposing of old carpet. Carpeters may over-charge you if they roll it into one job estimate.

- ✦ Save $3 to $5 a yard — on top of whatever the store is offering. Tell the carpet salesman you will pull up your old carpet instead of letting the installers do it. If you have a computer, visit *www.findhow.com* to learn how to do this.

- ✦ Ask family or neighborhood kids to help move your furniture. The carpet installer will charge much more.

- ✦ Install your carpet during the summer or winter. More people buy carpeting in spring and fall, so that is when experts charge top dollar.

# Budget-friendly remodeling

A new, fresh look for your kitchen and master bath would be great, but ripping out walls and spending $80,000 is not an option. Instead, try smaller, high-impact changes that can make these rooms pop.

- Replace your kitchen cabinet knobs with new hardware, and install rollout organizing trays and Lazy Susans that mimic the features of high-end cabinets.

- Clean your switchplates, curtains, and the rug or floor mat by the sink. If they still look old or outdated, purchase new ones.

- Replace your kitchen lighting with updated fixtures. Visit home improvement stores for under-cabinet lights that resemble hockey pucks and are easy to install.

- Repaint your kitchen and bathroom walls and trim.

- Change your bathroom faucets and cabinet hardware.

- Switch to white towels and bath mats and put light-colored paint on the walls for a spa look. Change your shower curtain, if you have one.

- Replace outdated or damaged bathroom towel racks, doorknobs, and toilet paper holders.

- Change old or outdated bathroom light fixtures, and update other bath fixtures like showerheads.

# Caution: this money-saver may cost you

Some home experts recommend granite tile countertops as a far less expensive alternative to the granite slab counter. But while these two countertops have a lot in common, they are not the same.

The grout between granite tiles is tough to keep clean, so these counters may require more cleaning time. Because granite tiles are thinner than a slab, they may also be less impact-resistant. And in some cases, potential home buyers may view granite tile as a step down from the granite slab.

# Improve your home with the ideal floor

You want the warm look of wood flooring for your home, but you cannot decide whether to spend the extra money on genuine hardwood flooring or go with a laminate floor that mimics the look of wood.

**TOP DOLLAR:** Hardwood flooring comes in two varieties, solid hardwood and engineered hardwood. Solid hardwood is made from a single plank while engineered wood features a wood veneer laminated over one or more layers of wood. Prices on these hardwoods can be up to $12 a square foot.

**VALUE:** Laminate flooring features either a wood veneer or a picture of wood laminated over a plywood or fiberboard base. It can pass for wood flooring but only costs up to $8 a square foot. This type of flooring can be cheaper to install and easier to live with. It resists sunlight-caused fading better than wood flooring. Laminate flooring is also wear-resistant, stain-resistant, scratch-resistant, and easy to clean.

**WHAT YOU GIVE UP:** Hardwood flooring can be refinished, adding years to its useful life. That means it lasts longer than laminate flooring and adds to your home's investment value.

# Secret weapon for decorators

Your camera phone can help you remodel, redecorate, and comparison shop. Use it to snap pictures of decorating ideas, products, or product features you see in shopping centers or elsewhere.

"I do this all the time to help me remember what things look like and to get my husband's opinion before dragging him out to the store," says Frances Harper. "It was a big help when we were replacing our bathroom vanity and fixtures. I took pictures of all the ones I liked in the different stores and later was able to compare how they would look in the bathroom itself."

This easy trick can help you make smarter buying choices, thus saving you time and money.

**DEEP DISCOUNT**

Cut out the furniture middleman, and pay yourself a 50-percent commission.

Just visit the furniture maker's factory outlet where you can find price discounts of 50 percent off. Many of these outlets are located in Hickory or High Point, North Carolina, so consider shopping there — especially if you need more than one piece of furniture. You can either take the furniture home yourself or have it shipped to you.

If you cannot visit a furniture maker's factory outlet, time your shopping to catch the best bargains near you. You can usually find the best local furniture sales in January and July.

## Buy furniture at rock-bottom prices

Here is a real estate industry secret you should know about. After all the homes in a new subdivision sell, the stunning furniture in the model home may be sold to the public — but at far cheaper prices than the same furniture in stores.

"I stumbled on a model-home sale while riding through a nearby neighborhood," says Mary Noble. "I couldn't believe the deals. I ended up buying artwork, an area rug, desk chair, and silk plants, along with some other beautiful things, for about $75. I only wish I had a truck available to move furniture. Next time I'll keep my ear open for sales like this so I can be more prepared."

If you would like to try this, look for new or nearly complete subdivisions in your area, and visit their model homes. Ask the real estate agent at the model home what happens to the furniture once the model home has sold. You may discover a way to buy some of the furnishings you have seen.

Also, keep an eye out for regular and charity auctions that feature furniture from model homes. Check the newspaper regularly since auctions may appear in news articles or the classifieds.

# Save money and control clutter

Every time you think you are almost organized, you find more clutter. How is this possible? Clutter does not just come from items you buy for yourself and your family. It also comes from your housewares, tools, furniture, and other products used to clean, decorate, or maintain your home. This clutter can get worse each time you bring home a new purchase. So before you buy anything for your house, ask yourself these questions.

+ Do I need this?

+ Do I have something like this already – or something I use for the same purpose?

+ Where will I place it or store it?

+ Will I use it? When?

+ If this replaces something I already have, will I bother to get rid of the old item?

+ Is this item of high enough quality to do what I need for years, or will I buy another one soon because this one broke or came up short?

+ Can this serve more than one purpose or have more than one use?

If you cannot remember all these questions, just remember the last two. They are two of the most important things to consider if you are constantly fighting the clutter battle or have very little space. If you limit your buying to the most important things, you will keep more money in your bank account and less clutter in your home.

# Spend less on repairs and replacements

Spare yourself the hassle and expense of avoidable repairs on electronics and appliances. Make them work well for longer with these tips.

**Refrigerator.** Wash the rubber gaskets that seal the doors with warm water and mild, bleach-free detergent. Rinse and let dry. Clean the compressor coils on the bottom or back of the refrigerator once a month.

**Personal computer.** Heat is like slow poison to computers. Make sure your computer has at least 6 inches of clearance on all sides so its ventilation system can keep it cool. Plug your entire computer setup into a surge protector to protect it from power surges.

**Dishwasher.** Check your dishwasher manual to see if the dishwasher has a filter. If so, find out how often the filter should be cleaned or changed, and follow that schedule. Dirty or damaged filters affect the dishwasher's other parts.

**Digital camera.** Protect your digital camera by storing it in its case when you do not expect to take a picture soon. But remember, dirt and grit in the case can damage your camera, so vacuum out your camera case occasionally with your vacuum cleaner's attachment for small spaces.

**Vacuum cleaner.** Any time your vacuum suddenly makes strange noises, starts to run oddly, or picks up unplanned objects, immediately turn off the vacuum and remove the item. Small objects can hamper the vacuum's workings or damage its parts. In addition, be sure to replace filters and bags at least once a year or to remove the canister and wipe it down with a sponge.

# How to shop without spending a penny

You can get things you need and get rid of the ones you don't, for free – and the store is closer than you think. In fact, just sit down at your computer and visit a "freecycling" site like the Freecycle Network.

Freecycle is an online community where people give items away for free. It's a no-hassle way to get rid of unwanted stuff. Local groups match up people who want to give or get free stuff, so landfills do not fill up with things that are still good. Join your local group, and you can "go shopping" for interior decor and home improvement items every day – and for many other products that may surprise you.

When someone posts an item you want, respond to that post with an email saying you want the item. Reply quickly or someone else may get there first. If the owner agrees to give you the item, simply work out an arrangement to pick it up. But that is not all freecycling can do for you. Your trash may be someone else's treasure. If you no longer need an item, but hate to throw it away, post it on your local Freecycle site and give it to someone who will appreciate it.

If you would like to try Freecycle or a similar group, visit one of these sites:

+ *www.freecycle.org*

+ *www.freesharing.org*

+ *www.freeuse.org*

**Safe & Secure**

Remember to take precautions like these when you use a giveaway site.

• Bring a friend with you when you pick up or give away an item.

• Avoid providing specific personal information such as your home address.

• Whenever possible, meet at a public location to transfer the item instead of inviting someone to your home.

# 3 cheap ways to organize your junk drawer

You could spend big bucks on a fancy organizer for your kitchen junk drawer, or you could try these money-saving ideas.

+ Ask a friend to save used baby food jars for you. Remove their labels, wash, and keep small items like twist ties or rubber bands in them.

+ Review the items in the drawer. Decide whether an egg carton or an inexpensive ice cube or silverware tray could be used to organize them.

+ Notice the packaging for items you buy. Items like berry baskets, cleaned butter tubs, small plastic containers, cleaned pill bottles, and small tea bag boxes can help organize items in your junk drawer.

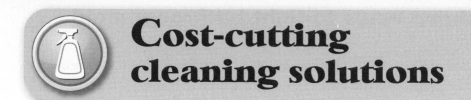

# Cost-cutting cleaning solutions

## Miracle worker no kitchen should be without

Baking soda is not just for the refrigerator anymore. Whether you have a dirty oven or a fire in your cooking pan, it's baking soda to the rescue.

**Try a 24-cent oven cleaner.** Use baking soda to clean your oven, and you will not only save money but do a lot less scrubbing, too. Just sprinkle baking soda over the bottom of your oven until lightly coated. Spritz with water from a clean sprayer until the baking soda is soggy, and let set overnight. When morning comes, either scoop the baking soda out of the oven with a spatula or wipe it away. The icky oven gunk should come up easily. Then just rinse.

This works because baking soda is alkaline, not acid, which makes it a good degreaser. Adding water and allowing the baking soda several hours to attack the dirt makes it even more effective. But that's not all. Ounce for ounce, baking soda is one-fourth the cost of a popular oven cleaner. Even if you only average two cans of oven cleaner a year, switching to baking soda can save you around $6.

**Use a homemade fire extinguisher.** Baking soda is cheap and small enough to store anywhere, so keep a large box of it within throwing distance of the stove. If a small grease fire flares up, stand back and quickly toss big handfuls of baking soda at the bottom end of the flames. Do not scrimp. The heated baking soda releases carbon dioxide to help smother the fire. In fact, that is why some fire extinguishers use baking soda in their firefighting solution.

Baking soda cannot put out all fires, so experts recommend you keep an all-purpose fire extinguisher in the kitchen, too.

# 3 cheap ways to fight bathroom mold

Brand name mold and mildew remover costs more than a gallon of gas. Try these instead.

+ Get mold and mildew off your shower curtain. Throw it in the washer with a half cup of bleach, or soak it for 15 minutes in a bathtub filled with water and one cup of bleach.

+ To erase mold from bathroom grout, mix equal amounts of water and household bleach in a spray bottle. Apply to grout, let sit a few minutes, and then scrub.

+ If you cannot use bleach, mix one-third cup of hydrogen peroxide with two-thirds cup of water, and spray that on the mold. Let set one hour and rinse.

**CASH SAVER**

Stubborn grout stains may tempt you to replace the grout between your kitchen or bathroom tiles, but one of these may give you clean grout for less.

• Fold a small piece of sandpaper in half and use the newly formed sandpaper edge to scrub the dirty parts of the grout.

• Rub dirty grout with a pencil eraser.

• Polish the stain away with a typewriter eraser.

# Discover 'sour power' for a sparkling clean home

You might be surprised to learn that vinegar is one of the secrets of professional house-cleaning services. They recommend tricks like these to help get kitchens and bathrooms squeaky clean.

+ Chlorine bleach may be a great disinfectant, but it can dull porcelain sinks and tubs. Dulled and roughened surfaces become tougher to clean. Fortunately, the acetic acid in white vinegar helps fight many kinds of bacteria. So shine up porcelain tubs and sinks by scrubbing them with vinegar. Then rinse with water.

+ Pour one to two cups of vinegar into your toilet, let sit for a few hours, scrub with a toilet brush, and flush. Acidic cleaners like vinegar are good at breaking up mineral deposits, rust, and stains that commonly appear in toilets, so this 25-cent toilet bowl cleaner will leave the porcelain sparkling. If you do not have time to wait, pour both vinegar and baking soda in the bowl, and scour with a brush.

+ Shine up a dull stainless steel sink with a cloth soaked in vinegar.

+ Mix one cup of vinegar into two quarts of water, and use this to scrub the walls and shelves of your refrigerator. Not only does it help clean the fridge, but it may also prevent mold and mildew.

+ Vinegar is also a must-have nontoxic, all-purpose cleaner. Mix it with an equal amount of water, and use this cleaner on almost anything except granite countertops, marble, and paint.

## Save big on window cleaner

Never pay for window cleaner again. For a regular-strength formula, mix one quart of water with one tablespoon of white vinegar for 32 ounces of cleaning power. A popular 32-ounce solution costs $4.19 while a tablespoon of vinegar costs about a penney, so you'll save at least $4.

For an extra-strength formula, mix a half teaspoon of mild dishwashing liquid, three tablespoons of vinegar, and two cups of water. Pour it into a spray bottle, and you're ready to go.

## Pennywise ways to get rid of odors

Forget special sprays and high-priced deodorizers. Switch to these and count up your savings.

✦ To deodorize your microwave, pour a cup of water in a large, microwave-safe bowl, and add lemon juice or chopped lemon rind. Heat this in the microwave until the water starts to boil.

✦ Put fresh coffee grounds in a small bowl or a paper lunch bag, and tuck it deep inside your refrigerator. Coffee may also work well in other enclosed spaces, such as kitchen cabinets or the cabinet where you keep your garbage can. Charcoal briquettes also absorb odors in enclosed spaces like refrigerators. Put several in a lid-free plastic container.

✦ To keep odors at bay in closets or rooms, try a large box of baking soda or a dish of vinegar. Smaller containers of vinegar or baking soda may work in refrigerators, drawers, and cabinets. Use baking soda anywhere a vinegar spill might cause trouble.

✦ For an odor-fighting spray, mix vinegar with water or use vinegar alone. Spray this regularly on smelly trash cans and any non-granite kitchen and bathroom surfaces. For a sweeter-smelling spray, mix two cups of hot water with a tablespoon each of lemon juice and baking soda.

No-Sweat Solution

Some cleaning jobs are so tough that only a store-bought cleaner will do. When that happens, you may prefer "green" products to protect your health. But very little regulation governs what qualifies as green, so businesses can label their products that way even if the product is somewhat toxic.

To avoid spending your hard-earned money on products that are not truly green, you could spend hours learning which ingredients are safe and which are toxic — or you could simply look for products that carry the Environmental Protection Agency's (EPA) Design for the Environment (DfE) seal. This means the product has been examined by the EPA and has the safest available ingredients to get the job done. If you cannot find a product with the DfE seal, check for the Green Seal Certified label.

# Simple no-polish silver solution

Make your sterling silverware gleam without paying a penny for polish. Find a large, flat-bottomed dish or pan, line it with aluminum foil, and spread your tarnished silverware on the foil. Avoid stacking silverware pieces on top of one another.

Add several inches of water, mix in one teaspoon of baking soda and one teaspoon of salt, and let sit for awhile. If the silver is badly tarnished and you are using a stove-safe pan, bring the water to a boil, add the silver, then boil for one to three minutes. Let cool, rinse the silverware, and dry with a soft cloth.

# Say goodbye to pricey screen cleaners

Use this cheap computer screen cleaning tactic from the experts instead of a special screen cleaner kit, and you could save yourself at least $5.

Find two soft, lint-free cotton cloths. Be picky because a rag, facial tissue, toilet tissue, hand towel, or paper towel may damage the LCD screen. A clean cotton handkerchief or cotton underwear is fine.

With the computer off, wipe dust off the screen with the dry cotton cloth. Wipe very lightly, because slight pressure may damage tiny wires hidden in the screen surface.

If the screen is unusually dirty, mix equal parts of water and vinegar, and spray the solution on the cloth. Never spray the screen directly because this may damage it. Wipe the screen very lightly using gentle strokes in the same direction. Dry it gently with the dry, lint-free cloth.

# Frugal secret: make your own gentle scrubber

Stop paying $3 to $4 for a bottle of soft-scrub cleaner. You can make your own at a fraction of the cost.

Pour one-third cup of baking soda into a bowl, and add just enough dishwashing liquid to make a paste. Apply this anywhere you would normally use a soft-scrub cleaner. This dries quickly, so spritz the area you are cleaning with a spray bottle of water, if needed. For small areas, non-whitening toothpaste can also be a good, gentle scrubber.

## Bargain tricks to unstick stickers

Easily remove a bumper sticker, window sticker, or kid's stickers with one of these clever money savers.

+ For hard surfaces that can take higher temperatures, heat the area with a hair dryer for a minute or two. Try to gently pull the sticker up. If that does not work, try a little more heat before attempting to pull the sticker up again. If the sticker comes away cleanly, you have just saved the $3 cost of a small bottle of adhesive remover.

+ If the sticker remains stubbornly fixed to the surface or comes up but leaves a mess, brush the area with a few layers of vinegar. Let dry for several minutes, and remove the sticker or its leftovers.

+ Coat a stubborn sticker in a glaze of mayonnaise, and let sit for awhile. This may be particularly effective if you cannot scrape the surface. The mayo should dissolve the gunky mess so you can simply rub it away.

Before you use vinegar or mayonnaise, test it on an inconspicuous spot to make sure these helpers will not damage the surface.

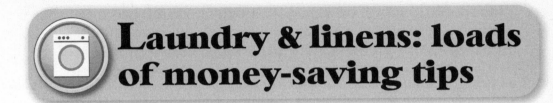

# Laundry & linens: loads of money-saving tips

## Zap stains while pinching pennies

Make your own dirt-cheap stain removers as an alternative to expensive commercial solutions.

**Lipstick.** It doesn't always stay on your lips, but these common household items can help wipe it away.

+ Work a little white toothpaste into lipstick-stained fabric, then launder as usual. Don't use gel toothpaste.

+ Rub petroleum jelly into lipstick traces left on linen napkins, then wash.

+ Apply a few drops of liquid glycerin to the stain, then treat with commercial stain remover or detergent. Wash in cool water.

**Ring around the collar.** Blame body oil for this greasy stain. Simply squirt a little shampoo on the collar and rub together before tossing it in the washer.

**Coffee.** Sometimes that first sip ends up on your shirt instead of in your mouth. Quickly rinse the stain away with cold water, then blot with a solution of one part vinegar to two parts water. Rinse again and wash.

**Ballpoint pen ink.** Stretch the smudged area over the mouth of a jar or glass. Slowly drip rubbing alcohol on the stain. As it drops into the jar, it will pull the ink out with it. Test a small area first to see if alcohol harms the clothing's color. Air dry.

**Red wine.** Sprinkle a hefty dose of salt on freshly spilled red wine to absorb it, then try to rub out the stain in cold water. For dry wine stains, try club soda or vinegar.

**Mustard.** Scrape off the excess with a dull knife, then soak the stain in a mixture of water and liquid dish detergent for 10 to 15 minutes. Rinse with warm water and machine wash on the warmest setting the garment can safely handle. Air dry. Repeat the whole process, if needed.

You can also try warm liquid glycerin. Rub it into the stain and launder as usual. Glycerin may help remove ketchup stains, too.

**Perspiration.** First, soak the garment in detergent and water. Wash it in the warmest water the fabric can safely take, and air dry. If the stain hasn't budged, it's probably caused by deodorant ingredients. Spray white vinegar on old stains. Next, treat them with a pre-wash stain remover or rub them with a bar of soap. Wash the garment again in the warmest water safe for it. For fresh deodorant stains, apply ammonia and wash.

# Clean laundry for half the cost

Save 50 to 90 percent on the cost of laundry detergent with easy "recipes" that let you make your own. Homemade detergent costs between 2 cents and 5 cents a load, compared to name brands at 20 cents a load. Even discount detergents from bulk-buying stores can run about twice as much per load as the homemade kind.

You'll find lots of recipes for do-it-yourself detergent, but most involve three ingredients — Borax, washing soda, and a bar soap such as Fels-Naptha, Ivory, or Zote. Wear rubber gloves while handling the ingredients, and avoid inhaling them.

**Liquid laundry detergent.** Shave down an entire bar of soap with an old grater. Add it to four cups of boiling water a little at a time, stirring until it dissolves. Pour three gallons of warm tap water into a large container, like a clean five-gallon bucket. To this, add half a cup of Borax, one cup of washing soda (not baking soda), and the stove-top soap solution. Stir until dissolved.

Tamp on a lid and let the mixture sit for 24 hours. Stir well, then pour into smaller bottles for everyday use. Shake it up before adding to the wash. Start with one cup of detergent per load.

**Powdered laundry detergent.** The recipe is roughly the same, only without water. Finely grate two cups of bar soap and mix thoroughly with one cup of washing soda and one cup of Borax. Use around two tablespoons per load.

No matter which kind you choose, make a small amount first to see how it works in your water, in your machine, and on your clothes before investing in a big batch. Liquid detergent may do better than powder for cold-water washing and for removing grease and oil. Powder, on the other hand, may better clean heavily soiled clothing.

Hard water may cause clothes to come out dingy-looking. In that case, add half a cup of baking soda during the wash cycle or vinegar in the rinse for a color boost. Do not add vinegar to a load containing chlorine bleach.

## Spot the best deal with this shopping secret

Store stickers that tell you the price of a product per unit usually help you find good deals. But one little item on the label can make it totally meaningless. When you see the phrase "2X" on the label of laundry detergent, ignore the per-unit price.

Products labeled 2X and 3X are more concentrated than the regular versions. They tend to cost more, but you need less of them. The per-unit price on these items doesn't make for the best measure of value. Instead, carry your calculator to the store. Divide the retail price by the number of loads each detergent claims it will wash. This will give you an apples-to-apples comparison of the cost of different brands.

## Stretch your detergent dollars

Make your detergent last twice as long and get your clothes just as clean by halving the amount you wash with. Most detergents these days are concentrated, so you need less to get the same cleaning effect. Products labeled "concentrated" or "ultra" contain less water, meaning a little goes a long way.

Lots of folks don't know this. They end up using twice as much detergent as they need. Cutting that amount in half could save you $80 a year. Plus, excess detergent makes your clothing stiff and dingy, not cleaner. The extra soap keeps water from releasing the dirt and stains in fabric. It also shortens the life of your washer.

Always use the bottle's cap to measure liquid detergent — don't eyeball it and pour. Caps today have small lines on the inside to help you get the right amount. Use the lowest line for most loads, unless your clothes are super dirty. Trace over hard-to-see measuring lines with a permanent marker to make them more visible.

Are you pouring money down the drain by using too much detergent? There are two ways to tell.

- Check the window. You shouldn't see soap suds during the wash cycle in a front-loading, high-efficiency (HE) washer. These machines take specially formulated low-sudsing soaps.

- Run a clean bath towel through a hot-water wash in a top-loader, but don't add detergent. Watch for suds to form. Any signs of soap are left over from the last wash, telling you to cut back.

Clean the built-up soap out of your washer by running an empty hot-water wash cycle with bleach once a month. Rid clothes of soapy buildup by adding a cup of white vinegar to the final rinse cycle. It naturally dissolves the chemicals in soaps and detergents. Don't use vinegar and bleach in the same load. The two together produce toxic fumes.

## Savvy ways to save on softeners

Stop spending a fortune on fancy fabric softeners and dryer sheets. You can make your own for pennies.

+ Add half a cup of vinegar to the final rinse cycle of each load.

+ Pour half a cup of baking soda into each rinse cycle for top-loading washers. Use one-quarter cup for front-loaders.

+ Dab a small amount of liquid fabric softener on a clean rag and toss into the dryer with wet clothes. This softens fabric and fights static cling.

## Laundry secrets fight shrinking budgets

Washing and drying your clothes the right way can significantly cut costs. You'll save on water, electricity, heating, bleach, and clothing wear and tear with these simple tips.

+ Wash only full loads, and you'll save up to 3,400 gallons of water each year.

+ Set the water for cold water rinses, not warm, to cut heating costs.

+ Get the same whitening with half as much bleach. Simply add one-quarter to one-half cup of baking soda to the wash with chlorine bleach.

+ Dry loads one after the other. They'll dry faster once the machine is warmed up. Start with delicate, lightweight clothing first, and do heavy towels last. They can handle the heat buildup.

+ Wash and dry similar fabrics together. They will dry more evenly and in less time.

+ Lengthen the life of your clothing and dryer. Use your machine's moisture sensor, if it has one, to avoid over-drying clothes.

+ Improve your dryer's efficiency. Scrub the lint filter once a month with an old toothbrush and dish soap to remove the film dryer sheets leave behind. And remember to clean lint from the filter after each load.

+ Line drying works well for some items, but put underwear, sheets, and towels in the dryer, if you washed them in anything other than hot water. Cold and warm water may not kill all the bacteria. Machine-drying helps finish them off.

✦ Wash and dry towels, sweatshirts, and other linty fabrics separately from sheets and smooth fabrics that tend to pill.

## Starch made simple, for less

Keep more money in your pocket by spraying on homemade starch. Dissolve one tablespoon of cornstarch into two cups of cold water, then pour into a spray bottle. Shake it well before each use.

Say goodbye to expensive aerosol cans and look for concentrated liquid starch. One 64-ounce bottle of Sta-Flo, for instance, claims to equal seven cans of aerosol. For a light starch, mix one part starch with two parts water and pour into a spray bottle. For crisper edges, mix equal parts water and starch.

**DEEP DISCOUNT**

Experts say you could save $60 a year simply by washing most of your clothes in cold water. Heating up the water accounts for up to 90 percent of the cost of washing. Most garments get just as clean in cold, especially if you use a detergent made for it like Tide 2X Ultra for Cold Water.

Save the hot water for cleaning very dirty or greasy clothes, and for washing towels, washcloths, bed linens, undergarments, and other clothing worn against the body. These may harbor bacteria that hot water can kill.

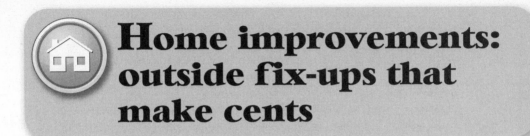

# Home improvements: outside fix-ups that make cents

## Increase the value of your home by thousands

One inexpensive upgrade may help you rake in more money when the time comes to sell your home.

A recent study sponsored by the Therma-Tru Doors company suggests the appearance of a home's entry can drastically affect the price people expect to pay for the house. People who were shown a house with a new, enhanced entry door estimated the home's price to be up to $24,000 higher than people shown the same home with a standard door.

The enhanced entry door included a new fiberglass door with decorative glass, sidelites, and a transom. It's an inexpensive upgrade compared to others you can make, and the study suggests you could get up to five times your money back when you sell your home.

Even if you simply replace your old door with a new steel door, research reported by *Remodeling* magazine suggests you will get 102 percent of your money back when you sell your home. Most home improvement projects cost far more but give far less of a return. Even an economical new entry door improves the look and curb appeal of your home, and that could save you extra money by ensuring your house spends less time on the market.

# Get home repairs without spending a dime

You might be surprised to learn that you can get home repairs — or any product or service — without shrinking your bank account. The secret is to barter or trade for something you want.

**Determine your trading power.** Bartering can be easier than you think. Say Margaret's handyman expresses an interest in the $60 item she was preparing to put in a yard sale, Margaret could offer him the item instead of paying his $60 hourly fee. Or Margaret's plumber comes to check her leaky faucet, notices a quilt she made, and mentions that his wife wants one. When the plumber tells Margaret he can replace her leaky faucet for $120, she could offer to make him a quilt worth $120 instead.

You may also have something to barter if you:

+ enjoy doing a chore that most people dislike.

+ have a hobby or skill you can offer or teach.

+ have time to run errands or do other tasks when others cannot.

**Learn the ins and outs.** To warm up your bartering skills, get an idea of the cash value of what you offer and what you want.

Newspaper ads, bargain bulletins, or researching online can help. But keep in mind that the value the other person places on it may be equally important.

Next, ask your friends, family, and colleagues if any of them do handyman work, home repairs, or other services you need – or if they know someone who does. Use the same method to find people with products you want. Then find out if that person would be interested in any items or services you can offer to trade.

When you barter, be sure to:

+ discuss the value of each item being traded and agree on a trade that is of equal value to both sides.

+ outline the details of the trade, including when and how long the trade will occur.

+ put the terms of the deal in writing. A written contract, even an informal one, is a good idea.

Keep in mind that some bartering is taxable, such as trades you profit from or trades between businesses. Many personal trades are not taxable, but check with an accountant to be sure.

## Surefire tip for longer paint life

Store your paint properly so you will not have to buy more when you need that color again. Before putting the lid on the can, cover the open top in plastic wrap. Then put the lid on. Use a mallet or piece of wood to rap on the lid, and make sure it is sealed shut. Check closely to be certain the lid is secure.

Grab a heavy-duty cardboard box lid, an old bucket or dishpan, or any leakproof container. Place it on the floor where you plan to store the paint, and place the paint can upside down inside the container. Storing the can upside down creates a tight seal that keeps the paint like new. Be careful to store the paint where it will not be exposed to extreme temperatures.

Try storing leftover paint in a clean, plastic peanut butter jar. This container will not rust and leaves less room for air to dry out your paint. The mouth is wide enough for a paintbrush, and you can hold the jar in one hand. Just remember to label it so you know exactly what type of paint you have.

# 4 worst home improvement projects

Some home improvements can actually lower your home's value because they may scare potential buyers away when you get ready to sell. That can mean fewer offers and more time waiting for a sale. Even worse, the remaining buyers may reduce their offers to make up for a home improvement they do not want. So resist making changes like these.

+ Adding a swimming pool. Many people do not want the cost or work of maintaining a pool and are afraid of the potential for lawsuits.

+ Changing your garage. Think twice before adding an extra bay to your garage or converting your garage into a home office. Too much or too little space for cars and storage may frighten buyers away.

+ Introducing unique renovations. Beware of adding extremely unique features like bell towers or castle turrets to your home. What looks like Cinderella's castle to one person may look like Dracula's castle to buyers. You may even get lowball offers as a result.

+ Installing a built-in Jacuzzi. This may require more maintenance than some buyers want, while others simply have no desire or use for a hot tub.

# Checklist for remodeling success

Taking the right steps before you begin a remodeling project can save you a lot of money, time, and hassle. Start with these.

+ Make as detailed a plan as possible for your remodel. Consider aspects like where you may need electrical outlets, how things should be laid out, which materials and fixtures you want, and the order in which remodeling tasks should be done.

+ If you need financing, shop around to determine how you will pay for the project.

+ Ask your insurer how the remodeling may affect your home-owners insurance, both during and after the project.

+ Contact the state and local licensing agencies to make sure the contractor meets licensing requirements, and ask the contractor for a copy of his license.

+ Check with the Better Business Bureau and government Consumer Affairs Office to see if complaints have been lodged against a contractor you are considering.

+ Ask for a copy of the contractor's certification of insurance, or get the name of his insurance company and verify that he is covered for worker's compensation, property damage, and personal liability.

**Safe & Secure**

Beware of contractors who only accept cash, ask you to obtain building permits, go door-to-door to find business, or cannot offer a phone number associated with a valid business. The Federal Trade Commission also advises you to avoid any contractor who:

• offers a discount if allowed to use leftover materials from a prior job.

• offers to fund your remodeling through his preferred lender.

• pressures you to hire him on the spot rather than allowing you time to think about it.

# Cheap projects that rev up home resale value

You do not have to spend a lot of money to spruce up your house and rev up its resale value.

HomeGain.com, a website for homeowners trying to maximize their home's value, surveyed more than 2,000 real estate agents around the country. They found that inexpensive improvements like these give you the biggest bang for your buck and may be worth thousands at resale.

+ Clean your home and clear away unnecessary furniture and clutter.

+ Add light by opening drapes, cleaning windows, and making sure your light fixtures work.

+ Clean up, trim, and landscape the yard.

+ Repair electrical and plumbing problems.

+ Replace or shampoo carpeting.

+ Paint interior walls a neutral color, and repaint your home's exterior walls.

You can also dramatically improve the look of your home's exterior by painting your front door. For $30 and an hour of your time, you'll have a simple update that will last for years. Experts recommend choosing a striking color like red.

# Tricks to picking a fabulous door

When your old front door warps and becomes drafty, it is time to bite the bullet and replace the door. But door technology now offers you more money-saving choices than ever before, so finding the right door may depend on which features are most important to you.

**TOP DOLLAR:** Wood doors start at $500 and may cost as much as $2,500. They are heavier and less likely to dent than other doors.

They are slow to show wear and tear, too. But wood doors also require regular varnishing or repainting and can warp when exposed to high moisture levels.

**VALUE:** Steel doors only cost $135 to $1,550 while fiberglass doors cost between $300 and $1,750. Fiberglass and steel doors both require less maintenance and will not warp. Fiberglass doors are also very durable, dent-resistant, and weather-resistant. And recent testing by *Consumer Reports* suggests a steel door can be just as good at keeping out the elements and adding to your home's security as other doors, but at a significantly lower price.

**WHAT YOU GIVE UP:** The look of luxury and the durability of heavy wood that takes a long time to show wear and tear.

# Make sure your pro isn't a con

The house of your dreams can turn into a remodeling nightmare if the contract does not protect you properly. Make sure your professional contractor isn't trying to "con" you in any way. Read your contract thoroughly, and perhaps even ask a lawyer to look it over. At the very least, be aware of the three clauses you must put in the contract and one "standard" clause you should never allow.

**Clause #1** – Spell out the details of exactly what needs to be accomplished during each stage of the remodeling, including the steps you think they ought to automatically include. Link payments to each stage.

**Clause #2** – Specify start and finish dates for the project. This can include some additional time for unexpected problems like severe weather but not enough to let the project drag on for many extra months.

**Clause #3** – Specify the brand, color, size, and quality of materials like appliances, fixtures, and anything else that will be used. Include the model number when possible.

Never allow the standard clause that lets the contractor substitute materials – even materials "of equal or better quality" – unless the clause also requires your written approval of the change before the item can be installed.

Make sure your contract also specifies or includes:

+ the contractor's full name, address, and telephone number.

+ the total cost for all work, including estimates or extra labor.

+ a detailed description of how change orders should be handled.

+ written versions of any verbal promises the contractor made.

+ a promise that the contractor will get all required permits.

You should not have to buy new paintbrushes every time you paint. The secret is to know how to clean and store paintbrushes so you can use them again.

If you painted with water-based paint, wash the brush in a bucket of warm water and detergent, and rinse under running water. If you painted with oil-based paint, clean the paintbrush in a shallow pool of paint thinner poured into a bucket. Rinse under running water. Then wash and rinse the brush the same way you would for water-based paint.

To store the brush, wrap it in aluminum foil or plastic wrap and hang it up. If this does not keep the bristles soft enough, coat the bristles in petroleum jelly or dishwashing liquid before wrapping the brush.

## Calculate the perfect amount of paint

Never buy more paint than you need thanks to this nifty trick. Use a tape measure to take measurements of the surfaces you plan to paint. Then calculate how many total square feet that covers.

+ If an area is rectangular, round each measurement up to the nearest foot or half foot. Then, multiply length times width.

+ If an area is irregularly shaped, divide it up into rectangles as precisely as possible. Figure the area of each rectangle, and add up all the figures.

Divide your total square feet by 425 to estimate how many gallons of paint you need. This may leave you with a little paint left over, but not an extra gallon or two. Besides, small amounts of leftover paint may be useful for touch-ups or cleanups later.

# 5 home repairs you should never ignore

Some home repairs can be put off, but others become more expensive, damaging, or dangerous the longer you wait. If you need any of these home repairs, do them now so you can avoid spending thousands more later.

**Cracks.** Beware of cracks in your home's foundation. If you find a vertical hairline crack and cannot fit the edge of a sheet of paper into it, just mark it with tape or a pencil and watch for spreading. But quarter-inch wide vertical or horizontal cracks — or any crack you can fit a No. 2 pencil eraser in — should be checked by a structural engineer, especially if you see bulging or buckling in your foundation. Foundation repair can cost more than $10,000, so do not wait.

**Gutters, grading, or drainage problems.** Anything that causes water to pool around your foundation can lead to foundation problems. That includes faulty gutters, improper yard grading, or other drainage problems. Get them fixed quickly.

**Mold and mildew.** Fix leaks promptly. Also, watch out for either colored wall or ceiling spots you cannot clean, or musty smells that begin about the same time as a rash of colds or allergies in your household. These may warn of mold inside walls or ceilings.

To clean moldy areas less than 10 square feet in size, wear heavy gloves, goggles, and an N95 respirator, and use a mixture of 10 cups of water and one cup of bleach. For larger areas or places that cannot be reached, contact a mold remediation company. Expect to pay about $3,000 per wall.

**Roof damage.** Your roof keeps water – and water damage – out of your home. Either have it inspected professionally or use binoculars to check for damaged, curly, or missing shingles.

**Termites.** Take steps to check for and prevent termites and other pests. Termites alone can do thousands in damage to your home.

**CASH SAVER**

If you have a computer, you can learn how to do just about anything yourself. A one-stop resource you shouldn't miss is the website *www.findhow*.com. You will find clear, detailed instructions from reputable sources to help you tackle repairs like fixing a gutter, take on home improvements like installing a kitchen counter, or ace other tasks such as making jam or packing for a trip. Or visit *www.fixitclub.com* for easy instructions on how to repair nearly anything around the house from coffee makers to clothes dryers.

# When hiring a pro can save money

Do-it-yourself (DIY) home improvements can often save money, but if you don't do the project right, it could end up costing you more. Hiring a professional tradesman or a handyman is sometimes a smarter move. The trick is to know who should do each job.

**Call a professional.** Anything that requires new wiring or plumbing, structural work, tree removal, or repairs to your air conditioner or furnace should be done by a professional. Mistakes in these areas could be costly to repair, not to mention dangerous, and you want to make sure the work can pass a home inspection.

**Rely on a handyman.** A handyman has less experience than a licensed electrician or plumber but is also less expensive. You may prefer him for jobs like installing ceiling fans, painting, replacing flooring, installing a new faucet, and unclogging drains.

The American College of Emergency Physicians has reported a recent jump in DIY injuries, so consider your risk of expensive injury before taking on a project yourself. Ladder injuries, for example, send thousands to the emergency room every year.

# Budget-friendly backyard tips and tricks

## Save big with self-seeding flowers

Imagine getting five years' worth of annuals at 80 percent off and only having to plant them once. Self-seeding annuals can do this for you because these low-cost "annuals" come back year after year. Examples of popular self-sowing annuals include Mexican aster *(Cosmos)*, pot marigold *(Calendula officinalis)*, spider flower *(Cleome spinosa)*, and snapdragon *(Antirrhinum)*. Discover what your garden center may not tell you about starting and caring for these cost-savers.

+ You may already have some self-sowers in your yard. In early spring, check for "volunteer" seedlings from flowers that you did not sow or plant. They may come from flowers you already have or from your neighbor's garden – and they cost nothing.

+ If you must buy self-sowing annuals, look for hardy annuals. Your best bets are native plants or plants from places with similar climate and soil.

+ Make sure your self-sowing area stays undisturbed. Plant your annuals where water will not wash the seeds away, and water gently enough to keep from washing the seeds away yourself. Mark the area so you will not accidentally clean it up, mow it down, or prepare it for different plants.

+ When you "deadhead" to remove dead flowers, be sure to leave a few untouched so you can harvest those seeds later. The more seeds you want, the less deadheading you should do.

+ You have three ways to get more flowers from self-sowers. You can let the seeds fall near the original plant for a clump of flow-ers. You can transplant any volunteer seedlings to wherever you want them once they develop three sets of leaves. Or you can collect the seeds that often hide behind fading flowers. Wait until these seeds have dried to harvest them. Then collect them in an envelope and keep in the refrigerator until time to plant.

+ Contact your county extension agent for more advice on the selection, care and overwintering of self-seeding annuals in your area.

## Slash your backyard costs

You can have the best-looking yard in town without all the watering and chemicals. Here is how to start.

Notice which plants in your yard, including grass, require the most watering, pesticides, herbicides, or fertilizer. These contribute the most dollars to your yard-care costs. Consider trading away these high-cost plants in exchange for plants native to your area. Native plants are less likely to need fertilizer, herbicides, or pesticides. Native plants also require less watering and care once they get established.

To find out which plants are native to your area, check with your state or local native plant society, visit your area cooperative extension website, contact your cooperative extension agent, or visit *www.plantnative.org*.

As you replace your high-maintenance plants with less costly substitutes, keep these tips in mind.

+ Ask your county extension agent which species of native plants can be planted close together to block out weeds.

+ When you cannot use a native plant, choose plants like daylilies that are famous for being tough to kill.

+ Opt for little or no lawn. The average suburban lawn gets 10 times as much pesticide per acre as farmland and accounts for at least 30 percent of water used, the National Wildlife Federation reports. Unfortunately, the cost of all that pesticide and water comes right out of your wallet. Replace grass with ground cover or with low maintenance native or ornamental grasses.

+ Choose drought-tolerant plants for parts of the yard that dry out quickly, such as unshaded areas in the southern or western sides of the yard.

+ Emphasize trees and shrubs in your landscape. Most of them require less care than other plants.

**Freebie Frenzie**

The best things in life are free, and that may include compost for your garden. Contact your city or county department for waste, sanitation, or recycling to find out if they have a program for free compost. The free compost may be available year round or on a certain day each year. Ask what requirements you must meet to get your compost, including what containers to bring, whether you must participate in related programs, and whether you must bring proof that you are a local resident.

# Dig up plant bargains

You can buy from the same plant nurseries as your neighbors but pay significantly lower prices than they do. Two simple secrets are all you need.

**Buy and plant in autumn.** This tactic can be successful whether you live in Georgia's warmth or in cooler climates like the Midwest. Experts say many plants, particularly perennials and trees, thrive after an autumn planting. This happens because the still-warm soil temperatures encourage better root growth than the cooler soil temperatures of spring. So contact your county extension agent to find out exactly when to do fall planting in your area.

Many garden centers and garden departments also have clearance sales during autumn to reduce inventory for the winter or make room for holiday products. Just remember that some of these clearance plants may be potbound or have other problems, so be sure to check the plant over carefully before buying or planting. Your new purchase may need a little tender loving care in order to thrive.

**Start them young.** If autumn planting is not right for you, but you still want a cheaper, store-bought plant, think small. Instead of buying the 10-gallon container, choose the same plant in a smaller size. The smaller plant will probably catch up to its larger siblings in a few years because larger plants take a while to recover from their extra time in containers.

**CASH SAVER**

Don't replace perfectly good lawn furniture just because it is dirty or rusty. Try one of these to make your old favorites look like new again and to avoid the sticker shock of new furniture.

- For plastic mesh lawn furniture or light-colored lawn chairs, mix two-thirds cup of household bleach and a tablespoon of detergent in a gallon of warm water. Apply to a small spot on the underside of the item, let sit for five minutes, and rinse. If no discoloration appears, use this technique on the entire item to make it sparkling clean.

- To remove light rust from metal lawn furniture, make a paste of lemon or lime juice and salt, and apply to rusty areas. Let sit for 10 minutes and scrub the rust off. Rinse and dry the areas you have treated.

# Harvest great deals on mulch

Get the mulch you need for cheap or even free. You will be surprised at how many ways you can do it.

**Use leftovers.** Contact local arborists or tree trimmers who frequent your area to ask if they will dump their leftover wood chips at your house.

**Benefit from your tax dollars.** Check with your local government's parks or public works department or your local cooperative extension agent to see if your local government offers wood chips or other types of mulch for free.

**Let sleeping dogs lie.** Leave pine needles and leaves where they are if they fall into beds or islands. Otherwise, collect them and redistribute them to the beds and patches where they can do the most good. Grass clippings can also be good mulch as long as they are free of herbicides, are allowed to dry before use, and are spread thinly.

**Always be ready.** Keep an old shower curtain, tarp, painter's drop cloth, or old bed sheet in your trunk for collecting mulch. You never know when you might stumble across a freebie.

**Reuse the newspaper.** Mulch with several sheets of newspaper or with shredded newspaper in your vegetable garden. Just be sure to put organic mulch on top of the newspaper so it will not blow away.

**Buy bargain bags.** Check your local garden centers or home improvement centers for a pile of deeply discounted, torn bags of mulch. Check to see how much mulch has been lost before you buy.

# 5 ways to cut your outdoor water bill

Even if you only have a stretch of lawn that is 20 feet by 20 feet, you may be spending up to $100 a year in watering costs alone — and that does not include the costs of watering trees, roses, shrubs, or a vegetable garden. Use these tips to reduce your watering needs without killing your grass or plants.

+ Instead of watering grass every day or week during hot weather, water when the blades curl at the tips; when they turn bluish green, gray green, or dull; or when the grass stops springing back into place when you step on it. Place an empty can where the sprinkler water will fall into it, and stop watering when the water measures 1-inch deep. Time how long this takes, and use a kitchen timer or wristwatch alarm to remind you to turn off the water.

+ Water in the early morning so you lose less water to daytime evaporation and wind.

+ Mulch flower beds generously to help them retain moisture in the soil.

+ Use a soaker hose to water trees, flower beds, vegetable gardens, and shrubs. You can also try "drip irrigation" that puts water straight into the ground. Just poke holes in the bottom of gallon milk jugs or two-liter soft drink bottles, fill them with water, and place around your plant.

+ Check for leaky hose connections, leaky hoses, and sprinkler leaks. Just a few small leaks in the garden hose or its connectors can waste hundreds of gallons of water in less than a month.

## Cash in on free water

You could be getting free water from your roof every time it rains. In fact, just one good thunderstorm could mean 50-60 gallons of free water for your plants. But you need a rain barrel to collect that rain, and those can be expensive. Fortunately, some cities give away free rain barrels or rain barrel kits or instructions on how to make your own rain barrel cheaply. Contact your water company and local government to find out what is available.

**No-Sweat Solution**

Try this bargain squirrel stopper. Instead of replacing your bird feeder with an expensive, squirrel-proof model, buy a cheap, silver slinky. Fasten one end of the slinky to the underside of your bird feeder and position the bottom circle of the slinky around the top of the feeder's supporting pole so it can drop to the ground. The slinky should surround the feeder pole from top to bottom. Reattach the bird feeder to the pole. Now the squirrels can no longer climb up to the bird feeder.

Of course, some squirrels may try to jump down to the feeder from a nearby roof or tree, so place the feeder well away from any potential "launch platforms." If you cannot move the feeder, make sure the feeder is metal, not plastic. Squirrels have chewed through plastic bird feeders.

# Smart and cheap lawn repair

Lawn-patching mixes and kits can save time because they combine grass seed with products that help retain moisture and fool hungry birds. But making your own lawn-patching mix may be cheaper if you already have the ingredients on hand. Just blend grass seed with peat moss.

If you need to buy those supplies, check their prices and compare the total cost to the prices of lawn-patching kits. Buying a package of peat moss and a small 1-pound bag of grass seed can cost around $10. Some grass-patching mixes cost less than $5 while others cost $10 or more. If a cheap grass-patching kit is available with seeds that grow well in your area, then you may be better off buying the kit.

On the other hand, if the product contains the wrong grass seed or if you already have good seed on hand, buying peat moss may be the cheapest way to go. This is one case where it pays to compare.

# Professional landscaping for less

You have always wanted to add raised beds, solve that drainage problem, or even landscape the yard for low maintenance — and now it is finally time. But landscaping can be tricky, and you may want professional advice.

**TOP DOLLAR:** Expect to spend $1,000 to $3,000 for a landscape plan from a landscape architect, while the cost of a plan from a certified landscape designer may cost between $375 and $1,350.

**VALUE:** Your local garden nursery can design you a landscape plan that may cost from $240 to $400. Some even offer them for free if you buy the plants from their nursery.

**WHAT YOU GIVE UP:** Landscape architects are college-educated, trained, and licensed professionals who understand all aspects of landscape planning, drainage correction, grading and erosion issues, and landscape-related construction. Certified landscape designers do not have the licensing and construction training of landscape architects, but they have expertise in designing with plants and can create a customized plan for your yard.

A landscape plan from a nursery may require purchases from the nursery, but you may also get discounts or rebates on their plants and supplies. You may receive a wonderful plan that works well for years or end up with a cookie-cutter plan that does not fully adapt to your yard's characteristics. Still, it can be a fairly inexpensive way to create a yard you can be proud of.

**No-Sweat Solution**

Having trouble keeping your grass looking nice? Maybe you should check your lawnmower blades.

Mowing should help keep your lawn looking sharp, but a dull blade can weaken turf, says Dr. Aaron Patton, assistant professor and extension turfgrass specialist for the University of Arkansas Division of Agriculture. "Sharply cut leaf blades increase turf health by improving recovery, decreasing water loss, and increasing photosynthesis," he says, adding that lawns mown with a dull blade heal more slowly, have greater water loss, and simply don't look as nice.

Diagnosing a dull mower blade is simple. If the grass blade has a single, clean cut across the top, the mower is in good shape. However, if the edge is ragged or there are signs of previous, incomplete strikes on the grass blade, there's a good chance the mower blades need sharpening.

"Sharpen mower blades at least twice a year or more often for larger lawns," Patton recommends.

# Home insurance: protection for less

## 5 steps to take after disaster strikes

You get what you pay for. At least that's what you'd like to think – especially when it comes to homeowners insurance. But to get what you deserve takes some effort on your part. After disaster strikes, here are five steps you must take to get everything your premiums paid for – or you could be left out in the cold.

**Take steps to stop further damage.** Board up broken windows or put a tarp over a leaky roof. Keep receipts for temporary fixes, like the tarp. But don't make any repairs or replace anything until meeting with an adjustor.

**Take photos.** You need to document the damage. But don't throw away damaged items before an adjustor sees them.

**Keep receipts for living expenses.** You should be reimbursed for temporary housing, meals, and other expenses while your home is being repaired. Your insurance company should cover the cost of these additional living expenses for up to one or two years.

**Make a list of destroyed or damaged items.** Provide evidence of what you owned and how much it was worth. You can speed up this process and limit disputes if you keep a detailed inventory of your possessions. If you don't have an inventory, you can use backgrounds of family photos to jog your memory and prove your losses to the insurance company.

**Keep detailed records.** Each time you talk with insurance employees, an adjustor, or a contractor, note the date, time, person's name, and contact details. Write down what was said or what happened. Keep copies of all receipts, correspondence, and paperwork. If you have trouble getting the claim paid, complain first to the insurance company. Then take your complaint to the state insurance department.

# Raise deductible to lower premiums

Think of your homeowners insurance premium and deductible as children on a seesaw. When one goes up, the other goes down. To find the perfect balance, learn the "magic number" for your deductible.

Your deductible should be at least $1,000. Jumping from a $250 deductible to a $1,000 deductible can save you 25 percent on the premium, and going from $500 to $1,000 can save you up to 15 percent. Even if you do make a claim, having a higher deductible can save you money in the long run.

With a higher deductible, you're also less likely to make small claims — which may get you dropped by your insurer. Just make sure you have enough money in the bank to cover out-of-pocket expenses.

**DEEP DISCOUNT** Looking for an easy way to save a bundle? Buy your homeowners, automobile, and liability coverage from the same company. This practice, known as bundling, may save you up to 15 percent.

# Discover discounts by the dozen

Like a baseball player, you want to be safe at home. But unlike the average major leaguer, you probably aren't worth millions. Luckily, making your home safer and more secure can also help lower the cost of your homeowners insurance.

Your insurance company may offer discounts if you take steps to protect your house from fire, storms, and thieves. Consider installing the following items to stay safe and save money:

+ storm shutters

+ smoke detectors

+ reinforced or fire-retardant roofing materials

+ fire extinguishers

+ sprinkler system

+ carbon monoxide detectors

+ hurricane-resistant windows or doors

+ deadbolt locks

+ burglar alarm

+ security system

The amounts of the discounts vary. For example, you may knock $200 off a $2,000 premium if you install hurricane shutters or roof tie-downs. Deadbolt locks can also save $200, while a central station burglar and fire alarm can pare your premium by $400. Update the plumbing, electrical, and heating systems, and you could save another $300.

Just being a nonsmoker may earn you a discount. If you're not lighting up cigarettes, you're less likely to set your house on fire. Being over 55 years old and retired also pays off. Because retirees spend more time at home, they're less likely to be burglarized and more likely to spot fires quickly. You also have more time to maintain your property and fix small problems before they become big ones.

Ask your insurer about these and other discounts. You could end up with some big league savings.

# 3 claims that put your policy in peril

Some home insurance claims come with more than the usual headaches. Just one of these claims can get your homeowners policy canceled. Read this before you file.

**Dog bites.** If your dog bites someone on your property, it could put you in the doghouse with your insurance company. In fact, the company will likely not renew your coverage. Just owning a dog — or a certain breed of dog — could put you at risk for higher rates, exclusion from liability coverage, or outright denial of insurance.

**Water damage.** It's bad enough if a pipe bursts and soaks your house. But your insurer may further dampen your spirits by dropping your policy if poor home maintenance was the cause. Old, corroded pipes or a shabby roof could signal risk of more water damage in the future — a risk your insurer may not be willing to take.

**Falls.** Your guest's stumbling may be blamed on your bumbling. If a fall was caused by dangerous conditions because you failed to maintain your property, your policy could be in jeopardy.

**CASH SAVER**

Don't get hosed by costly water damage. Washing machine hoses often leak or break, leading to water damage and insurance claims. Luckily, a simple fix can prevent this problem — and possibly save you money on your premiums. Check with your insurance company to see if it offers discounts for replacing rubber hoses with stainless steel. The stronger hoses should cost about $20 at your local hardware store. But, with a discount, you'll save much more than that on your premiums.

# 4 ways to fight for what's right

David beat Goliath, but that was a rare victory for the little man. More likely, you'll feel small and helpless when going up against your mammoth insurance company. But you don't have to give up — or grab a slingshot. Learn how to fight the big guys. Follow these four steps for dealing with insurers, banks, hospitals, and more.

**Understand the system.** Research how the industry works. Learn the language, so you don't fall for fancy double-talk and legalese. You'll be better prepared before making any phone calls. Using the right terminology will let them know you've done your homework.

**Keep track of paperwork.** Document everything — not just the original problem but all the hassles you encounter while trying to fix it. For homeowners insurance disputes, arm yourself with receipts for home repair and photos taken before the damage.

**Put it in writing.** Write a letter and get it to a supervisor or investigator as soon as possible. Include all the facts of your case, but keep it clear and short. You may have only a one- or two-month window to register a consumer complaint.

**Pull rank.** Go over the heads of customer service if the process is taking too long or you're not getting results. Contact someone higher up the company's chain of command. If that doesn't work, call your state insurance regulator, or try the consumer action department of a local newspaper, television, or radio station. Or at least threaten to. That might speed things along.

# Easy ways to take stock of your stuff

Comedian George Carlin had a classic stand-up routine called "Stuff" in which he joked that your house is just "a place to keep your stuff while you go out and get more stuff." But there is nothing funny about losing all your stuff in a fire, flood, or burglary.

Having a thorough inventory of your possessions before disaster strikes can help you document your losses and make sure you get everything you're owed from your insurance company. Here's how to do it.

+ Use a camera or video camera to make a record of what you own. Go room by room. Open drawers, closets, and cabinets. Don't forget about items in your attic, garage, and outdoor storage.

+ Make a detailed written list. Include serial numbers, make, model, purchase date, and price.

+ Update your inventory whenever you buy a valuable item. Keep receipts.

+ Store your inventory in a safe deposit box.

+ Download digital photos of your possessions to a flash drive or upload them to the Web for high-tech backup.

Helpful tools can make the inventory process easier. The IRS offers a free guide called Publication 584, *Casualty, Disaster, and Theft Loss*

*Workbook* that helps you log a room-by-room list of belongings. You can download it at *www.irs.gov* or order it by calling 800-829-3676. Free home inventory software is also available online at *www.know yourstuff.org* and *www.makelifeeasy.com.* You can even ask your insurer for a home inventory form.

# Tailor coverage to fit your budget

Deciding how much insurance you need can be tricky. But you can protect your home from most dangers without busting your budget.

**TOP DOLLAR:** Choose the most comprehensive policy, HO-5, which covers your home, other structures, loss of use, and personal contents against all risks unless it specifically excludes any. This policy costs about 15 percent more than HO-3, the most common homeowners policy.

Add umbrella liability coverage, which protects you from lawsuits and costly court judgments. An umbrella policy costs between $150 and $300 for $1 million of coverage. Get flood and earthquake insurance to guard against perils not included in your homeowners policy. The average cost of flood insurance is $500 per year, but it can cost as little as $112 in low-risk areas.

**VALUE:** Stick with the most common homeowners policy, HO-3, which protects your home, other structures, and loss of use against all dangers except the ones it specifically excludes – typically flood, earthquake, war, and nuclear accident. It offers enough coverage for fairly low rates. In a recent year, the average cost was $822. It also covers your home's contents, but only for named risks.

**WHAT YOU GIVE UP:** Personal property coverage due to certain risks, extra liability protection, and protection from unlikely natural disasters.

# Update your policy to trim costs

Circumstances change, and your homeowners insurance policy should change to keep up. Take a fresh look at your policy every year. You just might discover you spend too much on insurance.

If you got rid of any expensive items recently, drop them from your policy. Other items decrease in value over time, so you may want to reduce the amount of insurance you carry on them.

On the other hand, increasing coverage can save you money and headaches in the long run. If you've made any major purchases or additions to your home, make sure your policy covers them. You may need to add a rider or extra insurance for expensive jewelry, computers, artwork, and other items not covered by a standard homeowners policy.

Other upgrades include springing for extended-replacement coverage, which increases the amount you'll be reimbursed to rebuild your home by 25 percent for about $30 a year, and extending the loss-of-use period to 24 months in case rebuilding takes longer than expected.

## DEEP DISCOUNT

Your big backyard might increase the value of your home if you ever choose to sell it, but it shouldn't increase the cost of your homeowners insurance. That's because you don't have to replace your land after a disaster — just your house. When figuring out how much insurance to buy, remember to subtract the value of the land. Otherwise, you'll overpay.

## Find the CLUE to lower rates

The reason behind high homeowners insurance rates may seem like a mystery. But you don't have to be Sherlock Holmes to look for clues. You just need to pick up the phone or go online.

Insurers use a database called the Comprehensive Loss Underwriting Exchange (CLUE) to track insurance claim histories for both people and properties. They also use CLUE reports to determine the risk of insuring you and your home. Any claims made by you or the home's previous owner in the past five years can have serious consequences.

For example, if your home has a history of water damage, you might have trouble finding affordable insurance.

Like credit reports, CLUE reports can contain false information — and these errors can affect your rates. To see the same information your insurer sees, order your free CLUE report from LexisNexis. Go to *personalreports.lexisnexis.com* or call toll-free 866-312-8076.

You'll discover potential problems before they affect your premiums and learn how to correct or update your information. Mystery solved.

## Smart policies for flooding

You may be standing knee-deep in water in your living room, but don't be too quick to describe your water damage as a "flood." Remember, a standard homeowners policy does not cover flooding. When your insurance company hears the word "flood," it raises a red flag. Your policy probably does cover water from plumbing, heating, and air-conditioning systems, so be more specific when describing your problem.

To cover all your bases, you may want to buy flood insurance. If you live in a high-risk zone, you may even be required to carry it. You'll also pay higher rates because of the higher risk.

Even if you don't live in a high-risk zone, flood insurance could still be a good idea. Go to *www.floodsmart.gov* to check if your flood map has been recently updated. You may be able to buy a policy at a lower-risk rate before the higher rate kicks in. Just act quickly, because policies don't go into effect for 30 days.

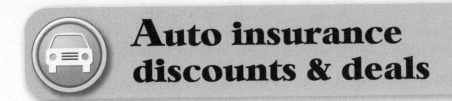

# Auto insurance discounts & deals

## 5 ways to slash your car insurance

Put the brakes on hefty car insurance bills with these simple strategies. They could help you save up to $100 a month.

**Shop around.** Comparison shopping will get you the best rate. Call several different insurance companies, or go online to get quotes. You can also contact an independent agent to search for you. Just make sure you compare "apples to apples." One policy may be cheaper but not provide the same coverage.

If you decide to go with a new company, make sure to cancel your previous policy. Don't just let it lapse. You may be on the hook for an extra month of payments.

**Raise your deductible.** A higher deductible — the amount you have to pay for repairs before the insurance money kicks in — means lower premiums. Boosting your deductible from $250 to $1,000 could save you between 15 and 20 percent, or up to $300 on a $1,500 premium. Just make sure you have enough cash in the bank to cover the higher out-of-pocket expenses.

**Drop some coverage.** It's possible to have too much insurance. You can probably drop collision and comprehensive coverage on an older car. This could save you 10 to 40 percent, depending on the make and model of the car. If your car is worth less than $1,000, consider dropping this coverage and saving up to $600 a year.

**Ask about discounts.** You'd be amazed how many discounts are available — but if you don't ask, you won't know about them. You may get a discount for age, for being a longtime customer or just for being a nonsmoker. If your car has anti-theft devices or air bags and other safety features, you may nab a discount. A clean driving record — no accidents or moving violations for three years — can also lower your payments. Get your homeowners and auto insurance from the same company, and you may earn additional savings. Most discounts range from 10 to 20 percent, which could save you up to $300.

**Maintain good credit.** Your credit score is a surprising factor when it comes to your auto insurance rates. But people with better credit tend to have fewer accidents and make fewer claims — just what insurance companies like. Check your credit report and correct any mistakes. Take steps to repair your credit if necessary. A higher credit score could mean lower rates on auto insurance.

# Small print may hide big costs

Read your auto insurance contract very closely. It will help you find potential pitfalls before it's too late. Find out the answers to the following questions.

+ Who is covered? You may think it's fine to let a friend or family member borrow your car, but are you sure? Some policies cover "named insured only." In other words, only drivers specifically named on the policy are covered. Consider a "family policy" instead if anyone else ever drives your car.

+ Are there restrictions on repairs? Some policies limit your right to choose your own repair facilities or use original equipment manufacturer (OEM) parts. Using generic parts may save you money, but it could also nullify your warranty. Look for the telltale phrase "as defined by us" in the Limits of Liability section of your policy. This lets your insurer insist on below-market repair rates, forcing you to either take your car to an approved repair shop or take it elsewhere and pay the difference yourself.

+ Can you settle disputes? Make sure you have an appraisal clause in your contract. This lets you seek an appraisal if the insurance company offers less for a totaled car than you think it's worth. It should also allow for a "court of jurisdiction" to name an arbiter in case the two sides can't agree.

Make fewer payments and enjoy lower auto insurance rates. If possible, pay your six-month premium all at once rather than in monthly installments. Insurance companies add an "installment payment service fee" to your monthly bill. These small processing charges can really add up. Avoid them with a lump-sum payment, and you may save up to $100 a year.

## Steer a course for savings

Better safe than sorry. Taking a safe-driver course can knock 5 to 10 percent off your auto insurance premium. In fact, some states require insurance companies to provide this discount. Courses are available through AARP, the National Safety Council, and other organizations. The course may cost as little as $12 – and the savings typically last three years. Ask your insurance company about this option.

## Hang up on higher premiums

After a minor fender-bender, don't be so quick to call your insurance company to ask if it's worth filing a claim. That one phone call could raise your premiums.

That's because the company will open a claim file as soon as you contact the claims department – even if you never follow through and actually file a claim. The more claim files you have, the more likely your premium will go up when it's time to renew your policy.

Only call your insurance company if you know the repairs will cost much more than your deductible. You may want to get a repair estimate first, just to be on the safe side.

# Rethink rental car insurance

Vacations can be costly enough without unnecessary spending. One way you can trim your vacation budget is to pass on rental car insurance. Often, this insurance merely duplicates coverage you already have. Why pay twice for the same thing? Take these steps when considering rental car insurance.

**Call your auto insurance company.** Ask if your policy pays for damage to a rental car or replaces it if it's stolen. Does it include administrative fees, towing charges, or loss of use to the rental company if you wreck the car? Remember, if you dropped comprehensive or collision coverage on your own car, you won't have it for the rental car, either.

**Contact your credit card company.** Your credit card may cover rental car damage or theft. Ask about the details of this coverage. If you have several credit cards, check with each one to see which has the best coverage — then use that one to pay for the rental car.

**Make changes.** If your current coverage seems lacking, you may be able to tweak it. Ask about adding a rental insurance rider to your auto insurance policy. You may even be able to temporarily add comprehensive and collision coverage for just the time frame of your vacation.

**Weigh your options.** Rental car insurance does have its advantages. Collision waiver damage insurance, which usually costs between $10 and $20 a day, helps you avoid dealing with your own insurance company and keeps any accident you have off your record. It may also make sense when you're driving in a foreign country.

## DEEP DISCOUNT

Age has its privileges — including a possible discount on auto insurance. Your rates may go down once you reach age 50 or 55. The discount often applies until age 70, when your rates may rise again because you're at increased risk for an accident. Luckily, low-mileage drivers may also earn a discount. Let your insurer know if you're driving less — and you may get to pay less, too.

# Keep yourself safe & secure

## Great deals on life-saving gadget

Personal emergency response systems (PERS) can save your life, especially if you live alone and are at risk for heart attack, stroke, falls, or other health emergencies.

PERS have three parts — a waterproof "help" button you wear at all times, a base unit hooked up to your telephone line, and an emergency response center. Press the help button during an emergency, and the base unit dials the response center. An operator will find out what is wrong and send someone to help you.

Unfortunately, you could pay a pretty penny for the added safety. Installation could cost anywhere from $200 to $1,500. Monitoring may run another $20 to $40 each month. Some companies charge a one-time activation fee as well.

A few phone calls could net you a PERS for next to nothing. Medicare and Medicaid won't pay for a PERS, but some insurance companies may cover it if your doctor deems it medically necessary. Check with your private insurer or Medicare Advantage provider.

If you can't get help there, call your state's department of social services, human services, or aging. Some state and social agencies subsidize the cost of PERS. The city of Independence, Ohio provides discounted Lifeline monitoring for local seniors, thanks to city funding and a grant from the Cleveland Clinic Foundation. Installation is free, and monitoring costs only $7.50 a month.

## No- and low-cost ways to burgle-proof your home

The average burglar will not spend more than four or five minutes trying to break into a home. Most burglars don't spend lots of time planning a robbery, either. They look for easy targets — empty-looking houses with easy access, low visibility from prying eyes, and something worth stealing. Don't give them what they're looking for.

**Free ways to beef up security.** Give burglars the cold shoulder with these no-cost improvements.

+ Place valuables out of view of windows, so thieves can't see them from outside. This includes expensive electronics, like computers and flat-screen televisions, as well as artwork, collectibles, and jewelry.

+ Keep doors and windows closed and locked, even when you're home. Unlocked doors and windows are among the most common ways robbers enter a home.

+ Get rid of the box from a big purchase, like a plasma television or new computer. Thieves will see it sitting on the curb and know you have something good to steal. Break it down and stuff it in the trash, or take it directly to the dump or recycling center.

+ Remove your name from the mailbox. A burglar can call 4-1-1 for your phone number, then dial it to see if you are home.

+ Call your local police department, and ask if they can assess the security on your home. Many departments have a crime-prevention unit and will send an officer to give you advice.

+ Prune shrubs and tall plants away from windows and doors, or remove them entirely. Otherwise, burglars can use them for cover while they break in. If you must have shrubs, plant ones with thorns or pointy leaves.

+ Lock up ladders in your garage or basement so burglars can't use them to climb through second-story windows.

**Cheap options to keep you safe.** These simple upgrades improve security for as little as $3.

+ Make deadbolts even sturdier. Buy a security-grade strike plate with 3-inch screws for under $3. Install them on every exterior door with a deadbolt lock.

+ Invest $5 in a peep hole. It's easy to install and can save you from opening up to potential intruders.

+ Mount a simple, $5 slide lock on the inside of your garage door to keep thieves from lifting it open.

+ Replace old flood lights with motion-detecting ones around doors and windows for as little as $13.

**Safe & Secure**

Fool would-be burglars by making your home look lived-in while you're away.

• Park your car inside the garage and lower the door even when home. The driveway won't look so obviously empty when you are gone.

• Hang old blinds or curtains on garage windows to hide the fact that your car is gone.

• Lower the volume on telephone ringers and answering machines so thieves can't hear them.

• Ask a neighbor to bring your trash cans in from the curb and collect your mail and newspapers.

• Plug lamps, televisions, and radios into timers that cost as little as $4. Set them to turn on and off so it looks like someone is home.

• Turn lamps on automatically at dusk with light-sensing socket converters for just $8.

# Guard your wallet against alarm system scams

Beware door-to-door alarm system salespeople. The Better Business Bureau (BBB) and other consumer experts want you to think twice before signing a contract, no matter how tempting the terms or persistent the seller. Take a look at these common sales pitches and how to respond to keep the upper hand.

+ "This is a limited-time offer." Tell them you need to think about it. Then check the security company's reputation with your local Better Business Bureau.

- ✦ "We're ready to install your system today." Consider this a major red flag. Insist on getting estimates from other companies before you make a decision. A reputable business won't mind waiting.

- ✦ "We'll install the entire system for free." Ask about hidden charges, like monthly monitoring fees. Get any promises in writing, and compare the quoted costs with those from other companies.

Ask who will monitor the system, if you are getting that type of system. Write down the name and phone number of the monitoring company, and check it out with the BBB.

In some states, security alarm companies must have a license to sell or install systems. Call your state's department of consumer affairs or similar protection agency, and ask about their licensing requirements. Make sure any company you hire meets the state's standards.

## Clever ways to hide valuables

Thieves have gotten wise to fake rocks and stashes of cash in the sock drawer. You can still take them by surprise. New, inexpensive "safes" look so much like common household objects that burglars will be hard pressed to tell the difference. Many retailers sell these, including Milestone Safety at 800-886-1560 and Amazon.com at *www.amazon.com.*

- ✦ The wall socket safe, for just $9, hides small valuables behind what looks like a normal electrical outlet.

- ✦ The book safe stows items inside a real, hollowed-out hardback for $14. It's best for people who have lots of books on their shelves already.

- ✦ A fake surge protector does the job, too, for $25. It plugs into the wall, like a real surge protector, but does not conduct electricity. Instead, the hollow inside holds small valuables.

- ✦ A hollow, tootsie-roll-shaped sofa pillow is perfect for stashing cash and documents for $25.

- ✦ The flower pot safe comes with a sealed container inside a real, plastic flower pot for under $30.

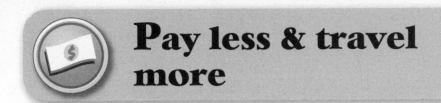

# Pay less & travel more

## Discover the deepest destination discounts

You and your family can't agree on where to go for vacation. That may actually work to your advantage when it comes to finding a bargain. Instead of pinpointing a destination and hoping to find a cheap deal, you can choose from dozens of discounts for all kinds of destinations.

Ask your travel agent what deals he has available for your travel dates — or do your own search on the Internet. Sites like *www.airfare watchdog.com, www.travel-ticker.com*, and *www.travelzoo.com* can help you discover great bargains. When you find the best deal for your family, you have also found your vacation destination. It is that easy.

## Cheap lifetime pass to the great outdoors

Enjoy a lifetime pass to natural beauty, unique attractions, and fun for only 10 bucks — for seniors only.

Most people pay $25 a car to enter Grand Canyon National Park, but you will pay nothing if you have an America the Beautiful Senior Pass. For a one-time fee of $10, you get a lifelong benefit that lets you enter national parks for free, even if they charge an entrance fee or standard amenity fee. Your pass also allows free entrance to three other adults with you and a 50-percent discount on some activities and services, such as camping and swimming within the park.

To get the America the Beautiful Senior Pass, you must be at least 62 years old and a United States citizen or permanent resident. You must request it in person at a national park. Call ahead and ask which discounts your pass provides at the park you plan to visit.

It happens every time you go on vacation. You reach your hotel and suddenly realize you forgot your toothbrush, failed to suspend newspaper delivery, or overlooked something important. But you can put an end to your absentmindedness if you use *www.dontforgetyourtoothbrush.com* to cover all the bases. This website helps you create a printable packing checklist from a list of possible options. All you have to do is check off the items you need.

What about remembering to water the plants or confirm your hotel reservations? The website offers a similar system of checklists for these tasks. Check off the items you want, and the site will send you email reminders at appropriate times. So just sign up for a free account to start using the site, and you may never forget to pack anything again.

## Clear your cookies to save on airfare

You just found a great airfare online, so you start to book your flight. Suddenly you are notified that your low fare is no longer available. Yet, when your spouse tries to book the same flight on his laptop, he successfully gets the low fare you originally spotted.

Other travelers have reported similar experiences, and many of them blame computer cookies. A cookie is a small file that contains information, such as items you buy. A website sends a cookie to your browser, which stores it on your hard drive. When you return to a website that sent a cookie, it retrieves the cookie and recognizes you. This makes certain things easier. For instance, a site might recommend items based on what you have bought previously.

Some travel experts claim that airline and travel sites use these cookies to track which flights you are interested in, so they can raise the fare when you start to book a flight. No one has ever proven these claims, and the travel industry says they are not true. Fares on travel and airline websites change frequently, so a fare may be equally likely to drop or rise while you book your flight.

On the other hand, if you do not like the fare you are offered, you can try deleting your cookies. Every browser offers a way to do this, so check your browser help files for instructions. But keep in mind, clearing your cookies may lead to a lower fare, but it may just as easily lead to a higher one.

**Safe & Secure**

Be prepared for the worst. Scan or take a picture of the front and back of your credit card, reservation documents, passport, driver's license, and other important travel documents. Turn that picture or scan into a file and send it to an email account you could easily access while on vacation. If anything is lost or stolen, you can pull the information you need from email and start making the necessary calls right away. Be sure to leave a copy of this same information with a family member in case email is not available.

# Cruise control — how to get your lowest prices ever

Take your dream vacation cruise for next to nothing. Whether you want to sail the tropical seas or visit Alaskan villages, one of these bargain tricks can help you rack up savings.

**Find the absolute best price on a cruise.** Visit *www.cruise compete.com*, and post your preferred cruising dates with a description of the cruise you want. Travel agents read that post and submit quotes to try to win your business. Your job is to review their offers and choose the best deal.

**Bon voyage for free.** Got friends? You can travel with your buddies for absolutely nothing. If you organize a group cruise for 15 friends or family members, the travel agent or cruise line may let you take the cruise for free. Determine where and when your group wants to cruise, and then find a good travel agent or cruise line that offers this deal.

**Freebie Frenzie**

You could buy maps at the expensive tourist stores near your travel destination, or you could get them for free. Visit *www.justfreestuff.com*, find the "User Favorites" area of the page, and look for a link to maps. When you click the link, a list of state map links appears. Find the state map you want, and either download a map to carry on your laptop or order a free paper map.

# 3 paths to a cheaper hotel rate

The Internet is not your only option for great hotel deals. Try these low-tech alternatives, and see how much you can save.

**Sample a hotel loyalty program.** Some hotels offer loyalty programs that may remind you of the frequent flyer programs offered by airlines. The benefits of the program vary widely. You may be offered extra perks, upgrades, complimentary nights, or discounts. But hotel loyalty programs start paying off much sooner than a frequent flyer program. Ask the hotel clerk if they have a free program for frequent lodgers.

**Skip the 800 number.** A hotel chain may offer a toll-free number for reservations, but that may not be where the best deals are. Instead, call the main desk of the particular hotel you want to stay in. That hotel may offer specials or discounts you cannot find on the hotel chain's main reservation system.

Just don't call between 9 a.m. and 1 p.m. local time, when the hotel clerk is busy helping people check out. The clerk can answer your questions about specials and discounts far more thoroughly when he is not swamped with customers.

**Try to haggle at least once.** You may not think of yourself as a world-class negotiator, but it never hurts to ask whether a lower rate is available. You may have better luck at independent hotels than at hotel chains. But leave your luggage in the car until after you negotiate. Otherwise, the hotel clerk may assume you have already decided to stay, even at the current price, and he will have no reason to offer you a lower rate.

# Slash your hotel bill with savvy discounts

Hotels constantly offer promotional discounts to gain your business, but finding them may take a little work. Here are several ways to lower the bill on your next hotel stay.

**Surf for specials.** Visit the hotel website to see if it is running a temporary special or limited-time offer you qualify for. If the hotel has both a chain website and a site for the individual hotel, check each one.

**Hunt for pit stop discounts.** Check visitor centers, restaurants, or gas stations for free travel guides or brochures. These may contain an ad or coupon for a discount at a nearby hotel.

**Pay before you stay.** If you know where you want to stay and can make your reservations at least one month ahead of time, ask about a pay-before-you-stay discount. These discounts may save you up to 40 percent, and they are more widely available than in the past.

The problem is you must pay the full hotel bill before you stay and, if you cancel, part or all of the bill may be nonrefundable. If you are willing to take the risk, make your reservation as early as possible. Some hotels offer larger discounts to people who reserve the room farther in advance.

**Max out your discount.** You may know to ask about a senior discount, but try this sneaky trick savvy seniors use to get rock-bottom prices. If the hotel has a website, check to see if you qualify for the senior discount. But when you call the hotel, first ask for the best price they can give you. Make sure you qualify for that price, and then ask for your senior discount.

Sometimes you cannot combine a senior discount with a best-price promotion, but you will not know until you ask. Besides, some promotions may save you more than your senior discount.

## DEEP DISCOUNT

Take one more step before you book a great hotel deal online, and you may save even more money. Print out the page and call the hotel's front desk. Tell them about the deal you found, and ask whether they can match it. If they do, you'll save the extra booking fee often charged by online sites. That is what happened to Linda Bennett.

"Several years ago, I found a great deal on Hotels.com," she says. "Then I called the hotel directly, told them the deal I found, and asked if they would match the price. They did. I came out ahead because I didn't have to pay the service charge."

# Sneaky hotel fees you can avoid

Your hotel bill is not only far higher than the rate you were quoted, but it also reads like a grocery list of fees – resort amenities, baggage holding, energy surcharge, minibar, and more. But just because you were not warned about these fees does not mean you can't fight back.

**Clarify charges at checkout.** Ask what each fee is for and how you benefit from it. Ask to waive fees you feel are unfair, particularly if you are charged for a service or product you did not use. The hotel may agree to waive at least some of the fees because many business travelers still pay these fees without protest.

**Be prepared for next time.** For a list of the fees you can expect, visit the hotel website, check the website where you plan to make reservations, or call the hotel. Ask the hotel about any fees you do not understand and request any unfair fees be waived. Ask them to send a written confirmation of your bill, and in the meantime, write down what fees the clerk agreed to waive, who you spoke with, and when the conversation occurred.

**Avoid extras during hotel stay.** You may be charged extra for what you think are complimentary services, so ask if you're not sure. If you want to be safe:

+ do not touch the minibar, store anything inside it or on it, or even lean against it.

+ avoid drinking any canned or bottled beverages supplied outside the minibar in your room.

+ do not use a laptop or desktop computer to access the Internet while inside your hotel.

+ skip reading the newspaper that appears outside your door.

Last, but not least, never use room service unless you're prepared for a hefty surcharge on your meal.

You could pay $80 for a bus tour in New York City — or pocket that money and take a walking tour for free. In fact, you can find plenty of free tours in New York City and many other places. You just have to know where to look.

Before you visit any city, contact its Chamber of Commerce or tourism board. You may find free walking tours or other free tours readily available. In fact, one location in New York City has even been known to offer free kayaking lessons and tours down the Hudson River.

If you want something different, consider a free factory tour. You can learn how goat's milk soap, grandfather clocks, or kitchen mixers are made — and often watch it being done. Visit *www.factorytoursusa.com* to find out about free tours near your vacation destination.

# Nab a bigger bargain for your family vacation

A week in a beach resort or a ski resort sounds perfect, but the hotels are so expensive. Perhaps hotels are not your only option. Take a look at alternatives such as renting a condominium or vacation home.

**TOP DOLLAR:** Hotels in resort areas vary but you will probably see a range of $99 to $229 a night during the shoulder season, the less-expensive weeks right before and after the peak season. During the peak season, rates are significantly higher.

**VALUE:** Condo rentals may range from $90 to $123 a night during the shoulder season in resort areas. Renting a house or condo can be a particularly good deal for a family or group, because they can split one rental cost instead of paying for two or more hotel rooms.

You may also have far more space in a rental, often including bigger bathrooms. What's more, most rentals come equipped with a full kitchen, so you can save money by cooking your own meals instead of eating at expensive, resort-area restaurants.

**WHAT YOU GIVE UP:** You know exactly what to expect from a hotel chain as far as rooms and services. But condominiums and rentals can vary widely in what they offer. Your rental may not come with house-cleaning service, room service, concierge, free continental breakfast, and daily linen changes. On the other hand, many condos or rentals provide bikes, cribs, a DVD player, washer and dryer, fireplace, swimming pool, and other surprising amenities.

But condos and houses are not always cheaper than hotels, particularly if your group or family is small. So compare the prices and amenities of both options. When possible, also read reviews of rental properties and hotels, and find out as much as you can before making a choice. For prices and details on vacation rentals at your vacation spot, visit *www.otalo.com* or *www.flipkey.com*.

# Secrets to stretching your road-trip budget

You can have a great road trip at a discount if you remember these tips.

**Pack your own food.** Drinks and snacks from convenience stores, vending machines, and tourist traps can be ridiculously expensive. Instead, buy soft drinks, bottled water, juice packs, trail mix, or other nonperishable snacks from your grocery store at home, and bring them on your trip. Pack the drinks in a cooler.

**Drive below the speed limit.** You'll save on gas and avoid the steep cost of speeding tickets.

**Eat out only once a day.** Do it at lunch. You can often order the same dishes at lunch as you would at dinner, but at a lower price. Also, visit *www.roadfood.com* to find interesting but informal restaurants along your route that usually do not cost an arm and a leg.

**Rent a room with a kitchenette.** Consider buying groceries and staying in a hotel room or rental with a kitchenette or at least a microwave and mini refrigerator. Compare the extra costs of the kitchenette and groceries to the total price of eating out. Go with the cheaper option.

**Use your bank's ATM machines.** Do not pay out-of-network fees just because you cannot find your bank's ATMs. Before you travel, check your bank's website, or call and ask whether your bank has ATMs along your route.

If your bank has no machines where you are going, check the back of your ATM card to see which network it uses. Search online for a map of in-network ATMs at your destination, or ask if your bank can provide this information. You may still be charged a fee if you use one of these ATMs, but your bank will probably waive part or all of that fee.

**No-Sweat Solution**

Do not pay extra for a bag of ice for your road trip. Instead, freeze mostly full bottles of water plus a few juice boxes. Use them to keep the food in your ice chest cool. When the ice melts, you can just drink the water and juice. This might also help you resist the temptation to buy overpriced bottled water or soft drinks while on the road.

# Best time to buy airline tickets

Want the best deal on airfare? Rick Seaney, CEO of *FareCompare.com*, states that the best time to buy tickets is at 3 p.m. Eastern time on a Tuesday afternoon. Here is why.

An airline that wants to put an airfare on sale usually posts the new rate late on Monday. As the hours pass, other airlines spot the discount and put their tickets on sale so they will not lose business to the discounter. Reservation networks usually have this sale information in their systems by 3 p.m., so that is when you will probably find more discounts to choose from.

And here is a bonus tip. Many airlines offer bargains either 21 days or 14 days before a flight, so be on the lookout for them. Otherwise, unless your airline specifically says you can purchase your ticket seven days in advance, buy it at least two weeks before your flight – or you may pay too much.

# 5 ways to get rock-bottom prices on airfare

Some airline ticket prices are so high they can leave you feeling rather ill. But don't take two aspirin. Instead, take these five tips on how to pay less, and you will feel much better.

**Broaden your search.** You can search for a good fare at the airline's website, or you can try an aggregator website, like *www.travelocity.com*, that sells tickets for many airlines. In both cases, be sure to look for a flexible date search. If you can leave or return a day or two earlier or later, you may pay a lot less.

**Visit the airline's website.** Unlike aggregator sites, most airlines do not charge booking fees for flights booked at their own websites. What's more, airlines often save their best deals exclusively for people who book at their websites. That does not mean you will not find airline deals on aggregator websites, only that the deals you find there may not be the best ones available from that airline.

**Seek out promo codes.** Sign up for email alerts, Twitter tweets, promotional codes, email newsletters, or frequent flyer programs from your favorite airlines. This may lead your airline to send you promo codes for bargains you cannot find anywhere else. Type the code into the special box on the airline's website, and you may get special discounts on a particular route or on any ticket you buy. Discounts can be as high as 50 percent off the standard fare. Also, sign up for fare alerts from a site like *www.airfarewatchdog.com* to monitor additional airlines, just in case.

**Beware discount-eating fees.** That incredible airline ticket deal you found may not include all the sneaky little fees. That is bad news because fees can add a lot to your cost. Check the fine print from your airline for signs of these fees. Also, visit the website *www.smartertravel.com* to download *Airline Fees: The Ultimate Guide* for the lowdown on which fees you can expect from your airline.

But do not stop there. Scour your deal's fine print to ferret out special prerequisites needed to qualify for the bargain, possible penalties for changes in plans, or other unpleasant surprises.

**Consider alternate airports.** Check for secondary airports near your arrival and departure airports. Low-cost airlines may offer cheaper flights to or from these airports.

# Save on flights by traveling light

Bag-check fees can really add to the price of your airfare. The secret to avoiding these fees is to pack light, preferably light enough to only need your carry-on bag. Start by following these tips.

✦ When choosing clothes for the trip, select mostly neutral colors such as black, gray, navy, tan, and white. This means you can mix and match nearly everything and wear items more than once. You can always hand-wash items before you wear them again.

To add color and camouflage the fact that you are wearing those pants a second time, use jewelry, belts, ties, and other lightweight accessories.

✦ Pack toiletries in travel size only. If you travel regularly, buy travel-size bottles you can fill and reuse.

✦ Wear your bulkiest shoes on the day you fly so you do not need to pack them.

✦ Roll up underwear and socks, and tuck them in your packed shoes so no space is wasted.

- To fit your clothes in a carry-on bag without causing creases and wrinkles, put individual items in tissue paper or dry-cleaning bags. Then pile and fold. For example, lay one shirt out flat, place a second shirt on top, put a third shirt on top of that, and so on until you have a small pile. Then fold the pile or roll it so it can fit in your bag.

For even more clever tips on packing light, visit the website *www.onebag.com.*

**No-Sweat Solution**

The trouble with lost luggage is that you may have to buy toiletries and clothes to tide you over until your luggage arrives. And in an unfamiliar place, you may have to shop in the nearest stores you can find, even if the prices are not cheap. But you can limit the damage to your wallet and your trip with two simple tactics.

- If you are traveling with someone, each of you should pack one outfit of clothing, including underwear, in the other person's bag. If you are traveling alone, put that outfit in your carry-on bag.
- Pack your prescription medicines as well as your most expensive, vital, or hard-to-find toiletries or other items in your carry-on bag.

# Find great deals on last-minute trips

You have some unexpected time off next week, and you sure could use a vacation. But you don't want to pay a ridiculously high price for your plane ticket. Don't worry. You can still find bargains if you use the right tools.

In recent years, the best bets for last-minute travel were aggregator websites that handled reservations for many airlines and hotels. But now, airlines hold back some deals and offer them exclusively on their own websites. So visit the websites of airlines that fly out of airports near you to check for last-minute deals that may suit you.

If you do not find one right away, sign up for the airlines' reward programs and email list to receive information on new deals as they become available. You can hedge your bets by visiting *www.airfare watchdog.com* to check for last-minute deals. Also, try visiting *www.hotelchatter.com* to find out if any new hotels at your destination are offering grand opening bargains.

Just remember to check on taxes, fees, prerequisites, and restrictions for any last-minute deal you want to book.

# Go the extra mile to save on car rental

Car rental companies can nickel-and-dime you to death, but a little extra effort may help you keep those costs down.

**Consider where you rent.** City and state governments often impose extra fees on airport rentals and on rentals from nearby locations that can be reached by the rental company's shuttle. Rentals near the city center or suburbs may cost at least 25 percent less.

But to find out for sure, run the numbers for yourself. Contact the rental car company, or visit *www.expedia.com, www.travelocity.com*, or *www.orbitz.com* to check rental car rates. Also, ask whether your hotel offers a shuttle to and from the airport. If it does, consider car rental options near your hotel.

**Pump your own gas.** The rental company may offer you an option to return the car without topping off the gas tank. Turn that option down, or you will be charged a fee that costs more than you would have paid for gas.

**Read the fine print.** Check your rental agreement carefully, and try to opt out of paying for things you will not use.

**Obey the traffic laws.** If you get a traffic or parking ticket, your rental car company may add fees to your bill.

**Think twice about insurance.** You may not need the insurance offered by the car rental company. For more information, see *Rethink rental insurance* in the chapter *Auto insurance discounts & deals.*

# Beware car rental no-show fees

The next time you rent a car, ask whether any fees or penalties might be added to the advertised rate. You may discover that the rental company will hit you with a costly penalty if you don't show up to claim your car.

Many companies are now charging this no-show fee, and it can cost you $50 or more. If the rental clerk does not mention it, be sure to ask. You may need to cancel as early as two days before your pickup time to avoid the fee. Hint – if she asks for your credit card, address, and phone number when you make the reservation, expect to be charged if you don't show up.

If your plans change due to an emergency, flight cancellation, or a death in the family, call the car rental company's customer service department, even if it is technically too late to cancel. Explain the situation, and ask that the fee be waived.

# Citywide travel for less

You only have a few days for your "bright lights, big city" vacation, so you want to get around as quickly as possible. You could take a taxi, but the fares are so expensive. Fortunately, the Hopstop website can help you use subways, walking, or buses to flit around the city with ease.

Just plan your itinerary, visit *www.hopstop.com*, and choose the city you want to visit. For each leg of your itinerary, type in your starting address, destination address, the time of day you plan to travel, and your travel preferences. Hopstop helps you find and map your best route.

# New cut-rate passport brings fantastic savings

You want to go on a Caribbean cruise or a road trip to Mexico or Canada, but your passport just expired. Fortunately, you may not need to pay full price for a passport. And you just may save $80.

**TOP DOLLAR:** A standard U.S. passport book costs $135 for travel anywhere in the world.

**VALUE:** Thanks to a 2009 law, you can buy a $55 passport card instead of the $135 passport book.

**WHAT YOU GIVE UP:** The opportunity for unrestricted travel by land, sea, or air. You can only use your passport card:

✦ when you cross the land border between the United States and Mexico or the land border between the United States and Canada.

✦ when you take a cruise or travel by sea between the United States and Bermuda, Mexico, Canada, or participating Caribbean nations.

You cannot use the passport card to go anywhere else. What's more, you cannot use the passport card to travel by air to Canada, Mexico, Bermuda, or any Caribbean nation. In other words, you still need a passport book for most international trips.

But if your out-of-country vacations are mainly road trips to Canada or Mexico or cruises to the Caribbean, you may get by with a passport card at its cheaper price. For the latest information about the passport card, its cost, and where you may use it, visit *www.travel. state.gov* and *www.getyouhome.gov*.

# New option for escaping bag fees

You have heard about airline fees for checked bags, overweight bags, and even for carry-on bags. But when the fees are at their worst, you may have your best chance to save money.

Before your next flight, call your airline or visit its website to discover how much it charges for the first and second checked bag and for overweight bags. Then calculate what you would pay to ship your bag using Federal Express, UPS, or the U.S. Post Office's Priority Mail Service.

Checking your bag is often cheaper, but not always. If your airline has high fees or your bag is likely to be overweight or oversized, you could save money. For example, an overweight 51-pound bag would cost $125 each way from Chicago to Florida on one major airline. But shipping your items in a special UPS luggage box would cost you $106 round trip. That's a savings that can't be beat.

# 3 surprising travel essentials

Some things you might normally leave at home can save money or help you cope with unexpected problems. Consider these examples.

+ Resealable plastic bag. Pack several of these in several sizes and you will discover uses for them. For example, fill a gallon bag with water, baby shampoo or a few squirts of detergent, and a washable item of clothing you want to wear again during your trip. Seal and shake the bag to wash the clothing, instead of paying at a laundromat.

+ Extra dental floss. Use as a clothesline, replacement shoelace, or even as thread.

+ Duct tape. Wrap some around a pen, and use it to repair luggage or other items, instead of buying repair supplies or replacements.

**No-Sweat Solution**

You have been stuck on the plane for nearly two hours, just waiting to take off or be let off at the gate. But don't worry, you may not be waiting much longer.

According to a new Federal rule, your airline must offer you water and snacks once you have been sitting on the tarmac for two hours as long as you are on a domestic flight operated by a United States airline. Working bathrooms and medical attention, if needed, must also be made available after two hours.

After three hours on the tarmac, you must be allowed to get off the plane except when exiting the plane would be unsafe or when letting passengers off would disrupt airport operations. The rules may be different for international flights, so ask about their policy before boarding.

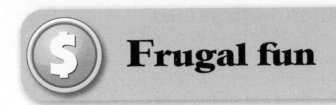

# Frugal fun

## Zero charge for zoos and more

Gaze at rare animals or works of art by taking advantage of something even rarer – a free pass. Use these tips to get free admission to museums, zoos, and science centers.

**Bank on it.** If you have a Bank of America credit or check card, you already have the key to getting in free. Bank of America's "Museums on Us" program gives you free general admission to participating museums, zoos, science centers, botanical gardens, and more on the first full weekend of every month. Just present your Bank of America card and photo identification, and you're good to go. Find out more details about the program online at *museums.bankofamerica.com*. You'll be able to view the schedule and locate participating attractions near you.

**Join the club.** Membership has its privileges. If you have a membership to a local zoo, aquarium, botanical garden, or museum, check the reciprocal membership list. Often, you can use your membership to get in free – or get a big discount on admission – to similar attractions in other metro areas.

**Check the calendar.** Most attractions, like museums and zoos, feature occasional free days for the community. Call your local attraction to find the schedule and learn about any restrictions. Free days may also be advertised on the attraction's website or in your local newspaper. Keep your eyes peeled for these great deals.

**Borrow a bargain.** Your library may have a city pass, which will get you into local attractions like zoos, aquariums, planetariums, museums, and art galleries for free. All you need is a valid library card, and you're free to explore the city's attractions at no charge.

# Close the book on high prices

Your bookshelves are groaning from the weight of all your books — and the high cost of new books is enough to make you do the same. Fortunately, you have several ways to get free books and clear out shelf space in your home.

**Sell your old books.** Put your old books up for sale to put a little cash in your pocket. You can always sell your unwanted books to your local used bookstore. But you'll find a wider market for your books on the Internet.

Sell your books online at websites like *www.cash4books.net* or *www.sell backyourbook.com*. Simply type in the book's ISBN number — a 10- or 13-digit number found on the back cover near the barcode — to get an offer. The website will even pay for the postage to ship the book. Another good resource is *www.bookscouter.com*, which searches over 40 book-buying websites to help you sell your books for the best price.

**Swap with other readers.** Trade books with fellow readers at these book-swapping websites. Just list the books you're willing to swap, and browse the website's list of available titles for those you might want. You will have to pay postage — either to mail a book or have one mailed to you — but no other fees.

+ *www.paperbackswap.com*

+ *www.bookins.com*

+ *www.bookmooch.com*

**Donate your books to your local library.** You can even list the donation as a tax deduction. Keep in mind that libraries often hold sales, where you can buy books dirt-cheap. When you're finished reading them, you can always donate them back to the library.

**Read them online.** Experience the classics in a new way — on your computer. You can read countless books for free at these websites.

+ *www.gutenberg.org*

+ *www.bartleby.com*

+ *www.bibliomania.com*

+ *www.classicbookshelf.com*

- ✦ *www.manybooks.net*

- ✦ *http://onlinebooks.library.upenn.edu*

Books won't cost you a cent or take up any precious shelf space. Just make sure your monitor is large and clear enough to let you read in comfort.

**Borrow e-books.** You already know you can borrow books from the library to save money. But now you may be able to borrow e-books without even leaving your home. Simply download the e-book from your library's website. The loan period is typically two weeks.

**Lend an ear.** Listen to your books instead of reading them. Download free audio versions of books in the public domain at *www.librivox.org*. You can listen to these classics on your computer or MP3 player.

# Language lessons for less than a euro

You don't have to travel to pricey Paris to bone up on your French. As long as you have an Internet connection, you can learn to speak French (or almost any language) for free!

The British Broadcasting Corporation – better known as the BBC – offers free online language courses. You can take lessons in French, German, Spanish, Italian, Greek, Portuguese, Chinese, Japanese, Arabic, Polish, Russian, and more. Go to *www.bbc.co.uk/languages* to get started.

You can also learn foreign languages at these helpful websites.

- ✦ *www.livemocha.com*

- ✦ *www.freelanguage.com*

- ✦ *www.word2word.com*

- ✦ *www.mangolanguages.com*

Because lessons are free, you can't beat the price. And that's a bargain in any language.

## Blockbuster savings on movies

Whether it's a comedy, drama, summer blockbuster, timeless classic, or independent gem, a movie can be magical. But a trip to the movie theater — with the high ticket prices and costly concessions — can make your money disappear.

Enjoy movies for free in the comfort of your own home. Just go to Hulu at *www.hulu.com*. Browse the alphabetical list of popular, classic, documentary, and obscure films. You'll also find a healthy helping of your favorite TV shows. And you can watch them all for free right on your computer.

Hulu isn't the only website that lets you watch movies and TV shows for free. Check out these sites for more viewing material.

- *www.fancast.com*
- *www.joost.com*
- *www.slashcontrol.com*
- *www.snagfilms.com*
- *www.veoh.com*

Another budget-friendly option is Netflix. For a monthly fee ranging from $7.99 to $9.99, you can watch unlimited TV shows and movies streaming from the Internet. You can watch on your computer or on your TV through your XBox, PlayStation 3, or Wii device.

You can also get DVDs by mail. You get one DVD at a time, and you can keep it as long as you like – so you don't have to worry about late fees. When you're finished watching it, mail it back in the provided postage-paid envelope. Then Netflix will mail you the next movie on your list.

Remember, you're charged the monthly fee even if you don't watch anything. So make sure you'll get your money's worth before signing up. A one-month free trial can help you decide. Go to *www.netflix.com* to learn more.

## Spend less at the movies

When you go to the movies, you don't want to be taken to the cleaners. Luckily, just being a senior can help you save money on movie tickets.

Movie theaters usually offer senior discounts. For example, at the Cinemark chain of movie theaters – located throughout the United States – a senior can save up to 35 percent off regular adult ticket prices. Go on a Monday, and the deal gets even better, thanks to a Seniors Day promotion that shaves an additional 10 percent off the price. You must be 62 or older to take advantage of this deal. Find a participating Cinemark theater near you at *www.cinemark.com*. Qualifying age and ticket prices may vary by location.

Even if you don't see a senior discount advertised at your local movie theater, don't be afraid to ask. You might get a deal anyway.

## Check out films for free

You love watching movies, but the cost of movie tickets and DVD rentals can really add up. Slash your movie budget while still enjoying great films. All you need is a library card.

Libraries have more than just books. You may be able to borrow movies and TV shows on DVD. Your library may have a more limited selection than a video store or online service, but you can still find plenty of classic, popular, educational, travel, and nonfiction films. Now all you need is some popcorn.

## Thrifty theater strategies

A night on the town in the Big Apple costs big bucks. But you can take in a Broadway show without taking out a second mortgage. Consider these options before enjoying a night of live entertainment.

**TOP DOLLAR:** Spring for a popular Broadway show at full price. Buy your tickets in advance, choose your seats, and plan your evening without any last-minute scrambling. Opt for prime seats, and tickets could set you back more than $130 apiece, plus service charges.

**VALUE:** Try one of these tactics to see a Broadway — or Off-Broadway — show for less.

+ Drop by a discount booth. The TKTS booth in Times Square sells tickets for up to 50 percent off. You do have to wait in line, and not all shows are available every day. But it can be a great way to snag affordable seats.

+ Rush at the last minute. Sometimes procrastinating pays off. Don't buy theater tickets ahead of time. Call the day of the performance and find out how many seats are available. Show up in time to buy "rush" tickets, usually sold about 15 minutes before the show at a fraction of the cost. Not all theaters sell "rush" tickets, so ask ahead of time.

+ Sign up for savings. Goldstar.com offers half-price tickets for a variety of plays, concerts, sporting events, and other fun activities in 16 cities, including New York. Go to *www.goldstar.com* to join, and you'll receive a weekly email list of available events.

**WHAT YOU GIVE UP:** Certainty. You need to be flexible with the cheaper options. For the discount booth and rush tickets, you need to go the day of the show. You may not get tickets to the show you really want to see or sit in the best seats in the house. But there are plenty of high-quality shows available for a good bargain.

Don't get worked up over high ticket prices. Volunteer to work instead. Many theaters let you see plays, concerts, and other events for free if you volunteer as an usher. Duties may include taking tickets, handing out programs, helping the patrons find their seats, and tidying up after the performance. Just make sure to wear comfortable shoes because you might have to stand during the show. Check with your local theater about this opportunity to spend time rather than money on entertainment.

## Pay less for a preview

Practice makes perfect — and perfect prices. Instead of paying through the nose for professional opera, symphony, or theater tickets, attend a dress rehearsal or preview performance. It's just like the real thing, only cheaper. By this time, the performers and crew have worked out all the details and technical aspects of the show. They just need an audience.

That's where you come in. Dress rehearsals let you enjoy quality entertainment at a steep discount — maybe even for free. Call local theaters to ask about pricing for these special performances. You may also see them advertised in your local newspaper.

## Watch TV for free — in the studio

Lights, camera, savings! Get an up-close view of your favorite television programs. If you're visiting Los Angeles or New York City, you can be a member of a studio audience. It's easy to get free tickets to watch live tapings of TV shows. Just go to one of these websites.

✦ TVTix.com. This site is packed with information about free tickets, taping schedules, studio tours, and how to be a movie extra, game show contestant, or talk show guest. It's based in California, but also has a link for tickets to shows taped in New York. Go to *www.tvtix.com*, or call 323-653-4105 to learn more.

- ✦ Audiences Unlimited. Find out how to be part of the audience for shows in the Los Angeles area, like "The Price is Right" and "Dr. Phil." Visit *www.tvtickets.com*, or call 818-260-0041 for more information.

- ✦ On Camera Audiences. This company offers opportunities to see a variety of popular shows, including "American Idol" and "Dancing with the Stars." To learn more, go to the website *www.on-camera-audiences.com*, or call 818-295-2700.

- ✦ New York Show Tickets. Snag seats to see David Letterman, "Saturday Night Live," and other shows filmed in New York at this website. You can also get discounts for Broadway shows, comedy clubs, museums, and other attractions. Check out all the deals at *www.nytix.com*.

You can also write to the Guest Relations departments of television networks to get free tickets.

## Group coupons give great deals

There is strength in numbers. There is also a strong chance of grabbing big discounts on restaurants, spas, massages, theaters, hotels, museums, and more. With group coupon websites, you can maximize your buying power to get more bang for your buck.

Groupon, the biggest of these sites, operates in more than 150 cities throughout the country. Go to *www.groupon.com* to join. Just provide your city and email address, and you'll receive a daily local offer. If enough people sign up for it, the deal goes into effect.

Simply click "Buy" before midnight to get in on the deal. Your card will be charged — if the minimum number of people buy in — and you'll get an email with a link to sign in and print out your voucher, which includes directions and instructions on how to redeem it. Let your family and friends know about these deals, so they can get in on the savings. After all, the more the merrier.

Groupon is not the only group coupon website. Try these others, which work the same way.

+ SocialBuy offers local deals for more than 50 cities. Visit *www.socialbuy.com* to start saving in your area.

+ Scoop St. focuses on deals in New York City. Go to the website *www.scoopst.com* to find big discounts in the Big Apple.

+ Angie's List features The Big Deal, which offers discounts all over the country. Go to *www.angieslist.com* and click on The Big Deal to sign up.

Group coupons come with some drawbacks. Some small businesses may get overwhelmed by responses and have a hard time fitting everyone in. You may not get the date you want or end up waiting a long time when you arrive.

Pay attention to expiration dates, and make sure you can take advantage of the deal during that time frame. Some places, like hotels, may only honor group coupons on certain nights or dates. If you have a problem, contact the coupon site's customer service to see if they can help.

## DEEP DISCOUNT

Stop the presses! You can say goodbye to costly newspaper subscriptions. Just go online to read the latest news — for free — from newspapers all over the world.

Most newspapers have online versions. Usually, a newspaper's website is easy to figure out. For instance, the New York Times website is *www.nytimes*.com. You can also type a newspaper's name into a search engine to find its website. Or just search for a city's name plus the word "newspaper." You may have to register at the site by providing your name and email address, but access is usually free.

You can also find links to thousands of online newspapers all in one place at the following websites.

• *www.newspapers.com*

• *www.findnewspapers.com*

• *www.allyoucanread.com/newspapers*

Sound too high-tech for you? Get your news the old-fashioned way by reading newspapers at your local public library.

# Treat yourself to terrific tunes

Sick of singing the blues over the high cost of compact discs? Then this should be music to your ears. Discover how to listen to great music absolutely free.

**Check it out.** Libraries are known for being very quiet – but they're one of the best sources of free music. In addition to books, many libraries lend out compact discs. The librarian may even let you listen to music on the premises – with headphones, of course. It's a great way to hear a wide variety of music without hurting your budget.

**Tune in online.** You don't have to go to the library – or even leave your house – to find free music. Just listen to Internet radio. All you need is a computer with a fast broadband Internet connection. You'll find stations from all over the world, playing every imaginable type of music from every decade. Whether you like big band, bluegrass, blues, jazz, R&B, folk, country, reggae, or classical, there is an online station for you. Visit these websites to search for Internet radio stations.

+ *www.radio-locator.com*

+ *www.radiotower.com*

+ *www.live-radio.net*

+ *www.live365.com*

+ *www.radiotime.com*

# Higher education offers lower prices

Living near a college can be a pretty smart move when it comes to low-cost entertainment. You can attend guest lectures, concerts, and student plays or recitals for reasonable prices – or even for free. If the college has a strong music or drama program, these performances can rival professional productions.

Want live music at your next party? Music schools or music departments can be a good resource. You may be able to listen to talented students play or sing for a fraction of the cost of professional musicians.

# Index

1035 exchange 96
401(k) account 43, 104

# A

AARP 31, 79, 109
Accounting of disclosures 60
Affordable Nutrition Index 20
Air bags 215
Air conditioner, repairing 250
Airfare, saving on 332, 340-344
Alarm system 329-330
Amazon.com 140
America the Beautiful Senior
  Pass 331
Annuals 307
Annuities 96
Antibiotics, free 158
Antiperspirant 200
Apple TV 126
Appliance
  maintenance 282
  rebates 269-270
  recycling 271
Area Agency on Aging 79
Arthritis, exercise for 159
Assets
  titling 114
  unclaimed 37-38
ATM card 57
  fees 74
  traveling with 340

Auction, online 38, 139-140
Audiologist 160
Audit, energy 253, 255
Automated phone system,
  bypassing 122
Automobile. *See* Car

# B

Back pain 164, 188
Bags, uses for 15-16
Baking soda, for cleaning 285
Balance transfer 84
Banking
  fees 71-76, 99
  living abroad and 152
  online 77-78
Bankruptcy 63, 93
Barrel, for rain 312
Bartering 298. *See also* Haggling
Batteries 6
Beans 17
  storing 19
Bedbugs 182
Beef 18. *See also* Meat
Beets, storing 19
Berries, storing 19
Bills
  errors in 154
  lowering 120, 123-124,
    153, 234
  paying online 80, 143-144

# D

Daily Money Manager (DMM) 78
Dairy 2
Date, sell-by 11
Deadhead 307
Debit card 57, 86
Debts
  of deceased 69-70
  weight and 178
Deductible 316, 323
Deductions, tax 52, 61, 106
Deli 2
Dental schools 157
Deodorant, homemade 200
Depression, light therapy for 188
Detergent, laundry 292-294
Diet
  Mediterranean 184
  plans 179
  tricks 178
Digital photos 230
Dining. *See* Restaurant
Directory assistance 234
Disability aids 187
Discounts
  after sale 276
  cash 81-82
  driving 325
  grocery 4
  hotel 334-336
  insurance 316, 323
  on beauty products 198
  on drugs 192-195
  on furniture 281
  on local attractions 349
  on medical treatment 168
  on paint 298
  on phone service 233-235
  on theater tickets 354
  on transportation 223
  restaurant 32
  scratch and dent 274
  senior 31, 142, 223, 250, 326, 331, 336, 353
  travel 331
Do Not Call list 62
Do-it-yourself (DIY) 302, 306
Dollar store 2, 5
Donations 106
Donut hole, and Medicare 172
Door, upgrading 297, 302
Drain, clogged 265
Drugs. *See also* Medicine
  discount cards for 193-195
  from Canada 195
  generic 191-192
  Medicare and 171-172
Drugstores 20
Dryer 261, 269, 273
Dust mites 183

# E

Earnings, lifetime 93
eBay 35, 38, 140, 242
Editing 35
Elder Cottage Housing Opportunity (ECHO) 149
Eldercare 114, 148
Electricity, saving 259-261
Electronics, recycling 119
Endcaps 4
Energy
  audit 255
  hogs 275-276

leaks 253-254, 256
savings 295-296
Entertainment, free 355, 358
Equifax 64, 89
Equipment, medical 187
Estate planning
  free legal advice 113-114
  funerals 111-112
  wills 115
Experian 64, 89
Explanation of Benefits 170
Eye care 161-163
  free exams 164
Eye doctors, types of 162-163
Eyeglasses. *See* Glasses

# F

Fabric softener 294
Fair market value 106
Fan, ceiling 249-250
Fannie Mae 136
Farmers market 1, 22
Federal assistance 155-156
Fees
  airline 342, 347
  ATM 74
  balance transfer 84
  car rental 345
  hotel 337
  late 75-76, 100
  overdraft 73, 99
  telephone 100
Fertilizer 26
Filter system 13
Finances
  help with 78

scams 56
Financial planner 55
Fire extinguisher 285
Firewood, cheap 253
Fitness, online 180
Flexible Spending Account
  (FSA) 105
Flooding 322
Flooring 280
Flowers, self-seeding 307
Focus group 36
Food
  nutritious 20
  organic 21-24
  pesticides on 23
  pet 24
  storage 18
Foreclosure, avoiding 133-136
Foreign country
  drugs from 195
  living in 152
  medical treatment in 167-168
  travel to 346
Formulary 190
Franchise 48
Fraud. *See also* Scams
  alerts 64
  business 55-56
  vehicle 203, 215
Freddie Mac 136
Freecycle 283-284
Freeware 229-230
Fruit
  growing 29
  pesticides on 23
  storing 19
Fuel. *See also* Gas
  when to buy 1
  gauge 206

Fuel *(continued)*
  premium 208
Funeral 111-112
Furniture, discounted 281


# G

Garage sale. *See* Yard sale
Gardening 25-27
Gas
  pumping 205-206
  saving money on 206-209
Gift cards 33, 68, 72, 142
Gift tax 107, 116
Glasses 161-162
Gold, selling 52
Grass. *See also* Lawn
  as fertilizer 26
  mowing 314
  watering 311
Graywater 266
Green products 288
Groceries, damaged 10
Grocery bags, uses for 15-16
Grocery list 14
Grocery store. *See* Supermarket
Groupon 356
Grout stains 286
Gutters 305
Gym membership 180


# H

Haggling 143, 160, 272, 335.
  *See also* Bartering

Hair color, homemade 199
Handyman 306
Hard drive 226
Health care
  costs, lowering 153
  credit card 175-176
  federal aid for 155-156
  living abroad and 152
  online 186
  overseas 167-168
  screenings, free 166
Health club 180
Health Savings Account (HSA)
  105
Hearing aid 159-160
Heel pain 181
Herbs
  growing 26
  to control pests 29
High-definition television
  (HDTV) 125
Hill-Burton program 156
Home
  buying 128
  cooling 249-250
  decluttering 282
  energy audit 253, 255
  foreclosure 133-136
  health care 147
  improvements 300, 302
  insurance 315-316
  remodeling 277-279, 297, 301
  repairs 305-306
  security 327-330
  selling 127
  sharing 149
Home business 44-48
Homeowner's Protection Act
  132

Joint, strengthening 159
Junk drawer, organizing 284
Junk mail 83, 124

# L

Laddering 94
Landline phone 233
Landlord 53
Landscaping 313-314
Languages, learning 351
Late fees 75-76, 100
Laundry 264
  detergent 292-294
  stain removal 291-292
Lawn 308, 311-312.
  *See also* Grass
Lawn furniture, cleaning 310
Lawnmower 314
Layaway 82
Leaks, energy 253-254, 256
Legal hotlines 113
Leisure. *See* Vacation
Lemons, storing 19
Letter of complaint 122
Life insurance 43
Lifestyle, healthy 177
Lifetime earnings 93
Light bulbs 257-259
Light therapy 188
Lights, holiday 6
Lint filter, clogged 269
Lions Club International 161
Lipstick stains 291
List, grocery 14
Living abroad 152
Living will 117-118

Loans
  401(k) 43
  modifying 134
  peer-to-peer 43
  piggyback 131
Locksmith 224
Long-term care insurance 174
Loyalty card 4, 9, 20, 334
Luggage, lost 343

# M

Magic Jack 235
Mail scams 61-63
Maintenance
  appliance 282
  car 210-215
  computer 225-226, 283
Makeup 198
Maps, free 334, 345
Marigolds 28
Market
  farmers 1, 22
  salvage 10
Massage 188
Mattress, sanitizing 183
Mayo Clinic 186
Meat. *See also* Beef
  gray 17
  stretching 17
  tenderizing 18
Mechanics, shady 55
Medicaid 147, 172, 175
Medical
  bills, errors in 154
  costs, lowering 153
  equipment 187

Taxes
  cutting 103-105
  deductions 52, 61
  free help 103, 109
  gift 107, 116
  IRA 117
  living abroad and 152
  property 101-102, 110
  sales 242
  software for 107-108
Telemarketing. *See* Do Not Call
  list
Telephone
  bill, lowering 234
  Internet service for 235
  scam 64, 239-240
Television
  live tapings 355-356
  recycling 119
  streaming shows 125-126, 352
Tennis ball, for massage 188
Termites 306
Theater 354
Theft, identity 58
Thermostat, programmable 252
Thrift store 241, 243
Tickets, airline 340-342
Tipping 34
Tires 210, 215, 217-219
Toilet, high-efficiency 263-264
Toothpaste 6
Tours, free 338
Toys 6
Training, computer 231-232
Transfer-on-death accounts 116
TransUnion 64, 89
Travel. *See also* Vacation
  budget 339-340
  discounts 331
  for medical care 167-168
  packing 342
  safety 333
Treasury bills 95
Trusts 116
Tutoring 35
TV. *See* Television

# U

Unclaimed assets 37-38
Unemployment 135
Utility
  bills, lowering 250
  energy audits 255
  savings 295
UVA/UVB rays 185

# V

Vacation. *See also* Travel
  checklist 332
  cruise 333-334
  deals 343-344
  rental 49, 338
Vacuum sealer 19
Valuables, hiding 330
Variable annuity 96
Vegetables
  blanching 30
  growing 29
  pesticides on 23
  storing 19
Vehicle Identification Number
  (VIN) 203, 224